The Opacity of Signs

The Opacity of Signs

Acts of Interpretation in George Herbert's *The Temple*

Richard Todd

University of Missouri Press
Columbia, 1986

University of Missouri Press, Columbia, Missouri 65211
Printed and bound in the United States of America

Library of Congress Cataloging-in-Publication Data

Todd, Richard.
The opacity of signs.

Bibliography: p.
Includes index.
1. Herbert, George, 1593–1633. Temple.
2. God in literature. 3. Theology in literature.
4. Christian poetry, English—History and criticism.
5. Reader-response criticism. I. Title.
PR3507.T43T63 1986 821′.3 86-6973
ISBN 0-8262-0609-3 (alk. paper)

∞™ This paper meets the minimum requirements of
the American National Standard for Permanence of Paper
for Printed Library Materials, Z39.48, 1984.

for
my
parents

Preface

George Herbert's status as one of the major poets writing in English in the seventeenth century is now amply recognized. The increasing literary and critical effort that has been devoted to his work, particularly since the early 1950s, has ensured that we no longer need to qualify that status by apologetic use of labels such as "metaphysical" or even "religious." Herbert's greatness has steadily been made available for all to see. At the same time, much of the critical effort since the commencement of the debate between Rosemond Tuve and William Empson in the 1950s, a debate central to the thesis of this book, has been directed toward demonstrating the nature and extent of Herbert's lyric gifts. More recently, commentators have explored the sometimes disturbing effects that those gifts can be said to exercise on his readers. The attention that has been paid to the rather more neglected area of intellectual backgrounds, without which it is impossible to arrive at a reasoned assessment of Herbert's lyric gifts and their effects on his readers, has until recently remained at the level of source study. Of course, there have been notable exceptions, and one must extol the scholarship of Tuve or, in the context of a more broad-based inquiry into seventeenth-century meditative poetry, Louis Martz. Yet it remains the case that the majority of significant contributions to our knowledge of Herbert's thought have taken the form of relatively isolated and unsystematic essays (many of them revealing and provocative) in article form rather than book form.

In the past few years there have been attempts at a larger-scale presentation of an intellectual background against which to account for Herbert's achievement. But as I point out in my first chapter, these have too frequently set out to contest a prevailing conception of an Anglo-Catholic Herbert that, although it was given authoritative currency in the 1950s by Tuve, Martz, and others, ultimately stems from T. S. Eliot's critical endorsement. Combative views such as those of Barbara Lewalski (1979) or Richard Strier (1983), presenting instead an uncompromisingly Protestant Herbert, seem to me to set out rather perilously from an ideologically oriented position: in their attempts to "claim" Herbert for the Reformation, for Calvinism, or Lutheranism, they perform an act of critical "kidnapping" no less exceptionable than that of John Donne more than a generation ago. Consequently, an Anglo-Catholic Herbert is "revised," and instead of his poetry's being allowed to speak to its readership in all its uncategorizable particularity, a fruitless debate reduces the inheritance of Eliot to little more than ideological terms. What is more, this perspective argues for an inhibited view of sixteenth- and seventeenth-century ecclesiastical orthodoxy and radicalism; while it shows awareness of the recent historiography of English Protestantism, it is at the same time curiously reluctant to accept the fuller implications of that historiography. Although Herbert scholars such as A. D. Nuttall (1980) and Heather Asals (1981) have properly been more cautious—that is to say, inductive and empirical—in their presentation of intellectual backgrounds, it has been left to a scholarly surveyor such as David Norbrook to show us something of the consequences that a truly revisionist approach to such matters might have for future readings of many poets besides Herbert. In his remarkable new study, *Poetry and Politics in the English Renaissance* (1984), he argues that the nature of the period's radicalism has been persistently misunderstood in our own time.

The state of affairs briefly sketched here prompts me to argue that there is room for this book. I have grown convinced that there are still disproportionately few full-length studies of Herbert that seek to account for the nature and stature of *The Temple* and its effect on present-day readers through inductive and systematic examination of one single aspect of his thought, as opposed to an ideological framework within which to view that thought. For in our eagerness to present Herbert to the late twentieth century as probably the most exquisitely accomplished and intelligent craftsman of the lyric in the English language, and to demonstrate the powerful and disconcerting effects that his lyrics exercise on our reading experience, we have lost sight of the Herbert who can be shown to have participated very fully *and eclectically* in the intellectual currents of his time: a Herbert who, in short, is a highly original thinker as well as a poet. In this book I therefore devote my energies to examining the consequences of Herbert's active reception of medieval and Renaissance recensions of a theory of signification developed by Augustine. I believe that to stress this aspect of Herbert's achievement is to illuminate both his lyric craft and his appeal to a twentieth-century readership, and in the following pages I offer an approach to his mind and art that springs from this conviction.

* * *

During the period that my work on George Herbert has been in progress I have incurred a number of debts, and it is a pleasure to be able to acknowledge them in this way. Among former teachers at University College London who did a great deal to initiate and encourage my interest in George Herbert are Basil Greenslade, Frank Kermode, Winifred Nowottny, Kenneth Palmer, John Sutherland, Keith Walker, and most of all Sarah Wintle, who supervised the doctoral thesis upon which the book is based. J. Max Patrick corresponded with me fully at that stage and generously shared his scholarship. Warren Chernaik, and more recently an anonymous reader for the University of Missouri Press, and Herbert's biographer the late Amy Charles (whose unexpected death in spring 1985 all Herbert scholars must deeply regret), went to great trouble to scrutinize earlier versions with the utmost rigor; other colleagues and friends in the Netherlands also kindly commented on former drafts or parts of drafts: August Fry, Hans Meier, Paul Sellin, Leendert Strengholt, and Peter de Voogd. Christina Latham-Koenig helped me prepare the translations from Latin originals. None of these people is of course responsible for defects that remain. I have received a great deal of kind hospitality from John and Lorraine Roberts while visiting in the United States. I should also like to thank Christopher Cooke for his support and efforts on my behalf at an earlier stage. Liesbeth Lenderink typed one entire version of the manuscript, and Katherine Manville more, probably, than she cares to remember; I am extremely grateful to both of them. I embarked upon final revisions in the idyllic surroundings of the Netherlands Institute for Advanced Study in the Humanities and Social Sciences (NIAS) at Wassenaar, near The Hague, to which I am glad to express my sincere thanks for resources of many kinds.

A shorter version of Chapter 5 has appeared in print previously, as part of Jacques B. H. Alblas and Richard Todd (eds.), *From Caxton to Beckett: Essays Presented to W. H. Toppen* (Amsterdam: Rodopi, 1979), and I am grateful for permission to reprint this material. The illustrations are taken from rare books among the holdings of the British Library, London, and the Bibliotheek Vrije Universiteit, Amsterdam; thanks are due to both institutions for their cooperation. A passage from W. H. Auden's "The Truest Poetry is the Most Feigning" (© W. H. Auden, *Collected Poems,* edited by Edward Mendelson) is reprinted by kind permission of Faber & Faber Ltd. (London) and Random House, Inc. (New York). My book forms part of research project no. LETT/83/8, Faculty of Letters, Free University, Amsterdam.

My greatest debts go beyond the scholarly and professional: I have received unwavering support from Winnie Kooy during a lengthy period of thinking, reading, and rewriting, and irresistible blandishments from Jennifer during a much shorter one.

R.T.
Amsterdam/Oegstgeest, the Netherlands
June 1986

A Note on References

I have chosen to quote from the first 1633 edition of *The Temple,* though the reader should consult Appendix 1 for a note on the textual situation. This 1633 edition is reprinted in facsimile by the Scolar Press (1973), though in a limited edition. Some readers may be unable to use either the 1633 text or the Scolar facsimile; they are referred to Appendix 2, which consists of a table of the poems in *The Temple* and their 1633 page numbers (I have used these in my text), together with the appropriate page numbers in the editions of Hutchinson, which is based eclectically on Bodleian MS Tanner 307, and Patrides, which is based largely though not entirely on the first 1633 edition. For fuller details of these editions, see the bibliography.

The 1633 edition of *The Temple* is flawlessly paginated, so that in citing it I have given page numbers only. For other less reliably paginated sixteenth- and seventeenth-century texts I give both page numbers and signatures, unless the former are too erroneous to be of use. In quoting from all sixteenth- and seventeenth-century texts, including *The Temple,* I have expanded contractions other than the ampersand, normalized "i/j" and "u/v," and shortened the long "s." However, where I have referred to nineteenth- and twentieth-century editions of patristic and scholastic texts (that is, from Migne's *Patrologiae,* the Quaracchi edition of Bonaventura, and the various editions of Aquinas), I have observed the editors' usages; in practice, Migne alone distinguishes "i" and "j."

I have used the following abbreviations:

ELH	*ELH: Journal of English Literary History*
GHJ	*George Herbert Journal*
NED	*New English Dictionary*
N&Q	*Notes and Queries*
PL	*Patrologiae . . . series Latinae* (ed. Migne; see Bibliography)
PMLA	*Publications of the Modern Language Association of America*
RES	*Review of English Studies*
SCN	*Seventeenth Century News*
SEL	*Studies in English Literature*

STC	*Short-Title Catalogue* (see Bibliography)
TLS	*Times Literary Supplement*

Latin texts are given in translation in the body of my text; the Latin is given in the relevant note. Unless otherwise stated, the translations have been specially prepared for the purpose.

Contents

1. Introduction

Reading George Herbert

According to Izaak Walton, George Herbert thought of his religious lyrics as "spiritual Conflicts."[1] Meant not only to apply to the poet's committal of his religious experience to verse, but also to convey something of the effect of that verse on its potential readers, the description that Walton attributes to Herbert will be familiar to most readers of *The Temple.* Despite more contemporary doubts about the literal truth of his *Lives*, Walton's description remains instructive.[2] It reminds us that despite all the developments that the history of thought has undergone during the past 350 years, and all that has been experienced in the related upheavals in religious belief and practice both inside and outside Herbert's Church, *The Temple* has continued to speak with remarkable persistence and accessibility to its readers. Indeed, since the revival of interest in George Herbert among literary critics earlier in this century, his poetry has provided a focus for some of the most sophisticated critical response that the entire literary canon in the English language has elicited. What is more, during the last ten to fifteen years a more rigorously intellectual interest in literary theory has emerged within the Anglo-American critical tradition, and it has prompted attempts to characterize a response to Herbert's poetry in terms of the process of reading itself. In Stanley Fish's now-classic statement in his *Self-Consuming Artifacts* (1972), for example, the reader may come to *participate* in a given poem:

It is time I think . . . to acknowledge the extent to which [the reader's]

1. Izaak Walton, *The Life of Mr. George Herbert*, p. 74.
2. For fuller details of the doubts, see, for example, David Novarr, *The Making of Walton's "Lives"*; J. Max Patrick, "Critical Problems in Editing George Herbert's *The Temple*"; and note 33 below. The forthcoming biography of Walton by Clayton Lein (Oxford University Press) is likely to do much to enhance our understanding of these issues.

> consciousness as well as that of the first person voice is the locus of a poem's action. . . . Just those problems which engage Herbert's protagonists engage his reader also. The poems are structured so as both to describe an experience and give one.[3]

Fish contends that the kind of experience he has in mind is one that he terms "self-diminishing": the experience of reading Herbert's religious lyrics may, in the end, be humiliating.

The idea that the reader participates in experiencing the lyrics in *The Temple* is integral to my undertaking in this book. The argument I develop is that Herbert's interpretation of his experience of relationship to God is revealingly analogous to the act of interpretation performed by the reader of his verse. Yet a formulation such as Fish's has proved controversial: to those of a more traditional turn of mind, its main danger must seem to lie in a temptation toward critical self-indulgence. Fish may have recognized this in his later monograph on Herbert, *The Living Temple* (1978), a book that is firmly seated in historical scholarship and relates the structure and experience of The Temple to a largely ignored tradition of contemporary Anglican catechistical thought. Yet at least one of his readers has censured him (albeit cautiously) for appearing to retreat from some of the implications of his earlier stance.[4] While advancement of the critical debate should always be firmly rooted in discourse whose terms reflect what Herbert would have understood, Fish's claims in *Self-Consuming Artifacts* nevertheless bring into focus some curiously unexamined assumptions that underlie much of the twentieth-century discussion of *The Temple.* How well qualified are Herbert's twentieth-century readers? Who are his "best" readers? George Herbert, as the subject of such questions, would doubtless have understood the convention of twentieth-century discourse that obliges us to reformulate them in the following specific, and more palatable, distillations: first, is it necessary to believe what he believed, and second, is it necessary to be steeped in the various traditions of thought that were still flourishing when he wrote, in order to appreciate *The Temple*?

3. Stanley E. Fish, "Letting Go: The Reader in Herbert's Poetry," p. 476.

4. Barbara Harman, *Costly Monuments: Representations of the Self in George Herbert's Poetry,* pp. 199–200n.

The major challenge to the idea that Christians are necessarily the best readers of Herbert's verse, an idea that critical discussion up to and including T. S. Eliot took for granted, came in 1975 from Helen Vendler, who asserted that Herbert's verse "is as valuable to those who share none of his religious beliefs as to those who share them all."[5] She was seconded by at least one of her reviewers: her former teacher I. A. Richards wrote that "the immense satisfaction" that unbelievers such as himself had acquired from Herbert's verse could not be doubted, and that a reader's status as an unbeliever should not be considered "disabling."[6] It is not my purpose to pursue this particular issue further. My argument assumes instead the centrality of the second question above: to what extent can or should traditions, whose influence on *The Temple* is readily demonstrable, be considered necessary knowledge for an appreciation, or even a fundamental understanding, of the lyrics? As we consider this second question, Richards's endorsement of Vendler's view of the first may recall the controversy aroused in the 1940s and 1950s by the work of another of his former pupils, William Empson, and its reception by the medievalist Rosemond Tuve. Readers of Barbara Harman's recent account of twentieth-century Herbert criticism in her *Costly Monuments* (1982) may be misled into thinking that it has responded to this controversy more systematically and centrally since the 1950s than it can really be shown to have done. I take the somewhat contrary view that, since Tuve's untimely death in 1964, the debate that she helped inaugurate has not advanced as far as is generally assumed, and that a return to its terms in the light of Fish's claims for reader participation is now due. Such a return, as I will argue, can initiate a historical and critical investigation that will illuminate the process of "reading" in *The Temple* in a manner, and with a discourse, that George Herbert would palpably have been capable of comprehending.

A brief summary of the debate is in order. In 1952, Rosemond Tuve published a study of the poetry of George Herbert in which

5. Helen Vendler, *The Poetry of George Herbert*, p. 4.

6. I. A. Richards, review of Vendler, *The Poetry of George Herbert*, p. 1417.

she offered a reading of his poems in the context of a received liturgical and typological tradition.[7] She was not the only critic to have stressed the idea of tradition in reading *The Temple*,[8] but her study was particularly important in that it was a polemic work, arguing against methods of criticism that attempted to account for the poems more or less exclusively in terms of close analysis and a twentieth-century modernist sensibility. Tuve's principal quarry was Empson's reading of Herbert in *Seven Types of Ambiguity* (1930). Yet while Empson later conceded that parts of his reading might have been over-ingenious, he remained on the whole unconvinced that Tuve's scholarly findings had actually made any great difference to the substance of his account.[9]

Empson's indifference to Tuve's insistence that knowledge of traditional material available to Herbert was not merely desirable but actually necessary to a reading of his verse implies a certain view of reader participation in the poetry of *The Temple*; yet the extent to which Empson himself would have been prepared to concede this remains unclear. In effect, in taking him to task for referring to Herbert's conduct of "The Sacrifice" as "unique," Tuve was forcing a concession since, as he himself later admitted, Empson had not been willing to recognize the close relation between "The Sacrifice" and earlier liturgical treatment of the paradoxes with which the poem deals. Yet having conceded to Tuve that this relation rendered absurd his claim that the poem was unique, since Herbert had not invented the theological and typological paradoxes, Empson characteristically persisted with his claim that Herbert's *expression* of those paradoxes was, if not unique, then certainly singular. Tuve, however, still felt obliged to contest Empson's assumptions; in her view, what he was calling attention to was an expressiveness that Herbert, working within a liturgical tradition, could not ever have intended; Empson was

7. Rosemond Tuve, *A Reading of George Herbert*.

8. See also, for example, Rosemary Freeman, *English Emblem Books*, and Malcolm M. Ross, *Poetry and Dogma*.

9. See William Empson, *Seven Types of Ambiguity*, pp. 262–70, in which he discusses Herbert's "The Sacrifice"; also his comments in "Donne and the Rhetorical Tradition," p. 735, and in the "Note" to the 1973 edition of *Seven Types of Ambiguity*, pp. 16–17.

failing to admit that he was reading Herbert's words with the spiritual and mental equipment of the twentieth century. Tuve did not question the validity of this act but wished it to be recognized as "creation," in that the critic should be seen as the author of a "new poem" and not as what she considered a commentator on the original. Empson's reply to this view of the critic's role was to draw a distinction between the poet's handling a traditional theme and his making explicit certain powerful paradoxes inherent in that theme. In short, Empson urged that Herbert had managed to achieve the latter rather than the former in "The Sacrifice" and that such an achievement should support the claim to novelty in the poem. For Tuve, however, that novelty was not Herbert's, but Empson's. Within this argument lies what Harman calls "a disagreement about the ontological status of the poem (is it free-standing or implicated in its past?)";[10] Empson's sense of novelty implies active, creative participation by the reader, whereas Tuve's view that there could be no novelty where there is tradition implied what she called a willingness "to learn Herbert's language."[11] Clearly, Empson's view admits the possibility of a participation that Tuve's, by its insistence on an almost Eliot-like surrender to the poet's past, does not. At the risk of gross oversimplification, we might summarize these two subtle positions by saying that where Tuve would have us "read" Herbert's poetry, Empson would, in a sense, have us "write" it.

Can these positions be reconciled? The answer that I develop in the following pages arises from my strong conviction that the essentials for any such inquiry are to be found in a judicious combination of both historical scholarship and recent critical notions of reader participation. Examination of Herbert criticism to date has convinced me that the balance has been neither frequently attained nor consistently held: ideas of reader participation have not yet been used to throw sufficient light on what we know of the thought of Herbert's age, and the continuing need for a firm grasp of that thought in any approach to Herbert's lyric verse has only

10. Harman, *Costly Monuments*, p. 10.
11. Tuve, *A Reading of George Herbert*, p. 203.

intermittently been recognized since the 1950s. In the pages that follow I examine a sense of relationship between God, the poet, and the reader that is characteristic to Herbert's verse and that has its basis in what we know of his thought and reading. In the next chapter I trace a historical background for what had become a firmly traditional belief by Herbert's time: that in a fallen world God reveals himself to man indirectly, by means of signs. To fallen man, communication in any more direct sense than the significant is not possible. The idea itself is scriptural, but it received particular exegetical attention, as I will show, in the writings of Augustine and in medieval and Renaissance Augustinian thought.[12]

My argument, then, rests on the assumption that the poetry of *The Temple* is illuminatingly approached in terms of Herbert's interpretation of his experience of relationship with God, in his role as God's reader. Interpretation is necessary precisely because of man's fallen nature: he is *homo significans* for whom all communication, with God and with his fellow men, must take place through the medium of signs. In the third chapter I argue that what is particularly characteristic about Herbert's specific apprehension of relationship with God is nevertheless entirely consistent with tradition, for Herbert conveys with characteristic force the idea that the signs that should convey divine presence may, and indeed frequently do, seem so far from clear as to suggest instead his absence. Although the idea is constantly couched in personal terms, its applicability to mankind in general is equally persistent in *The Temple.* In fact, man's state is seen to be such that lack of clarity in the face of an apprehension of God's signs, a property I term "opacity," is regarded throughout *The Temple* as inherent in the way Herbert, as God's well-intentioned but reluctant reader, perceives God's signs in his fallen condition. Only when this condition is spontaneously transformed into one of spiritual health can these signs be discerned with anything approaching clarity, but whether the ability can be maintained in

12. 1 Cor. 13:12. I use the phrase "particular . . . attention" with care, admitting that Augustine's treatment is to be seen in the context of Neoplatonic influence behind his writing and is not *sui generis.* Needless to say, this assumption will also underlie the argument of the next chapter.

the present life other than in a state of mystical or visionary ecstasy remains far from sure. Although it has long been accepted that at one of its many levels *The Temple* can be read as the halting and uncertain progress toward achievement of this visionary state, a progress the reader may follow, my final business in this book is to urge that this is not all that can or should be said concerning the twentieth-century reader's experience of Herbert's religious verse.

My approach demands proper investigation of the meaning of a concept of signs that reveal only opaquely until spiritual vision is granted. Such an investigation will demonstrate our need for an understanding of the ways in which Herbert conceptualizes, through his lyric expressiveness, man's attaining spiritual vision by making sense of the opacity of signs. The fourth and fifth chapters, which serve as companion pieces, pursue more systematically the suggestion that emerges from the third, namely that as one gradually discerns the substance of an opaquely significant experience of a relationship with God, through both world and Word, one's experience may be tantamount to a reading experience. Accordingly, I examine Herbert's interpretative understanding of the concepts of Providence and Grace through his "readings" of the books of Nature and Scripture respectively. From these we see that Herbert's characteristic strategy for making sense of the opacity of signs is nothing less than the sacramental offering up to God of his discoveries as they are portrayed in his lyrics. In this way, I show that the metaphor of the reading process, conscripted to represent the strategic discernment of signs that for the most part persist in remaining opaque, springs from a tradition of thought with which Herbert would have been entirely familiar. But this is not all. The metaphor also provides grounds for documenting a parallel between Herbert's relationship with God and the reader's relationship with the poet. The divine text, as I argue in the fourth and fifth chapters, is discovered in its natural and scriptural forms but remains largely opaque, as the processes of Providence and Grace remain for the most part inscrutable. This leads to a concession that all the poet can ultimately do is to offer up his discovery to God. My argument in the final chapter rests on the assumption that to hold that God provides a text at least partly opaque to the poet is at the same time necessarily to suggest that the poet's text is similarly apprehended by its reader. God is therefore seen as standing to the poet as the poet stands to the reader. The poet's act of sacramental offering results in a text that is itself a work of artful creation such as he has discovered in the divine text. It is the very artfulness of the literary text of Herbert's *The Temple* that elicits an analogously interpretative response by the reader, who is confronted with a sense of significant opacity used rhetorically or expressively by the poet. In the final chapter, accordingly, I consider the ways in which Herbert's reader is obliged to come to terms with this response.

In what follows I take issue with Rosemond Tuve's assumption that the discovery and creation of meanings must be activities different in kind to poet and reader or critic. Instead I propose that the reader's interpretative response to a Herbert lyric may proceed from an impulse analogous to the one that underlies the poet's sacramental offering of the experience of relationship to God in a given poem, in that neither may satisfy man's deepest hermeneutic urges. However, I am not merely convinced that it is possible to dissent from Tuve while at the same time maintaining a historical perspective; in fact, I prefer to emphasize my position by asserting that it is the balance that I am urging between historical scholarship and critical notions of reader participation that is vital in enabling the present-day reader of Herbert's poetry to accept, with Empson, the idea of novelty in tradition. Such a reader is confronted with the disturbing notion that interpretation of a particular poem, and the sacramental offering that it enacts, may *both* be considered as acts of resigned abandonment, even renunciation and surrender, given the exigencies of communication between God and man after man's Fall. This book therefore falls into two parts. In the first, consisting of the second through the fifth chapters, I maintain a historical perspective as I explore the traditional background for the role of signs and the opacity of their character in the relationship between God and the poet. In the second part, consisting of the final chapter, I apply the notions that emerge from the first part to the relationship between poet and reader and to the act of reading *The Temple* in the twentieth century. It is my fundamental assumption, however, that the two perspectives are not merely analogous: they are ultimately inseparable.

* * *

Having invoked a tradition that received patristic attention, we are obliged to consider whether Herbert was familiar with it—in other words, to ask what Herbert read. Rosemond Tuve's examination of Herbert's reading remains one of the most thorough and scholarly, although the fine studies of Louis L. Martz and Joseph H. Summers, both of which appeared shortly afterward, can be said to have been comparably influential.[13] But all three authorities do more to create a general intellectual context than to address the matter of specific titles in Herbert's library, and in fact little concrete evidence has emerged, or is likely to. As a result, critical discussion during the 1960s and 1970s tended to supplement the deductions of these scholars rather than offer any startlingly new ideas. In 1979, however, Barbara Lewalski, in her *Protestant Poetics*, proposed what she termed a frankly "revisionist" view: "the major seventeenth-century religious lyrists [*sic*] owe more to contemporary, English, and Protestant influences than to Counter Reformation, continental, and medieval Catholic resources."[14] Although this view was refreshing and challenging, it did anticipate a dangerous situation in which subsequent discussion could become trapped in "either/or" categories. It is therefore alarming to find Richard Strier prefacing what is on the whole a balanced account of Herbert's verse with remarks such as these: "Meditation and typology remain topics deeply rel-

13. Jerry Leath Mills, "Recent Studies in Herbert," p. 113, claims that "the majority of recent studies [of Herbert] respond, in terms of either refinement, modification, or reaction, to ideas advanced by Summers, Tuve, and Martz." See Joseph H. Summers, *George Herbert: His Religion and Art*, and Louis L. Martz, *The Poetry of Meditation: A Study in English Religious Literature of the Seventeenth Century* (the 1962 edition of Martz is used throughout). But cf. also John R. Roberts, *George Herbert: An Annotated Bibliography of Modern Criticism 1905–1974*, p. ix.

14. Barbara K. Lewalski, *Protestant Poetics and the Seventeenth Century Religious Lyric*, p. ix.

evant to Herbert's poetry, *but they have now been freed from medieval and Counter-Reformation contexts*" [emphasis added].[15] It is hard to reconcile this with the more temperate tone of Strier's conclusion, and we must admit the possibility that poets such as Herbert were more eclectic in their reading and thinking than critics such as Lewalski and Strier would have us believe. However, there is some encouraging evidence to suggest that not all Herbert's most recent commentators are content with the polarities that are implied in the debate that Lewalski's work has regalvanized, if not actually initiated. A. D. Nuttall, for example, has provocatively seen in Herbert's poetry "a fundamental if largely unconscious critique of Calvinism," and more recently still Heather Asals has proposed a return to a view of Herbert as "a specifically Anglican poet," clearly sensing a need to detach him from some of the implications of Lewalski's view.[16] In view of the uncertainties that such recent work reflects, one of the most urgent needs for the literary and historical study of Herbert and his contemporaries in the near future is for a greater preparedness to accept the fullest implications of recent historical scholarship; it is evident that influence-study discussion of the English religious poetry of the period remains seriously hampered by an insular, twentieth-century sense of dichotomy between theological and even political aspects of seventeenth-century Catholic and Protestant thought and practice.[17]

One of the few, and by this token major, pieces of evidence in

15. Richard Strier, *Love Known: Theology and Experience in George Herbert's Poetry,* pp. xvi–xvii, although cf. p. 253.

16. A. D. Nuttall, *Overheard by God: Fiction and Prayer in Herbert, Milton, Dante and St John,* p. 75; Heather Asals, *Equivocal Predication: George Herbert's Way to God,* p. 5. Whereas Ilona Bell, " 'Setting Foot into Divinity': George Herbert and the English Reformation," argues (p. 222) a "rebellious" attitude to Catholic meditation, John E. Booty, "George Herbert: *The Temple* and *The Book of Common Prayer,*" offers a reading along the lines of orthodoxy to Anglo-Catholic doctrine and practice.

17. However, it is encouraging to note that David Norbrook, *Poetry and Politics in the English Renaissance,* has proposed a genuinely revisionist view of the question, arguing convincingly with reference to the work of Christopher Hill and others that the nature of sixteenth- and seventeenth-century religious and political radicalism has been persistently misunderstood in our own century. See also Patrick Collinson, *The Religion of Protestants,* pp. 79–83 and *passim.*

Herbert's own words as to the nature of his reading is found in his will, which indicates that he possessed the works of Augustine.[18] Mary Ellen Rickey, in contrast to other commentators, demonstrated many veiled classical allusions in *The Temple*:[19] yet the "clamorous and greedy bookish requests" (*Works*, p. 367) that Herbert made to his stepfather Sir John Danvers in 1617 or 1618, while he was still at Trinity College, Cambridge, were, by his own account, for "those infinite Volumes of Divinity, which yet every day swell, and grow bigger" (*Works*, p. 365). While an intimate knowledge of the Bible, the liturgy, and other sources cited by Tuve goes without saying, Herbert's somewhat expansive statement in his prose treatise *The Countrey Parson* fails to argue any specific patristic or scholastic influence: "The Countrey Parson hath read the Fathers also, and the Schoolmen, and the later Writers, or a good proportion of all" (*Works*, p. 229).

In the 1960s Arnold Stein, building on our knowledge of Herbert's possession of Augustine, attempted to supplement the received account. He argued that the Christian "plain style" of *The Temple* indicates a familiarity with the rhetorical principles laid down in Augustine's *De Doctrina Christiana*. We must admit that, although the argument is in itself convincing, Stein's application of these principles to Herbert's metrics is less so; as Helen Vendler conceded, current prosodic notation does seem inadequate to describe many of Herbert's effects.[20] This is not a new problem; it is remarkable how straightforward a task it is to affirm that Herbert was influential in the later seventeenth century, yet how difficult it is, short of citing the metrical psalm translations of Sidney,

18. F. E. Hutchinson's Oxford edition will be referred to throughout what follows as *Works*. Here the reference is to p. 382. (See also note 29 below). In addition, Herbert seems certainly to have owned copies of contemporary writers such as Luigi Cornaro and Juan de Valdés (*Works*, pp. 291–320), as well as the Franciscan writers Lucas of Bruges (*Works*, p. 382) and the somewhat earlier Girolamo Savonarola (see Martz, *The Poetry of Meditation*, p. 282). But Tuve's "Note" on the materials available to Herbert (*A Reading of George Herbert*, pp. 204–210) should nevertheless be consulted.

19. Mary E. Rickey, *Utmost Art: Complexity in the Verse of George Herbert*, pp. 1–58.

20. Arnold Stein, *George Herbert's Lyrics*. Cf. the comments in Vendler, *The Poetry of George Herbert*, p. 280.

the religious verse of Donne, and possibly also that of Southwell and Alabaster, to point to *poetic* sources within the late sixteenth- and early seventeenth-century English literary canon upon which Herbert himself could have drawn. Attention to this problem must constitute a research priority in the near future. A customary explanation is to hold, with Martz and others, that Herbert turned Sidney's secular poetic to sacred use; the influence of the Shakespearean sonnets, though less frequently asserted, also seems demonstrable. Herbert's influence on Vaughan and Crashaw was admitted by these poets; yet in studying the many lesser-known seventeenth- and eighteenth-century imitations of Herbert, variously discussed by Summers, Vendler, and others, a reader perhaps too often has the feeling that what appealed to these imitative poets was Herbert's piety rather than any real interest in or understanding of his poetic or the subtlety of his prosody.[21] This is interesting in that it suggests that the idea of reader participation in religious lyric poetry such as Herbert's should be seen less as startlingly novel than as requiring proper and rigorous definition within an existing historical framework.

Of course it would be misleading to claim that no satisfactory account has been offered of the nature of Herbert's prosody, nor any historical explanation suggested for its particular character. In 1972 Coburn Freer presented an urbane survey of English metrical psalm translations of the sixteenth and early seventeenth centuries,[22] and although he endorsed Martz's belief (Martz, p. 273) that the elegant Sidneyan metrical psalm is a close poetic influence on *The Temple*, Freer argued that Herbert was also in debt to a more popular literature of metrical psalms, suggesting that Herbert's sporadic syntactic awkwardnesses and lumpish meters were best seen as parodying this literature. Such parody, how-

21. See C. A. Patrides, ed., *The Critical Heritage, passim.*

22. Coburn Freer, *Music for a King: George Herbert's Style and the Metrical Psalms.* Critics who have more recently explored relationships between *The Temple* and the psalms include Noel J. Kinnamon, "A Note on Herbert's 'Easter' and the Sidneian Psalms," and "Notes on the Psalms in Herbert's *The Temple*", and Martin Elsky, "Polyphonic Psalm Settings and the Voice of George Herbert's *The Temple*." There is a comprehensive discussion in Chana Bloch, *Spelling the Word: George Herbert and the Bible,* pp. 231–305.

ever, if present, is to be seen as serious in intention, and there is no doubt that Herbert's only actual setting, of Psalm 23, is metrically exquisite. Freer (p. 133) admitted Herbert's "extraordinary care" with the craft of the popular metrical psalm, and Rosemond Tuve had previously indicated serious purpose behind parodic writing in *The Temple*.[23]

Even if Arnold Stein was not wholly successful in accounting for Herbert's prosody, there can be no doubt that he convincingly showed the importance to Herbert of Augustinian views on style. In yet another fine essay, Tuve demonstrated the influence throughout *The Temple* of Augustine's theology of love,[24] and scholars such as Perry Miller and Ruth Wallerstein had already drawn attention to a general revival in the seventeenth century of both Augustinian theology and rhetoric.[25] While the present approach to Herbert's verse stresses participation by the reader, the historical sense I am pleading will be buttressed by the account that follows of an Augustinian theory of signs and its reception into medieval and Renaissance thought. My aim in offering such an account is to contribute—in some spirit of disagreement with critics such as Lewalski and Strier—to a view of Herbert that can be illuminated by consideration of patristic and medieval tradition, but that in no way attempts to underestimate the need for a historical understanding of seventeenth-century English Protestantism. Augustine's conception of man as *homo significans*, although not new in itself, was expressed in a manner that clearly appealed to later thinkers; I suggest that we may be enlightened by tracing the development of this thought into the Middle Ages and Renaissance, particularly in the writings of the Franciscans of the period. Such writings will in their turn be seen to illuminate the experience of reading *The Temple*.

* * *

23. See Rosemond Tuve, *Essays by Rosemond Tuve*, ed. Thomas P. Roche, Jr., pp. 207–249.

24. In Tuve, *Essays by Rosemond Tuve*, pp. 167–206.

25. Perry Miller, *The New England Mind: The Seventeenth Century*, and Ruth Wallerstein, *Studies in Seventeenth Century Poetic*. See also Mark Taylor, *The Soul in Paraphrase: George Herbert's Poetics*.

The groundwork that such an account presupposes requires some preliminary theoretical remarks. Since this book offers a particular view of the experience of reading George Herbert's *The Temple,* I am obliged to indicate more precisely how such a view differs from that advanced in Fish's *Self-Consuming Artifacts.* Although I share Fish's interest in the activity of reading *The Temple,* I have set out from somewhat different assumptions. We have become familiar with the notion that every literary text, when received by its reader, constitutes an act of communication: every text is subjected by its reader to a process of interpretation. To see the activity of reading in this way is to concede the notion of a "semantic autonomy," and it has been argued that to regard a "piece of language" that constitutes any text as "a public object whose character is defined by public norms" is to take an insufficient view of the business of reading; rather, we should see a given text as representing "the determinate verbal meaning of an author."[26]

In the light of the term "semantic autonomy," let us return briefly to the dispute between Rosemond Tuve and William Empson over the use of the word *unique* to describe Herbert's handling of a traditional theme in what may or may not be a traditional way in a poem such as "The Sacrifice." Tuve, anxious to avoid the complications of trying to extricate, as she put it, "what-the-poem-'really'-means," declared that she was "frankly interested in what Herbert meant."[27] My assumption throughout is that if we are indeed to ascertain "what Herbert really meant," we are confronted with the need to document our attempts in terms of the effects that Herbert's meanings exercise on their present-day readers, whose self-conscious participation in documenting their response is solicited in this book. Of course, it is possible to attack a conceptualization of "semantic autonomy" on the grounds that it too easily encourages complacent or insufficiently focused critical doctrines, such as T. S. Eliot's belief in the descriptive adequacy of

26. E. D. Hirsch, Jr., *Validity in Interpretation,* pp. 224, 226. The notion of a "piece of language" is Empson's; see *Seven Types of Ambiguity,* p. 19.
27. Tuve, *A Reading of George Herbert,* p. 32.

"what the poem means to different sensitive readers."[28] However, Eliot's formulation as it stands is rendered more rigorous once the reader self-consciously begins to dramatize his or her experience of a given text. Thus Stanley Fish quite rightly attaches great importance to Herbert's words in "The Flower" (1633, p. 160):[29]

We say amisse,
This or that is:
Thy word is all, if we could spell. (19–21)

Fish uses Herbert's words in this poem to illustrate his belief in the "self-diminishing" nature both of Herbert's experience of the cosmos and of the reader's experience of Herbert's text. Yet it is also defensible to suggest that the words comment dramatically on their writer's own interpretation of the phenomenon that gives rise to them; that is to say, in affirming the relativity of interpretations by conceding the possibility of interpretative error, they can be seen as documenting the poet's act of interpretation.

There is in fact support throughout *The Temple* for the self-conscious documentation of an act of interpretation: the experience described in "Love-joy" (1633, p. 109) provides an excellent example. This little poem is of such immediacy to my argument that it might almost have served as an epigraph to this book:

As on a window late I cast mine eye,
I saw a vine drop grapes with *J* and *C*
Anneal'd on every bunch. One standing by
Ask'd what it meant. I (who am never loth
To spend my judgement) said, It seem'd to me
To be the bodie and the letters both
Of *Joy* and *Charitie*. Sir, you have not miss'd,
The man reply'd; It figures *JESUS CHRIST*.

The poem is used by Tuve in the second part of her *Reading* to dem-

28. Hirsch, *Validity in Interpretation*, p. 4.

29. Unless otherwise stated, the text of *The Temple* used throughout this book is that of the first edition of 1633. See "A Note on References" and Appendix 1; see also under *Herbert* in Bibliography. References to the first 1633 edition are given wherever possible in the body of my text; the date 1633 is followed by the page number(s) in question.

onstrate the benefits of learning the language of symbols in which Herbert was steeped. Once the reader knows this language, she argued, he becomes aware of the associations between the grapes and the Passion of Christ. The pains of the crucifixion were frequently expressed by means of the figure of the winepress. Christ was traditionally figured as being pressed to death, and his blood, thereby released, becomes sacramental. I will discuss seventeenth-century treatment of emblematic and figurative conventions such as this more fully in Chapter 5; what is important for present purposes is Tuve's claim that the twentieth-century reader's familiarity with the "language" that such conventions imply enables him or her to gauge the poet's "tone of voice" correctly and "accurately take his meanings even across intervening centuries."[30]

Tuve's claim remains a high one and must be examined, albeit briefly at this stage, for we cannot gauge the tone of voice in this poem without at the same time pointing to the interpretative drive it elicits ("One standing by / Ask'd what it meant"). The acts of interpretation it documents are made relative by the existence in the poem of both the narrating poet, the "reader" of the window, and "One standing by," whose query elicits the narrated response: "It seem'd to me / To be . . . ." This documentation ("I [who am never loth / To spend my judgement]"), with its beautifully equivocal play on *spend,* exhibits an acutely aware self-consciousness. One of the ways in which we as readers can participate here is in our unfolding realization, shared with the narrating poet, that the interpretation given of the sign in the window is both right and wrong. "Joy" and "Charitie" are in one sense correct answers, since they are signified by "J" and "C"; yet the apparent endorsement in the reworded answer "Jesus Christ" is puzzling. In the sense that "Jesus Christ" can be expressive of joy and charity, the poet's answer was clearly adequate. Yet the restatement simultaneously suggests that the answer was in some

30. Tuve, *A Reading of George Herbert,* p. 134. Stanley E. Fish, *The Living Temple,* pp. 27–29, offers an account of this poem in terms of traditional catechistic procedures.

other way far from adequate. But although *spend* can certainly imply slickness on the poet's part, the eagerness to interpret does not in itself represent a mistaken impulse. Tuve's insistence on a knowledge of the sacramental associations that underlie the sign specifically in question (that is, the grapes) may obscure a process that the sign *as sign* invites poet and reader to contemplate. More damagingly, it seems to obscure the immediacy of the process in which the reader participates. In *The Living Temple*, Fish rightly places emphasis on the way that the spending of judgment in this poem is something in which the reader participates. It does not seem sufficient, however, merely to suggest that there is a "catechistical" sense in which the poet's (and reader's) two answers, when "properly understood," in Fish's words, "imply each other";[31] the truth of Fish's insight is also applicable to the "significant" sense of the poem's two answers. Accepting this, we can go further than Fish does and assert that the answer given at the end of the poem, JESUS CHRIST, possesses significance of an order such that the poet and reader are told *more* about "Joy" and "Charitie" than could have been learned without that spending of judgment. JESUS CHRIST "figures" these other signs by making sense of them, too, as signs. If we are prepared to admit the process as strategic, we shall see that the discoveries that the reading of a sign permits can, and indeed do, include discoveries about the nature of the signs in themselves, and that this realization is crucial to an understanding of Herbert's poetic.

We cannot leave consideration of these theoretical issues without reminding ourselves that devotional poetry such as that in *The Temple* is tantamount to creating a spiritual personality of the poet. The ease with which we as readers indulge in this act may blind us to what it suggests of our reading habits. Aside from scattered comments by various admiring imitators and other later contemporaries of Herbert,[32] and from Barnabas Oley's remarks in Herbert's *Remains* (1652), the first and the most celebrated documenting of the creation of Herbert's spiritual personality

31. Fish, *The Living Temple*, p. 29.
32. See Patrides, ed., *The Critical Heritage, passim.*

occurs in Walton's *Life*. It is true that Walton's work has been seen in more just proportions during the last half-century,[33] but idealized though it may be, it is really no different in kind from that creative activity in which all of Herbert's readers indulge. As readers, we have learned to regard Herbert's "experiential" poems as fictions, and consequently to conjecture a poetic personality enacting or undergoing fictional experiences. We identify this personality as having a recognizable voice, whose changes of mood—from hope to despair, lament to praise—may be traced and even accounted for. It is easier for us to examine why this voice resorts so frequently to an expressive or addressive mode, and to label it "Herbert," than it is for us consistently to embark on such an exercise in the case, for example, of the speaking voice in Donne's *Songs and Sonnets*. From this point of view, Herbert's voice has more in common with those of Elizabethan sonnet sequences. Of course, there are historically attested biographical details of George Herbert,[34] but despite their availability, it is hard to see how we could postulate the characteristic spiritual personality whom we understand as "Herbert" from them alone, or from the surviving letters. We seem strangely reluctant to admit that a spiritual personality bearing the name *George Herbert* is an inevitable result of the creative act of reader participation, of engaging with

33. John Butt, "Izaak Walton's Methods in Biography," seems to have been among the first to express skepticism about Walton's account. Joseph H. Summers, *George Herbert*, pp. 28ff., calls attention to Walton's tendency to paraphrase Herbert's poems; David Novarr, in *The Making of Walton's "Lives,"* judiciously appraises Walton's biographies and examines their underlying ideology. J. Max Patrick, "Critical Problems in Editing George Herbert's *The Temple*" is more forthright and suggests that quotations that Walton attributes biographically to Herbert frequently have no firmer basis in fact than that they are Walton's own paraphrases from *The Temple*. Patrick is the first to extend this skepticism into a claim for the authority of the 1633 text. The case remains controversial (see Appendix 1), but I have accepted it.

34. See Amy M. Charles, *A Life of George Herbert*, and Summers, *George Herbert*, pp. 28ff. The edition of *The Temple* by G. H. Palmer depends, in its rearrangement of the poems in a supposedly chronological order, on an extrapolation from these details. Palmer's reordering of the poems has for a long time been discredited, but his edition remains valuably annotated. At the same time, a recent study such as Diana Benet's *Secretary of Praise: The Poetic Vocation of George Herbert* demonstrates the potential strengths of an approach to Herbert's verse through spiritual biography.

the text of *The Temple*.[35] Yet such an admission is essential to the reader's attempt to interpret the signs conveyed by that text. In stressing the reader's self-consciousness in reading, we are conceiving of our engagement with Herbert's poetry in terms of a dramatization of our experience of the text, thereby enabling ourselves to compare what we do with Herbert's interpretation of the signs that constitute his experience of relation to God.

Such an admission accounts for this book's concentration on the majority of experiential poems in *The Temple* at the expense of the few homilectic poems, and of the almost certainly early poem that ends the collection, "The Church Militant." It is true that careful attention to poems such as "The British Church" and "Church-rents and schismes" can tell us much about Herbert's place in seventeenth-century English Protestantism; yet they and the homilectic poems lack a certain immediacy for most twentieth-century readers, although the longest of them, "The Church-porch," has recently fallen into sympathetic and discerning hands.[36] The ensuing discussion is therefore almost exclusively confined to the section of *The Temple* from "The Altar" to "Love" [III], that is, with the largest of the three subdivisions in *The Temple*, entitled, in both extant manuscript versions and in the 1633 editions, "The Church." I will refer throughout the text, however, to the title of the entire volume, since this title is far more suggestive than "The Church" and keeps its readers mindful of a structure easier to sense than to describe. The existence of several attempts to describe it suggests a rich superimposition of many ideas,[37] so

35. There is an interesting fictive instance of this process in Ford Madox Ford's tetralogy *Parade's End*. At times in *No More Parades* and *A Man Could Stand Up* Ford imagistically presents Christopher Tietjens's shell-shocked reminiscences, one of which is of George Herbert, whose parsonage at Bemerton (the name cannot at first be recalled) is connected for Tietjens with "the renaissance of Anglican saintliness."

36. Sheridan D. Blau, "The Poet as Casuist: Herbert's 'Church-Porch,'" and Robert B. Hinman, "The 'Verser' at *The Temple* Door: Herbert's *'The Church-porch,'*" in *"Too Riche to Clothe the Sunne": Essays on George Herbert*, ed. Claude J. Summers and Ted-Larry Pebworth, pp. 55–75.

37. Both Martz, *The Poetry of Meditation*, pp. 288–320, and Summers, *George Herbert*, pp. 73–94, devote chapters to the structure of *The Temple*. See also Elizabeth Stambler, "The Unity of Herbert's *Temple*"; John D. Walker, "The Architectonics of George Herbert's *The Temple*"; Valerie Carnes, "The Unity of George Herbert's *The*

that the overall order of the poems may best be thought of, as Amy Charles has remarked, as "personal, intuitive, and allusive."[38] I have assumed throughout that it is indeed pointless to tamper with the order and that at least part of the impulse to tamper arises out of confusion between two notions of "order," both applicable to a reading experience of *The Temple.* The quality that T. S. Eliot, commending the style of the sermons of Lancelot Andrewes, called "ordonnance, or arrangement and structure,"[39] must be distinguished from the largely speculative order of composition of the poems. I have assumed throughout that we would be mistaken to subscribe to the fullest implications of views of overall design in *The Temple,* which run the risk of surrendering a sense of historicity.[40] I shall tacitly be maintaining, nevertheless, that it is consistent to my purpose that discussion of Herbert's poems in a given order must rest entirely on dramatic, or poetically self-conscious, grounds.

In later chapters I test that assumption in a number of ways; before I can embark upon discussion of the lyrics of *The Temple,* however, I must lay the promised groundwork in a consideration of an Augustinian theory of signs, one that appealed in interesting and various ways to a number of medieval and Renaissance thinkers.

Temple: A Reconsideration"; and John R. Mulder, "George Herbert's *The Temple*: Design and Methodology." More recently, Fish, *The Living Temple,* pp. 154ff., has postulated an "aesthetic of the unfinished."

38. Amy Charles, "The Williams Manuscript and *The Temple*" p. 60. Accordingly, it has proved fruitful to seek order in smaller sequential units within *The Temple.* A fine recent example of this approach is Joseph Summers, "From 'Joseph's Coat' to 'A True Hymne.' "

39. T. S. Eliot, *For Lancelot Andrewes: Essays on Style and Order,* p. 15.

40. See, for instance, John R. Mulder, "*The Temple* as Picture," in "*Too Riche to Clothe the Sunne,*" ed. Summers and Pebworth, pp. 3–14.

2. Augustinian Theory

Divine Signs as "Visible Words"

Augustine

In Book 10 of the immensely influential *Confessions,* Augustine externalizes and dramatizes the consequences of attempting to postulate the Divine in any other way than through things perceptible by means of his senses; as a result, what he observes he concludes to constitute the evidence of a Creator. This Creator cannot be perceived directly, yet he is considered to exist, and consequently everything that can be perceived comes to be interpreted as evidence for his existence. Augustine scoured the natural world for God:

> I asked the Earth, and it said I am not he; and all things that are in the Earth confest the same. I asked the Sea, and those deep bottomes, and the creeping creatures; and they answered, *we are not thy God, seeke him above us.* I asked the subtle Ayre, & this Ayre, with all the Inhabitantes thereof sayd, *Anaximenes is deceaved, I am not thy God.* I askt the *Heavens,* the *Sun,* the *Moone* & the *Stars; neither are we* (say they) *the God that thou seekest.* And I said to all these creatures which are subject to my senses, *Concerning my God you have told me that you are not he; Tell me now somwhat of what he is?* And they cryed out with a loud voyce, *It is he, that made us.*[1]

The theme is recurrent in Augustine: the created world can be

1. Interrogavi terram, et dixit, Non sum; et quaecumque in eadem sunt, idem confessa sunt. Interrogavi mare et abyssos, et reptilia animarum vivarum, et responderunt: Non sumus Deus tuus; quaere super nos. Interrogavi auras flabilles, et inquit universus aer cum incolis suis: Fallitur Anaximenes, non sum Deus. Interrogavi coelum, solem, lunam, stellas; neque nos sumus Deus quem quaeris, inquiunt. Et dixi omnibus iis quaes circumstant fores carnis meae: Dixistis mihi de Deo meo quod vos non estis, dicite mihi de illo aliquid. Et exclamaverunt voce magna: Ipse fecit nos (Ps. 99:3). Augustine, *Confessionum S. Augustini* 10, vi; *PL* 32, col. 783. The translation is that of Sir Toby Matthew (1620), pp. 472–73 (see *Augustine* in Bibliography).

directly observed but the Creator cannot; he can be only inferred from the evidence of the senses.

> For I see those things which my God has made, but I cannot see my God himself who made them.[2]

And elsewhere in the *Enarrationes,* Augustine conceives of a Divine

> who is everywhere secret, yet known to all; whom no-one is allowed to know, yet of whom no-one can be unaware.[3]

The notion that a knowledge of the Divine cannot be arrived at by any more direct means than through contemplation of created things persists in later writing influenced by Augustine. Although we cannot claim that it originated with Augustine, we can certainly say that wherever it occurs it marks a thinker as standing in an "Augustinian tradition" of spirituality.

According to Augustine, signs were created by God, who confers upon reality its potential for significance.[4] To its very nature, a theory of signs concedes an interpretative role to man; in the theological Augustinian conception, man was considered capable only of discovering and using signs. Their significance was "given"; man did not in any sense invent it. The authoritative statement in Augustine's writings for the idea that God communicates with his creature man by means of signs seems to be the distillation of Neoplatonism in *De Doctrina Christiana.* In Book 4 of this work Augustine contrasts the eloquence of words with the far greater eloquence of divine truth. Before he does this, however, Augustine makes an important distinction:

> All teaching is by means of either "things" or signs, but it is through signs that things are learned. Now I have defined as "things" objects

2. Video enim quae fecerit Deus meus, non autem video ipsum Deum meum qui fecit haec. Augustine, *Enarrationes in Psalmos* 41, vii; *PL* 36, col. 467.

3. Qui ubique secretus est, ubique publicus; quem nulli licet ut est cognoscere, et quem nemo permittitur ignorare. Augustine, *Enarrationes in Psalmos* 44, ix; *PL* 36, col. 952.

4. Augustine, *De Doctrina Christiana* 2, ii (3), etc; *PL* 34, col. 37, etc. See J. A. Mazzeo, *Renaissance and Seventeenth Century Studies,* p. 6, etc. In what follows I have drawn extensively on Mazzeo's work. See also Grover A. Zinn, Jr., "Book and Word: The Victorine Background of Bonaventura's Use of Symbols," pp. 147–48.

> which are not primarily communicative, such as sticks, stones, sheep and suchlike. But I do not mean that particular stick which we read that Moses threw into the bitter water to make it drinkable; nor that stone which Jacob used as a pillow; nor that ram which Abraham sacrificed in place of his son. For those, although they are things, are also signs of other things. Furthermore, there are other signs which are communicative in their use, such as words. For no-one uses words unless they wish to communicate. From this it is clear what I mean by "signs"—that is to say those things which are primarily communicative. Moreover each sign is also in some way a thing, for that which is no thing is nothing at all. It is however not the case that every thing is a sign.[5]

Signs include both the verbal and the nonverbal; it is the latter that can allegorize by approximating some conception of the Divine, and this realization accounts for what Augustine refers to elsewhere as "a kind of eloquence in events rather than words."[6] In communicating with each other, however, we customarily use verbal signs; still, there are a few occasions when we may use nonverbal ones:

> Generally speaking, of those signs which men use to communicate their feelings to each other, some are visual and some are aural, and a very few involve the other senses. When we nod we are only communicating *visually* that which we wish our audience to understand, and certain people convey many things by using gestures; actors communicate in addition by using the studied movements of all their limbs, and with their eyes alone can almost tell whole stories; military standards and flags indicate visually the wish of their leader. All these things are as it were visible words. However as I have said most signs are aural, especially words. Trumpets, flutes and harps often give not only pleas-

5. Omnis doctrina vel rerum est vel signorum, sed res per signa discuntur. Proprie autem nunc res appellavi, quae non ad significandum aliquid adhibentur, sicuti est lignum, lapis, pecus, atque hujusmodi caetera. Sed non illud lignum quod in aquas amaras Moysen misisse legimus, ut amaritudine carerent (Exod. 15:25); neque ille lapis quem Jacob sibi ad caput posuerat (Gen. 27:11); neque illud pecus quod pro filio immolavit Abraham (Gen. 22:13). Hae namque ita res sunt, ut aliarum etiam signa sint rerum. Sunt autem alia signa quorum omnis usus in significando est, sicuti sunt verba. Nemo enim utitur verbis, nisi aliquid significandi gratia. Ex quo intelligitur quid appellem signa; res eas videlicet quae ad significandum aliquid adhibentur. Quamobrem omne signum etiam res aliqua est; quod enim nulla res est, omnino nihil est: non autem omnis res etiam signum est. Augustine, *De Doctrina Christiana* 1, ii (2); *PL* 34, cols. 19–20.

6. Non verborum, sed rerum eloquentia. Augustine, *De Civitate Dei* 11, xviii; *PL* 41, col. 332.

> ant sounds but significant ones. Yet all these signs are very few in number compared with words. For words are by far the most important tools which enable men to communicate what they have in their minds—if of course they wish to give themselves away.[7]

Augustine's concept of *verba visibilia* ("visible words") is of particular interest since it reflects his feeling that communication by nonverbal signs is somehow nobler: the examples he gives of signs involving the senses of smell, taste, and touch are notable in being taken not from everyday communication on the part of men, but from episodes during the Incarnation of Christ (cf. Mazzeo, p. 6):

> Our Lord himself gave a particular sign by means of the perfumed ointment with which his feet were bathed; and communicated his will by the Sacrament of eating his body and drinking his blood, and when the woman touched the hem of his garment and was healed, it was not lacking in significance. But the great majority of signs by which men express their thoughts are words.[8]

Greek thought characteristically takes this further than Augustine does in order to arrive at a feeling that silence is actually nobler than words; words thereby become a form of communication that results from, and consequently draws attention to, man's fallen nature. Thus the earlier Greek Father, Ignatius, went so far as to state that the Incarnation was itself a descent, from silence to

7. Signorum igitur quibus inter se homines sua sensa communicant, quaedam pertinent ad oculorum sensum, pleraque ad aurium, paucissima ad caeteros sensus. Nam cum innuimus, non damus signum nisi oculis ejus quem volumus per hoc signum voluntatis nostrae participem facere. Et quidam motu manuum pleraque significant: et histriones omnium membrorum motibus dant signa quaedam scientibus, et cum oculis eorum quasi fabulantur; et vexilla draconesque militares per oculos insinuant voluntatem ducum: et sunt haec omnia quasi quaedam verba visibilia. Ad aures autem quae pertinent, ut dixi, plura sunt, in verbis maxime. Nam et tuba, et tibia, et cithara, dant plerumque non solum suavem, sed etiam significantem sonum. Sed haec omnia signa verbis comparata paucissima sunt. Verba enim prorsus inter homines obtinuerunt principatum significandi quaecumque animo concipiuntur, si ea quisque prodere velit. Augustine, *De Doctrina Christiana* 2, iii (4); *PL* 34, col. 37.

8. Nam et odore unguenti Dominus, quo perfusi sunt pedes ejus, signum aliquod dedit (John 12:3, 7); et Sacramento corporis et sanguinis sui praegustato, significavit quod voluit (Luke 22:19, 20); et cum mulier tangendo fimbriam vestimenti ejus, salve facta est, nonnihil significat (Matt. 9: 21): sed innumerabilis multitudo signorum, quibus suas cogitationes homines exerunt, in verbis constituta est. Augustine, *De Doctrina Christiana* 2, iii (4); *PL* 34, cols. 37–38.

words;[9] the silence is luminously revelatory, and words, as always, are only representations.

Whether or not George Herbert was familiar with all these ideas, there can be no doubt that they illuminate our reading of a poem such as "The Bag" (1633, pp. 145–46), a poem that customarily attracts attention largely on account of the bizarre conceit of Christ's sidewound as a "postbag" in which messages may be conveyed to God. Though conceitful treatment of the wound is traditional,[10] Herbert's treatment in his poem is intense and unusual enough to have provoked, from Robert Graves, an early reading as controversial as that offered by William Empson.[11] The strangeness of Herbert's conceit tends to draw the reader's attention away from the treatment of Christ's Incarnation, so that traditional features of the poem are less often noticed. We should not be distracted by the poem's remarkable presentation of scriptural narrative, although we may note that it conflates the language of the Nativity with that of the parable of the Good Samaritan so as to present Christ's time on earth as beginning in an "inne" and as ending with his settling mankind's account with his own life:

When he was come, as travellers are wont,
    He did repair unto an inne.
    Both then, and after, many a brunt
    He did endure to cancell sinne:
    And having giv'n the rest before,
Here he gave up his life to pay our score. (19–24)

We shall see that conflation of this sort is characteristic of Herbert. What it may distract us from is a realization that the Incarnation, in addition to being a "putting-on" of flesh, is seen in this poem to involve Christ in the loss of divine attributes that the human mind

9. Cited by Mazzeo, *Renaissance and Seventeenth Century Studies*, pp. 22–23.

10. In addition to the widespread sacramental typology—"as sinne came, so Sacraments might flow" ("The Sacrifice" [1633, pp. 19–26], 247)—see the *Soliloquies* attributed to Bonaventura (London, 1655) for a meditation on the wound being "opened to suffer thee to enter therein" (p. 88; sig. E7^v).

11. See Robert Graves, *Poetic Unreason and Other Studies*, pp. 57–63. Graves read the poem in sexual terms, and, as Vendler remarks, citing Graves's reading, Christ is more than once given female attributes by Herbert. See Helen Vendler, *The Poetry of George Herbert*, p. 292.

can only figure as, in Herbert's words, "majestick robes of glorie." Christ does nothing less than divest himself of these ennobling qualities when, while riding in the heavens, he

> Resolv'd to light; and so one day
> He did descend, undressing all the way.
>
> The starres his tire of light and rings obtain'd,
> The cloud his bow, the fire his spear,
> The sky his azure mantle gain'd.
> And when they ask'd, what he would wear;
> He smil'd and said as he did go,
> He had new clothes a making here below. (11–18)

The distribution of spiritual attributes among the stars, cloud, and sky certainly recalls the episode in Christ's passion evoked in "The Sacrifice":

> They part my garments, and by lot dispose
> My coat, the type of love, which once cur'd those
> Who sought for help, never malicious foes:
> Was ever grief like mine?[12]

The point I want to stress, however, is that the initial resolution to "light" is made in revelatory silence; it is not until the actual descent to earth begins that Christ speaks (18). Prior to this, questioned by his celestial beneficiaries, Christ is portrayed as having "smil'd." This supremely communicative Augustinian "sign" is followed by an indirectly reported reply, and it is not until Christ has received the "blow upon his side" (29) that there is any direct speech. From this point on the narrative treatment of the Incarnation is at an end.

"The Bag" offers grounds for suggesting Herbert's familiarity in general terms with the Augustinian belief that man was incapable of conveying the supreme eloquence of the thing itself (*res*) but must fall back on the different order of eloquence of words (*verba*), and that in submitting to the Incarnation the Divine, too, submitted to this inability. According to Augustinian belief, then, Christ descended from silence to a world of words in assuming human

12. "The Sacrifice" (1633, pp. 19–26), 241–44.

form. Elsewhere in *The Temple* we may discern a more specifically conceived relationship between verbal articulacy (as necessarily mediating communication between God and man) and the incarnational notion of "dressing." In "Ephes. 4. 30." (1633, pp. 128–29), Herbert writes:

> Almightie God doth grieve, he puts on sense. (16)

Heather Asals has recently written of this aspect of Herbert's expressiveness, relating "Christ's putting on of humanity and humanity's putting on of Christ" to Herbert's poetic vocation, and referring to an immediate scriptural source for the incarnational notion in Rom. 13:12, where the reader is exhorted to "put on Christ."[13] Yet this is not all that needs to be said: we cannot doubt a clear connection in Herbert's mind between such an exhortation, his desire for poetic and moral harmony, and the "dressing" of man as priest. This hieratic ritual is typified in the Old Testament figure and narrative of Aaron and undertaken in Herbert's poem of that name (1633, pp. 168–69) by gracious means, enabling its speaker to mediate between God and his fellow men.

Man's role in relation to communication with God is therefore interpretative: Augustine's thought clearly implies that in order to be apprehended by man at all, God must somehow both divest himself of certain qualities and assume others, including communication through words. Where man was not involved, we may imagine that God was conceived of not only communicating in senses other than the verbal but also being communicated with in ways other than the interpretative. We may suppose that the very existence of words and signs should be seen as a function of man's fallen nature and the act of interpretation as consequently inevitable. Indeed, we might adduce Michel Foucault's assertion that "the function proper to knowledge is not seeking or demonstrating; it is interpreting."[14] But, having done so, we would need to stress that Foucault's remark is helpful to have in mind only as long as we remember that what was being interpreted, for Augustine and his

13. Heather Asals, *Equivocal Predication: George Herbert's Way to God*, pp. 38–39.
14. Michel Foucault, trans., *The Order of Things* (*Les Mots et les Choses*), p. 40.

followers, had to do with the existence of a transcendent realm, to which the signs that are a function of man's fallen nature constantly and frustratingly draw attention. The signs are frustrating because they have the effect of suggesting that what characterizes the transcendent realm, of which man may occasionally catch glimpses, is something that cannot be known; yet knowledge must continually strive toward it. The goal, if it could be attained, would be the supreme eloquence of *res*. The use of *verba*, of significant communication, provides man with a perpetual reminder of his fallen nature by allowing him these glimpses, forcing him to interpret. Yet although man is compelled toward acts of interpretation, his acts must constantly be predicated by a sense of opacity, of the unclear and the obscure. Even if man attempted to "read" those things that were not verbal words, he was nevertheless, for Augustine, engaging in an act of interpretation. Every sign, including the verbal, was a thing, since in the Augustinian scheme it existed by virtue of its Creator; but every thing was not necessarily a sign, *though it could be read as a sign*. As such it was capable of taking on sacramental significance, as a communication from the Divine.

From Augustinian theory, therefore, it was possible to arrive at a notion of two kinds of signs: verbal and nonverbal. Clearly, the Scriptures contained the verbal kind, although nonverbal signs were also to be found there, as in Augustine's examples of significance in the senses of smell, taste, and touch. There was, too, a more general kind of significance in the Scriptures. This would later come to be seen more explicitly in typological terms, and we cannot doubt the typological interpretation that Augustine was pointing toward in speaking of "a kind of eloquence in events rather than in words." Indeed, attitudes to the scriptural canon from the time of the Apostles onward tend to regard all other people and events described in Scripture as "types" of Christ and of his life and death,[15] for this way of looking at the Scriptures could be supported by the teaching of Christ himself, reaching sophisti-

15. See, for example, Heb. 3:1–6; 5:1–10, etc.

cated levels in the Church Fathers beginning with Ambrose.[16] In fact, Christian typology is unique, and A. C. Charity presents an extremely useful working definition. He offers two definitions of typology itself,

> neither of which applies commonly to the use of the word in non-theological writing. Typology, in the first of these senses, may be defined as either the broad study, or any particular presentation, of the quasi-symbolic relations which one event may appear to bear to another—especially, but not exclusively, when these relations are the analogical ones existing between events which are taken to be one another's "prefiguration" and "fulfilment." The second definition is a comparatively dogmatic and idealistic one, intended to apply only to a Christian typology, though, with only the last two words omitted, it might serve the same dogmatic purpose for the Old Testament as for the New: according to this definition, Christian typology is "the science of history's relations to its fulfilment in Christ." (Charity, p. 1)

Typology should be seen as distinct from allegorism because of its dependence on a historical framework of revelation (Lampe and Woollcombe, p. 40). People and events in the Scriptures were capable of interpretation in this particular way: they could be seen as a nonverbal representation of the reality the Scriptures described in verbal terms.

This nonverbal signification could be applied not only to the Scriptures but also to the world that the Scriptures describe. The external world that man perceives also had potential for significance, and the reader of Augustine may be struck by the familiarity of Foucault's rhetoric: "The face of the world is covered with blazons, with characters, with ciphers and obscure words—with 'hieroglyphics'. . . . And the space inhabited by immediate

16. A celebrated example is Christ's adducing the episode (Num. 21:9) of the brazen serpent: "As Moses lifted up the serpent in the wilderness, even so must the Son of man be lifted up" (John 3:14). See in particular the studies of Jean Daniélou, such as *The Lord of History,* trans. Nigel Abercrombie, and *From Shadows to Reality,* trans. Dom Wulstan Hibberd; also G. W. H. Lampe and K. J. Woollcombe, *Essays on Typology,* and A. C. Charity, *Events and their Afterlife: The Dialectics of Christian Typology in the Bible and Dante.* In *The Lord of History* (p. 140), Daniélou cites the definition in Aquinas, *Summae Theologicae Ia,* q. 1, art. 10, the import of which (see ad. 1) is that typology is not a meaning of words but a meaning of things.

resemblances becomes like a vast open book; it bristles with written signs. . . . All that remains is to decipher them" (Foucault, p. 27). For Augustine the whole created world was nothing less than a set of symbols of the Divine; it was a sublime poem whose words were created things and whose silent voice was the voice of its Creator.[17] This is Augustine's restatement of Neoplatonism in terms of a mystical theology in which every "thing"—that is, every created thing—had become a metaphor for what is unseen and incomprehensible.

Augustine's conceit of the world as a sublime poem was taken up by later writers. It emerged in Alan de Lisle and reappeared in the *Imitatio Christi*; the natural world was seen as a book that man could read.[18] The literary topic represents a particular refinement of the Augustinian conceit and is expressed by two later thinkers, Hugh of St. Victor (ca. 1091–1141) and Bonaventura (1221–74), in ways that seem to have especially close bearings on the seventeenth century in general and Herbert in particular.[19] Hugh later came to be regarded as *alter Augustinus* ("the second Augustine"), and the catholicity of his interests placed him very high in the estimation of the Franciscan scholastic Bonaventura.[20]

17. See Mazzeo, *Renaissance and Seventeenth Century Studies*, pp. 11 and 24; Mazzeo cites Augustine, *Epist.* 55, vii (13); *PL* 33, cols. 210, and *De Civitate Dei* 11, xviii; *PL* 41, col. 332.

18. E. R. Curtius, *European Literature and the Latin Middle Ages*, trans. Willard R. Trask, pp. 319–23.

19. Ruth Wallerstein's discussion of medieval expressions of the Book of Creatures includes the Victorines and Bonaventura, though not in the context of the dichotomy between this book and the Book of Scripture that I see as characteristic of these writers; see her *Studies in Seventeenth-Century Poetic*, pp. 203–213, etc. In what follows I discuss the notion of dichotomy in Hugh and Bonaventura in the belief that the twofold book constitutes by far the most persistent and influential expression of Victorine and Bonaventurine book symbolism. I am, however, aware that in certain other (and arguably less definitive) works, these writers distinguish a third book, the Book of Life, which, properly read in heaven, illuminates the other two (see Zinn, "Book and Word," pp. 151 and 163).

20. Bonaventura, *Opusculum de reductione artium ad theologiam*, p. v; *Opera Omnia* 5, p. 321. Cited in D. E. Luscombe, *The School of Peter Abelard*, p. 184. A seven-volume folio of the works of Bonaventura appeared in Rome between 1588 and 1596, and another was printed there in 1609. A folio of Hugh's works appeared at Venice in 1588, and there were further printings at Mainz and Cologne in 1617; all were three-volume editions. Neither the British nor Bodleian libraries possesses any single edition of Hugh's *De Sacramentis* or Bonaventura's *Breviloquium* dating from after the first quarter of the sixteenth century. This information is not con-

Hugh of St. Victor

Hugh accepted the Augustinian idea that an invisible Creator was apprehensible by man from the signs of a visible creation. Aware that there are different degrees of creation, including the nonsentient, the sentient but not rational, and the sentient and the rational, Hugh transformed the Augustinian idea into a systematic hierarchy. Yet there are certainly elements of a hierarchy in Augustine, as the passage from the *Confessions* 10 indicates. In the *Meditations* later and erroneously ascribed to Augustine, the writer, realizing that man's rationality sets him apart from the rest of creation, provided an instance of what was later to become a celebrated topic; other users of the "ladder of ascent" include Bonaventura himself (in his *Itinerarium mentis ad Deum*) and the sixteenth-century Jesuit Robert Bellarmine. Here is a passage from the *Meditations*, translated by Antony Batt (1624):

> Lett my minde . . . passe beyonde what soever is created: lett it runne, and ascende, and flie, and soare above them all, lookinge stedfastlie with the eies of faith (as much as is possible) on him that hath created all thinges. For this cause, I will make (as it were) steppes or stayres in my hart, and by them I will ascende unto my soule, and from my soule into my understanding, and from thence unto God, who remaineth over my head. (p. 102)[21]

The essence of Hugh's hierarchy, however, lay in a distinction between the order of creation and that of cognition: in fact the one is exactly the opposite to the other. The order of creation suggested that those things were farthest from their Creator by means of which man first came to know the Creator. Given that all creatures are signs, man began to arrive at a knowledge of the Divine by

---

tained in extant *STC*'s. See also Wallerstein, *Studies in Seventeenth Century Poetic*, p. 51.

21. Transeat . . . animus, et transcendat omne quod creatum est, currat et ascendat, volitet et pertranseat, et in eum qui creavit omnia, quantum potest, oculos fidei dirigat. Faciam gradus ascensionis in corde meo et per ipsam animam meam, ascendam ad Deum meum, qui capiti meo desuper manet. Augustine, *Meditationes* 27; *PL* 40, cols. 921–22. The attribution is not now indubitable, as it was in the seventeenth century, though Migne includes it in an appendix to Augustine's works.

means of the lowest, least sentient, creatures, progressing through the merely sentient to the rational. Nonsentient corporeal creatures, viewed as representations of their Creator, signified only from a distance and resembled only partly; rational creatures, having been created in the image of their Creator, exhibited most completely, in terms both of their innate, given properties and of their capacity to interpret signs, their potential for clearly demonstrating the existence of the Creator. The uniqueness of the rational creature, man, was implicit in his conceptualization as the image of God.[22] Hugh considered that the significance of things was much greater than that of words:

> Few words can have more than two or three meanings, but any one "thing" can mean as many other things as may be inferred from its own visible or invisible properties.[23]

This conception of the language of things, that is, of "visible words," is rich but not unlimited. The theory of signs that Augustine developed, insofar as it applied to the Scriptures, had come, by the twelfth century, to be regarded in such a way that it was the words of Scripture that were thought of as conveying literally, whereas its things, by figuring other things, were thought of as conveying spiritually; both significations were given by God, but it was the latter that were the more flexible. By the time that Aquinas came to state it,[24] the idea was well established. From it, many Fathers, including Hugh, were able to deduce that those things that convey the meaning of sacred things are themselves sacred, and the belief that certain things were capable of rich sac-

22. For this account of Hugh I rely chiefly on Zinn, "Book and Word," pp. 143–69; though see also George L. Scheper, "Reformation Attitudes toward Allegory and the Song of Songs," p. 553.

23. Paucae voces plusquam duas aut tres significationes habent, res autem quaelibet tam multiplex potest esse in significatione aliarum rerum, quot in se proprietates visibiles aut invisibiles habet communes aliis rebus. Hugh of St. Victor, *De Scripturis et Scriptoribus Sacris praenotatiunculae* 14; *PL* 175, col. 21. Cited by E. H. Gombrich, *Icones Symbolicae*, p. 212n.

24. See Thomas Aquinas, *Quaestiones quod libetales* 7, art. 14, p. 145; "Videtur quod in eisdem verbis sacrae Scripturae non lateant plures sensus." Cited by Gombrich, *Icones Symbolicae*, pp. 13–14.

ramental signification may be regarded as of particular importance to Hugh.

For Hugh, literal signification corresponded to the body of man and was apprehended as the "outer" (*foris*); spiritual signification corresponded to man's soul and could be apprehended as the "inner" (*intus*).[25] For my purposes this formulation is extremely important. As might be expected of a writer familiar with the work of Augustine, Hugh conceptualized the perceived universe as a book written by the finger of God.[26] Man was capable of observing this book but could not take in its meaning. The outer was accessible to him because he could actually see it, but seeing the outer did not necessarily enable him to understand the inner. The former perception was tantamount to considering the beauty of the universe; the latter, if it could be achieved, to realizing that the universe had been created and to wondering at the wisdom of the Creator. The rational creature alone possessed the facility for interpreting what he perceived and alone had the potential for arriving at an inner reading of the universe, perceptible as the creation of God. All sentient creatures saw the outer; the rational creature man, who was the image of God, differed from the merely sentient in his capacity both to see the outer and to understand—potentially, at least—what it represented. For Hugh, in fact, the work of creation was a twofold book. The outer book contained what was apprehensible only by the sentient (or by the sentient part of man); the inner one contained what was apprehensible only by the spiritual (the angels and the spiritual part of man). Consequently, man's place was unique. When Sir Walter Raleigh referred to this uniqueness in the seventeenth century, he gave Gregory Nazianzen (ca. 323–83) as its authority; but the expression is comparable with Hugh's. Man was

> internally endued with a divine understanding, by which he might contemplate and serve his Creatour, after whose image he was formed, and endued with the powers and faculties of reason and other abilities, that thereby also he might governe and rule the world, and all other

25. Hugh of St. Victor, *De Sacramentis* 1, ix, 2; *PL* 176, col. 317.
26. Hugh of St. Victor, *Eruditiones didascalicae* 7, iv; *PL* 176, col. 814; see Zinn, "Book and Word," p. 156.

> Gods creatures therein. And whereas God created three sorts of living natures, (to wit) Angelicall, Rationall, and Brutall; giving to Angels an intellectuall, and to Beasts a sensuall nature, he vouchsafed unto man, both the intellectuall of Angels, the sensitive of Beasts, and the proper rationall belonging unto man; and therefore (saith GREGORIE NAZIANZENE:) *Homo est utriusque naturae vinculum, Man is the bond* and chaine *which tieth together both natures*: and because in the little frame of mans bodie there is a representation of all the parts thereof, therefore was man called *Microcosmus*, or the little world.[27]

Herbert's lines in "Mans medley" (1633, pp. 123–24) offer a remarkable echo of Raleigh's expression:

> To this life things of sense
> Make their pretence:
> In th'other Angels have a right by birth:
> Man ties them both alone,
> And makes them one,
> With th'one hand touching heav'n, with th'other earth.[28]

Hugh, too, had related man's uniqueness to the twofold book:

> And man is set in the middle, having both inner and outer senses. His inner senses are invisible, his outer ones visible; the inner ones being controlled by the mind, the outer ones by the body.[29]

In his interpretation of the cosmos, the creation of God, man had therefore to aspire to the role of mediator between the inner and outer books. In so aspiring, he was attempting to emulate and even to imitate Christ's Incarnation in its mediatory aspect. The implications of this particular conceptualization of man as the image of God were profound: man had both a unique and a general place in the created order because he could mediate between

27. Sir Walter Raleigh, *The History of the World*, p. 30 (sig. $D3^{v}$). The marginal note is "*Greg. Nazianz. Epist. Omnis in homine creatura, & coelum & terra*". There is a reference to Hugh on the very first page of Raleigh's work, though as always the problem in treating such citations as primary sources lies in our knowing very little of the extent to which these sources were disseminated through commonplace books.

28. Lines 7–12. "Pretence" (8) is a genuine claim to ownership; it does not connote usurpation here (cf. *NED* 1a, 3a).

29. Et positus est in medio homo ut intus et foris sensum haberet. Intus ad invisibilia, foris ad visibilia. Intus per sensum rationis, foris per sensum carnis. Hugh of St. Victor, *De Sacramentis* 1, vi, 5; *PL* 176, col. 266.

the visible and the invisible. Other Herbert poems, notably "Providence," strongly suggest awareness of these implications.

What emerges from Hugh's important distinction between God's two works? Man, standing before God's creation, saw it as the outer book; in his fallen state he could not do more. But he was capable of being inwardly renewed, and in such a state he could read the inner book also. God's work of creation contained both an inner and an outer book: in his fallen state man could read only the outer; however, by means of God's other work, the work of "restoration" recorded in the Scriptures, he could discern the meaning of the inner book of the work of creation. Only the man who was inwardly renewed could properly read God's outward signs in the universe, and such a reading implied inner understanding: it was only through the work of restoration that man could again perceive what he once perceived—the "symbolic" or "significant" dimension of the universe, the work of foundation (cf. Zinn, p. 157). Bonaventura's doctrine of the Fall of Man was to make this plain. Hugh's formulation is considerably more complex than this brief account suggests, but its complexity does not detract from his emphasis on a "restored," healthy interpretation of the cosmos on man's part.

It is evident that Hugh was anxious to regard the teaching laid down in the *De Sacramentis* as definitive. If the reader found any disparities between it and any of Hugh's other disseminated works, he wrote; and if perhaps anything had to be corrected in the others, the reader might adjust the disparities according to the norm provided by the *De Sacramentis.*[30] This apparent desire to crystallize developing theory encourages Hugh's reader to give the work special attention. It does contain the most carefully argued formulation that Bonaventura is likely to have received of Victorine interpretations of the communications of the Divine through the cosmos and through the Scriptures to man, the reader of signs.

30. *De Sacramentis* praef.; *PL* 176, cols. 173–74.

Bonaventura

Bonaventura's own formulation of the dichotomy between the books of Scripture and Nature depends on the Victorine distinction between *intus* and *foris*. Bonaventura's terminology is of a more scholastic nature than Hugh's: he is almost exactly coeval with the Dominican Aquinas (1225–74), though he represents a scholasticism of a more Franciscan temper than the Aristotelian influence of the Dominican scholastics. But the influence of Hugh is undubitable. There are references to the *De Sacramentis* in Bonaventura's own gratifyingly short "summa," the *Breviloquium*, which contains the salient points of the vast *Commentary* on Peter Lombard's *Sentences*. For Bonaventura, divine perfection was expressed in two books, an inner and an outer. In stating this, Bonaventura built on Hugh's notion of man, *positus . . . in medio*, who had at least the potential for reading both the inner and the outer, and was thereby unique among God's creation:

> The first principle made the sensible world in order to make himself known so that as it were by a trace and a mirror man should be led back to loving and praising God the creator. In accordance with this conception there is a double book: one written in an inner fashion, which is the eternal art and wisdom of God, and the other written in an outer fashion, that is, the apprehensible world. Since there was one creature whose sense was wholly inner for an understanding of the inner book, that is, the angel, and another whose sense was wholly outer, that is, the brute animal, so for the perfection of the universe there ought to be a creature with the two senses mentioned above to understand the book written in both inner and outer fashion, that is, of the wisdom of God and his work. And because in the person of Christ the eternal wisdom and his work are one, he is said to be the book written in both inner and outer fashion.[31]

31. Primum principium fecit mundum istum sensibilem ad declarandum se ipsum, videlicet ad hoc, quod per illum tanquam per speculum et vestigium reduceretur homo in Deum artificem amandum et laudandum. Et secundum hoc duplex est *liber*, unus scilicet scriptus *intus*, qui est aeterna Dei ars et sapientia; et alius scriptus *foris*, mundus scilicet sensibilis. Cum igitur esset una creatura, quae sensum habebat *intus* ad cognitionem libri *interioris*, ut Angelus; et alia, quae totum sensum habebat *foris*, ut quodlibet animal brutum: ad perfectionem universitatis debuit fieri creatura, quae hoc sensu duplici esset praedita ad cognitionem libri scripti *intus et foris*, id est Sapientiae et sui operis. Et quia in Christo simul concurrit aeterna Sapientia et eius opus in una persona; ideo dicitur *liber scriptus intus et foris*. Bonaventura, *Breviloquium* 2, xi, 2; *Opera* 5, p. 229.

Christ in the Incarnation was the perfection of what man strives toward. Christ perfectly reconciled, and man attempts to reconcile, the *liber intus* (the Book of Divine Ideas, which the angels were solely equipped to read) with the *liber foris* (the Book of Appearances, beyond which the sentient creatures could not read).

Bonaventura gave strong emphasis to the Fall of Man. His doctrine of the Fall[32] stressed that, whereas the prelapsarian Adam knew everything without ever having learned anything, postlapsarian man was condemned to seek and find knowledge empirically, through the use of senses, memory, and experience. Postlapsarian man was unable to reconcile the inner and the outer books. Bonaventura's best modern commentator, Etienne Gilson, recognizes that to Bonaventura the Fall is "the decisive event that governs the whole history of humanity."[33] Gilson admirably summarizes Bonaventura's expression of this event:

> By the very fact that God permitted man to read both books, He permitted him to choose between them. Two expressions of the divine essence were offered to man's intellect, and two imitations of the divine perfection were offered to his will; man could contemplate God in the clear mirror of his ideas or see Him across the endlessly varied symbols of things. But by reason of this free choice, man found himself in a condition of unstable equilibrium. Apt to see in things what the animal cannot see in them and the angel has no need to see in them, he could be solicited by a curiosity necessarily unknown to beings more perfect or less perfect than himself. . . . From the moment he attributed subsistence to things and relied upon his senses to study them in themselves, man could no longer attain any stable object or immutable truth; hence he was to be abandoned to himself in the midst of things good but incomplete and incapable of satisfying either his thought or his desires. Such was the fall: an act of curiosity and pride. (pp. 436–37)

The point to be noticed about the inner book in this formulation is that it was regarded as the "clear mirror" of divine ideas. Once man's choice had been made, and he had in effect "fallen," this

32. See Bonaventura, *Commentaria . . . in secundum librum Sententiarum magistri Petri Lombardi* 23, ii, 1; *Opera* 2, pp. 537–38.

33. Etienne Gilson, *The Philosophy of St Bonaventure,* trans. Dom Illtyd Trethowan and F. J. Sheed, p. 434. I rely chiefly on Gilson for this account of Bonaventura.

clear mirror was no longer available. This meant that man did not clearly perceive God's subsequent appearances to raise him from his fallen state. Given that the original, prelapsarian books "accommodated"[34] the Divine to man's comprehension, subsequent "theophanies" to postlapsarian man (as E. H. Gombrich terms them)[35] were interpreted only dimly and with difficulty. Gilson summarizes the effect of the Fall on man's perception of the two-fold Book of Nature:

> As long as he remained in the state of original justice, he possessed the knowledge of all creatures and, regarding them as so many images or representations of God, he was led by them to praise God and adore Him and love Him. So doing, man not only attained his own end, but enabled the universe to attain its. A world which exists only to show forth God to the mind of man achieves its purpose only if man's mind sees God in it—*et ad hoc sunt creaturae et sic reducuntur in Deum*—for this creatures exist and so they are brought back to God. But once man turned from wisdom to look for natural knowledge and claimed to discover a meaning for the world intrinsic in the world itself, he was attempting an absurdity and seeking the meaning of a book which had lost its meaning. (pp. 438–39)

Man was unable to discern clearly the mirror of divine ideas, and he was unable any longer to read the Book of Nature properly because he had turned from cause to effect and tried to make sense of cause simply by observing effect. Yet, in itself, effect was now incomprehensible to him: "It is of the nature of fallen knowledge—when it reasons *as* fallen—to be unaware of its own fallenness" (Gilson, p. 434). Furthermore, the universe that had been created for the sake of man's own soul, and that man been able to use, not only to preserve his life but—primarily—as his means of acquiring wisdom, had been affected in its entirely by man's Fall in such a way as to lead both to its separation from God and to its apparent meaninglessness in the eyes of postlapsarian man (Gilson, p. 438). This state of affairs is poignant: man's perceptions are inadequate, yet they are all he has. Bonaventura did, however,

34. I accept here the *New Catholic Encyclopedia*'s definition of "accommodation" as the "adaptation of the Divine to the possibilities of man and the conditions of his existence" (vol. 1, p. 80).

35. Gombrich (*Icones Symbolicae*, p. 151) uses the term to indicate the divine choice for the form in which he wishes to appear to man.

point out in both the *Breviloquium* and the *In hexaemeron* that partial recovery at least had been made possible by the theophany granted in the Book of Scripture. He equated this with the work of "restoration" far more directly than did Hugh. Working in a tradition accepted into Western Christianity by Augustine, Bonaventura regarded the Book of Scripture as having been written encyclopedically;[36] it acted as a kind of dictionary that enabled man to recapture something of the prelapsarian sense of the universe and man's place in it. Perhaps Hugh's sacramental emphasis is not quite so marked in Bonaventura; at any rate, Scripture "restores to us some part of the knowledge held and lost by Adam" (Gilson, p. 440).

As a result of man's Fall, then, there was a shift in the opposition between two parts of the Victorine "work of foundation." The situation before the Fall had been that there were two books, *intus* and *foris*. Man had been unique among sentient creatures in that, like the angels, he could read the "language" of both; the sentient creatures other than man could read the *foris* but not the *intus*. After the Fall, in which man in a single act of curiosity and pride unwarrantedly placed prior emphasis on the *liber foris* (where no emphasis at all should have been placed), the clarity of the *liber intus* became impossibly clouded: man's epistemological error had rendered it illegible and therefore meaningless. It was for this reason that God graciously provided the Book of Scripture. Its role was to act as a substitute for the lost *liber intus*, enabling man to interpret once more the cosmos, his place in it, and the altered relation that now existed between himself and God. The *liber foris* remained, affected by man's Fall to an extent that made it, too, largely illegible, but now there at least existed a possibility of deciphering it with the aid of Scripture. Scripture pointed toward, and indicated both typologically and actually, the culminating events in the work of restoration, that is, the Incarnation. In itself it was a guide: "In the general economy of the work of restoration, Scripture helps to restore to the universe its original signification" (Gilson, p. 441).

36. See Beryl Smalley, *The Study of the Bible in the Middle Ages*, p. 26.

Bonaventura's doctrine of the Fall of Man led him to restate, in the *Breviloquium,* Hugh's dichotomy between the work of restoration and the work of foundation. The Divine revealed himself to man in a twofold manner: as an "effective principle" through the *liber foris* (or, as in the *Breviloquium,* the *liber creaturae*) and as a "redeeming principle" through the *liber scripturae.* Hugh's "foundation" had become "effect," and his "restoration" had become "redemption."[37] The restatement was the result of Bonaventura's exposition of the Fall, so that his theoretical viewpoint was developed from a far more postlapsarian perspective than was Hugh's. Bonaventura's restatement now permitted a memorable opposition, between the topics of the Book of Nature (or Book of Creatures) and the Book of Scriptures, although it perhaps caused a certain loss in the richness of the Victorine concept of "restoration." However, we should bear in mind that Bonaventura, writing in the thirteenth century, may have desired to be unequivocally clear about the matter of redemption after the previous century's doctrinal controversies, insofar as these had centered around the heretical beliefs of Peter Abelard and their rebuttal by Hugh in the *De Sacramentis.*[38]

Conclusion

An Augustinian tradition of sign theory can be traced into the thought of the Middle Ages. In the writings of Hugh of St. Victor and Bonaventura the tradition develops into a twofold expression of a significantly revealed relation between God, man, and the rest of creation. This expression takes the form of two books. Man is regarded as unique among God's creatures in possessing at least the potential for "reading" the signs that these books contain. However, that potential has been severely, though not irreparably, damaged as a consequence of the Fall. Man no longer possesses intuitive gifts for apprehending the Creator and his own

37. Bonaventura, *Breviloquium* 2, v, 2; *Opera* 5, p. 22.
38. See D. E. Luscombe, *The School of Peter Abelard,* pp. 183–97.

place in the created order: instead, sense experience must be deployed in a semiological approach to what is perceived.

We must now turn to the ways in which Renaissance thinkers and writers developed this idea further. We shall see that several of them paid particular attention to man's depleted "reading" ability, and demonstrated their fascination at what (figuratively speaking) we may term man's "illiteracy." We shall see, too, that their work represents a way of thinking that appealed strongly to Herbert's poetic sensibility and takes arrestingly individual expressive forms in his work. In the next chapter I introduce the related topics of Renaissance interest in man's "illiteracy" and the manner in which Herbert's poems of suffering and grief illustrate his own documentation of sensory unreliability and perceptual error.

3. The "Hidden" God

Perceptual Error, Grief, and Suffering

There is no shortage of evidence to suggest that the line of thought traced in the previous chapter extends, in varied and interesting ways, into the sixteenth and seventeenth centuries. Indeed, it is Augustinian sign theory that in its implications underlies Renaissance orthodoxies as apparently various as the so-called ladder of creation and ideas of God's mercy in affliction.

The first of these is exemplified in a writer such as the Franciscan Bernard Ochino (1487–1564). Ochino's writings are of particular interest to students of seventeenth-century Anglicanism, since they were more than once translated into English in the sixteenth century.[1] One reason for this dissemination may lie in Ochino's exile from Italy, associated with his conversion to Protestantism in the 1540s. The works of such a convert were undoubtedly attractive to promoters of Reformation theology in England, and in Ochino's writings we may observe a particularly interesting combination of thought clearly acceptable to Protestant theology yet equally clearly derived from a scholastic Franciscan basis.[2] Ochino's most popular works seem to have been his sermons. In one of these, entitled "Howe to know God by hys creatures," the reader is exhorted not to be led aside by undue admiration of the creatures: unless we exercise caution, "thys ladder . . . to clyme

1. According to the *STC*, six editions of Ochino's sermons were published in English between 1548 and 1580.

2. Harold J. Grimm, *The Reformation Era 1500–1650*, pp. 281–82, and Roland H. Bainton, *Studies on the Reformation*, pp. 159–60, point out the resemblance of Ochino's to Savonarola's spirituality. In stressing similarities between medieval and Protestant Reformation theology, I find much of my argument here at variance with Barbara K. Lewalski's *Protestant Poetics and the Seventeenth Century*.

unto God is peryllous." But although God "some what discovereth him selfe by hys creatures . . . So he which entereth into this world . . . must of force know the maker thereof to be the God omnipotent."[3] Elsewhere, Ochino demonstrates both familiarity with the apposition of "creatures" and "Scriptures," and the view that the creatures as well as the Scriptures are significant means to a spiritual end. The writings of another and more influential Continental reformer, Peter Martyr (1500–1562), who left Italy with Ochino in 1542, suggest that such a view of "significance" is not unique to Ochino. This is all the more interesting in view of the probability of Martyr's direct influence on the sixteenth-century Anglican church through John Jewel (1522–71) and, consequently, Richard Hooker. According to Martyr:

> It is to be noted, that whereas God is a nature so dissevered from anie matter, as he cannot sensiblie be perceived; yet he hath been accustomed by signes and certeine sensible woords to declare himselfe. And those signes, which from the beginning have declared God unto us are creatures.[4]

As far as ideas of God's mercy in affliction are concerned, these appealed most obviously in the sixteenth century to thinkers of a more Calvinistic turn of mind but depend equally firmly on an expression of the need to read God's signs correctly. According to Calvin himself, "God ceasseth not to be mercifull unto us when he sendeth any affliction unto us,"[5] and the paradigmatic scriptural example of divinely permitted affliction was provided by Job. It could be deduced from a study of Job's afflictions that a disturbing experience of the Divine could be interpreted in such a way as to prompt self-discovery:

> God . . . hath a regarde of our ablenesse to beare, and according as wee bee practized with the induring of troubles, so sendeth he them too us

3. *Certayne Sermons of . . . Bernadine Ochine,* sigs. Aviii^r-Bi^r.

4. Peter Martyr Vermigli, *The Common Places . . . Translated and partly gathered by Anthonie Marten,* p. 12 (sig. C6^v). The chapter (1, ii) from which the quotation is taken is entitled "Of the naturall knowledge of God by the things created: & wherunto this knowledge tendeth" (p. 10). See Joseph C. McLelland, *The Visible Words of God: An Exposition of the Sacramental Theology of Peter Martyr Vermigli,* p. 47.

5. *Sermons of Master John Calvin, upon the booke of Job. Translated out of French by Arthur Golding,* p. 29 (sig. Bvii^r).

> smaller or greater. But when wee bee once as it were inured with them, then maye he the better lay full lode uppon us: for he hathe also given us wherewith too beare it oute. . . . But our afflictions are meane and sweete, if a man compare them with the afflictions that are spoken of heere. Therefore let us conclude, that God sheweth him selfe curteous and very pityfull towardes us, seeing wee bee chastized so gently at his hande, and that he keepeth such a measure as wee bee not racked too the uttermost, nor he useth so greate and excessive rigour as wee see heere in the person of Job.[6]

Calvin's associate Beza shares this belief; glossing Job 1:12 ("And the LORD said unto Satan, Behold, all that he hath is in thy power; only upon himself put not forth thine hand"), he concludes:

> Here we see how that God in trying and exercising those that be his, doth alwayes keepe a good measure. For he knoweth our strength beeing indeede the authour of it him selfe, above the which he will never suffer us to bee tempted.[7]

In fact, for one seventeenth-century writer, "Afflictions are Gods mould in which He casts His children."[8]

* * *

George Herbert's poems of suffering and misery are particularly amenable to consideration in terms of the expressive consequences of a view of man's consciousness as fallen. The fictions they present permit us as readers to see how it is that Herbert manages strategically to get across, by means of his exploitation of the limits of significant communication, his sense of relationship to God. What follows in this chapter depends on the realization that Renaissance responses to the sufferings of Job are to be seen as both standing directly in a tradition of Augustinian sign theory and exemplifying clearly the emotional, nonintellectualistic reading of divine signs that characterizes Herbert's poetry too. Herbert's poems of suffering depict his speakers at their remotest

6. Ibid., p. 38 (sig. Ciii^v).

7. Theodore Beza, *Job expounded by Theodore Beza, partly in manner of a Commentary, partly in manner of a Paraphrase*, sig. E4^v.

8. Joshua Henshaw, *Horae Succisivae, or, Spare Houres of Meditation*, p. 117 (sig. F9^r). There is still a copy of this volume in the church at Little Gidding, and it is very probably one of the books bound by Nicholas Ferrar's sisters.

reach from God, so that God frequently appears absent, deaf—or even dead—to the poet's cries. To consider these poems now will assist in our attempt at characterizing the ways in which Herbert expressively conveys the notion of man's "illiteracy," a concept upon which the argument of the next two chapters will depend. Those chapters' discussion of Herbert's poetic response to the topic of the books of Nature and Scripture will allow us to see his speakers approaching closer to God by rationalizing the significance of their experience in terms of apprehending the divine workings of Providence and Grace, respectively. In order to succeed in this strategy, however, Herbert's speakers must first learn that what are being experienced in moments of desolation *are* actually apprehensible in terms of their status as signs. Only then will they be able to read what Peter Martyr calls God's "signes and certeine sensible woords."

Let us return to Calvinistic commentary of Job's suffering. Job's experience could be seen not as symptomatic of "a certaine mutation and changeableness" on God's part; instead,

> truly God is one & the same to us both in wealth & woe, never changing his fatherly good will towards us, never abusing his rule over his children, no not then, when he exerciseth them with most grievous trialls to his owne glory; but most liberally crowning their patience, as the end of the story doth shew.[9]

How is it possible to draw this conclusion from such sufferings as Job's? We can seek an answer through examination of the impulse that Calvin, Beza, and others demonstrate in making sense of Job's experience; that is, we may watch them interpreting explicably what at first sight seems inexplicable. In the scriptural narrative God permits Satan to afflict Job with the loss of his children and possessions and with a loathsome skin disease. The rest of the Book of Job contains, through the advice of Job's three friends, and finally in conversation with God, Job's interpretation of his experience. Studying this interpretation of an experience that initially refuses to yield to explanation, we may observe changes in the attitudes and perception of the interpreter himself. It is useful to

9. Beza, *Job expounded by Theodore Beza,* sigs. F7^{v} and I6^{r}.

have in mind the term *accommodation* for what happens here: if the inexplicable persists in remaining inexplicable, the faculties and processes of interpretation may themselves yield and broaden, so that "interpretation" comes to include the accommodation of inexplicable phenomena to a framework within which they will, eventually, either become explicable or at least comfortably coexist with the interpreter. The perceived phenomena may change, in that they become adjusted to the perceptions of the interpreter.[10] In what follows we may be able to see this process in operation in some of the lyrics of *The Temple*. Herbert is frequently confronted with experience that at first sight appears meaningless. He must learn to interpret it as having "significance": it comes to be seen as a divine sign or "visible word." It is generally acknowledged that in their entirety the lyrics of *The Temple* are characterized both by an extraordinary sensitivity to the variability of spiritual moods and by a scrupulous precision in recording and reenacting those moods. The poems of suffering reflect great instability, and their fictions enact this instability specifically by means of attempts to catch the fleeting moment of joy and more generally through what Helen Vendler has so finely described as their "provisional" quality.[11] By this she refers to the way a poem by Herbert may be rewritten as it progresses so that the whole manner of his documentational reliability is ironically questioned, not only by the reader but self-consciously by the poet as well. Consequently, more than one account of an experience may coexist in a given poem, with arresting discrepancies between the various versions as a result.

The "provisional" quality in Herbert results from a fictively expressed unreliability affecting his sense-experience and is particularly apparent in the poems of affliction or misery. In poems such as these, which document what Herbert often refers to as his "griefs," the reader is made to feel that communication between the poet and God has been so seriously disrupted that God is con-

10. I take it that this is fundamentally in disagreement with E. D. Hirsch, Jr., *Validity in Interpretation* (see Chapter 1 above).

11. Helen Vendler, *The Poetry of George Herbert*, pp. 25ff.

ceived of and portrayed in terms that are far from divine. Indeed, we are reminded more of the unresponsive mistress celebrated by Elizabethan sonneteers writing in the Petrarchan tradition, but of course there are sacred as well as secular antecedents for expressiveness of this kind. Herbert's reader will be reminded not only of the sufferings of Job, but also of those of the Psalmist, of whose agonies some of these poems contain loose paraphrases.

In many ways Herbert's most Job-like poem is the famous "Affliction" [I] (1633, pp. 38–40), which details illness and the death of friends. We can see in certain other poems, such as "Submission" (1633, pp. 87–88), "The Size" (1633, pp. 131–32), and "The Rose" (1633, pp. 172–73) (arguably a rewritten version of "Submission"), an assured familiarity with what Calvin calls "such a measure as wee bee not racked too the uttermost," though in these poems the "measure" is seen in terms of joys present in moderation, rather than those of suffering. However, in "The Temper" [I] (1633, pp. 46–47), one of the senses of the title[12] is realized in Herbert's cry, with its reference to a reluctance to submit to the agonies that malleability seems to demand:

> O rack me not to such a vast extent;
>   Those distances belong to thee. (9–10)

"Affliction" [I] reveals a mood of particular bewilderment. It is a challenge to its reader for a number of reasons. Unlike most other poems of its kind in *The Temple,* it is conducted for the most part in a past-tense narrative, a form we usually associate in Herbert with moods of greater assurance than we find here. The end of the poem ("Ah my deare God! though I am clean forgot, / Let me not love thee, if I love thee not") is notoriously perplexing and was cited by William Empson as an example of "ambiguity by tautology."[13] Certainly, some such sense as "Do not permit me to love you (as your lover) if I do not truly love you" is present in these lines. And as Vendler has pointed out, the poem is unusual even

12. These are comprehensively explored by Fredson Bowers, "Herbert's Sequential Imagery: 'The Temper,'" pp. 202–213.
13. William Empson, *Seven Types of Ambiguity,* pp. 215–16.

in terms of a tradition of reproaching God, since it does not allow God a response.

While the response of the kind we find elsewhere in *The Temple* is missing here (there is no poem for a divine hand to complete, for instance, nor is there irruption into the form of a kind that destroys the human construct yet completes the poem), it is worth bearing in mind that what Vendler sees as "re-invention" results in "Affliction" [I] from Herbert's sensory inability. This inability leads to perceptual error, so that the various roles given to God in the poem may come to be seen as functions of Herbert's own disordered perceptions. The lack of response allowed to God would then be consistent with the strategy Herbert chooses; the perceptual errors that constitute his apprehension of God in this particular poem are all qualified, one after another; each attempts to correct the one preceding it and each is reenacted so that, in Vendler's words, "they show Herbert's care and accuracy in describing his own notions of God as they changed from episode to episode" (Vendler, p. 43). The expressions of what Herbert perceived God to be are all realized visually. Perceptual disorder, in that God apparently changes from what he seemed to be before and does not in any of these disguises show those qualities we traditionally associate with the Divine, is expressed as a function of Herbert's sight. This has not been "cleared" by the end of the poem, and the last lines do not expand that view, so that the multiple perspective is highly ironic. The limitations of viewpoint have the effect of making the various postures and roles of God seem more "real" than they would be had the poet's sight been cleared. An understanding is conveyed from a position of weakness.

In a recent essay, Anne C. Fowler discusses all five "Affliction" poems in *The Temple* and draws some useful distinctions between the second, third, and fifth, in which Herbert "chooses to explore the subject of affliction through an intelligence very close to that of his own adult self" and consequently show him as continuing "to keep feelings at bay," and what Fowler sees as the very different expressive mode of "Affliction" [I] and [IV].[14] These two poems

14. Anne C. Fowler, "'With Care and Courage': Herbert's 'Affliction' Poems," in

are unlike the other three in that they "represent versions of a self far less mature and more disordered. These personae are often incoherent, wrong-headed, spiritually deficient. Their perceptions of the world are bizarre and unreliable. They unequivocally blame God for their misfortunes, their contentions are unreasonable, and their tones often unpleasant."[15]

These characteristics result from a separation of the stances of poet and speaker and from what Fowler calls an "ironic interplay" between the two. The exploited disparity between poet and speaker may therefore be seen as one of Herbert's strategies for conveying the idea that in a state of affliction, what is apprehended and expressed as God's capricious behavior in deserting and betraying his creature may in fact be susceptible to interpretation as being itself a "sign or visible word."

A poem of suffering such as "Affliction" [I] is so personal that the impulse to treat it as spiritually autobiographical is virtually irresistible. Fowler's insight, however, may guard us against too ready an identification of poet and speaker, although in remarking that in "Affliction" [I] "Herbert's situation is worse than Job's: he is answered only by silence. God has forgotten him,"[16] Helen Vendler is clearly untroubled by such reservations. However closely Herbert identifies himself with his speakers, his portrayal of the silent or absent Divine prevails in his poems of suffering. "Deniall" (1633, pp. 71–72) is a favorite of critics who are eager to show Herbert's musical ear and his delight in felicitously resolving cadences, and it opens with a characteristic statement of inability on the speaker's part and a lack of response on God's:

When my devotions could not pierce
Thy silent eares. (1–2)

The speaker does not have the ability, though he apparently has

"Too Riche to Clothe the Sunne": Essays on George Herbert, ed. Claude J. Summers and Ted-Larry Pebworth, pp. 129–30. Another recent approach to the "Affliction" poems, Daniel Rubey in "The Poet and the Christian Community: Herbert's Affliction Poems and the Structure of *The Temple,*" pp. 105–123, seeks to relate the movement discerned in them to larger structural concerns in *The Temple.*

15. Fowler, "'With Care and Courage,'" p. 130.

16. Vendler, *The Poetry of George Herbert,* p. 44.

the desire, to communicate with God, yet God appears not to answer. Walter Ong has remarked that belief in a person is ultimately an invitation for that person to respond. Belief in God is to look for a response from him; he is not just an object of belief with whom belief terminates.[17] If this is so, then the notion that God's "eares" are silent is disturbing to Herbert's speaker; at any rate, he constantly returns to it during the course of the poem:

> O that thou shouldst give dust a tongue
> To crie to thee,
> And then not heare it crying! all day long
> My heart was in my knee,
> But no hearing. (16–20)

Here the voice of the curiously dismembered speaker is, as it were, disfigured with grief. Displaying a fundamental lack of direction, the voice's speaker does not know where to look and would be unable to look even if he did know. For a moment these two elements converge in the phrase "unable to look right" (23), only to become detached, operating as what I can only term an analogy of distortion: because the soul's broken flower cannot look "upward" in the direction of its Creator, it looks unnatural:

> My feeble spirit, unable to look right,
> Like a nipt blossome, hung
> Discontented. (23–25)

Running through the the lyric is a more traditional figure, however. As in "The Temper" [I], the untuned lute[18] is associated with the idea of racking and stretching, and in "Easter" (1633, p. 33) it comes to suggest an imitation of Christ (7–12). In "Deniall" the figure of the untuned lute gives point to the device of the unfinished cadence whose resolution is deferred to the end:

17. Walter Ong, *The Barbarian Within, and other Fugitive Essays and Studies*, p. 56 (cited by Margaret Blanchard in "The Leap into Darkness: Donne, Herbert and God," pp. 43–44).

18. See Rosemond Tuve, *A Reading of George Herbert*, pp. 144–45; also Paul R. Whiting, "Two Notes on George Herbert," p. 131, and H. Neville Davies, "Sweet Music in Herbert's 'Easter,'" pp. 95–96.

O cheer and tune my heartlesse breast,
Deferre no time;
That so thy favours granting my request,
They and my minde may chime,
And mend my ryme. (26–30)

The asked-for response of the Divine is felt to be possible; whereas according to the words it is still being requested, it seems by the end of the poem already to have been granted, or so the prosody indicates. Health, figured by metrical smoothness (deviant trochee becomes conforming iamb), is restored within the action of the poem, and the unrhymed last line is thus dramatically subordinated to the pattern of the whole. "Deniall" contains a spectacular resolution to the problem of divine silence, because it can be heard, and so reexperienced, when read aloud. It constitutes, in fact, a poetically enacted documentation of Herbert's experience. It can be contrasted with other readings offering resolution of a conditional kind, such as the last line of "Mattens" (1633, p. 54) ("Then . . . I will climbe to thee"), precisely because in "Deniall" the resolution, although still conditional, is *enacted* in the poem. Yet any such resolution, however satisfying to the senses, must nevertheless remind its reader of the Fall of Man, since it implies knowledge that can only be conveyed by means of the senses. Indeed, the more satisfying the resolution, the more it will underline man's essentially postlapsarian knowledge of a relation to God. This potentially humiliating realization is central to Herbert's poetic: it contains the concession that the best technical means he can employ to express a relation that can only be realized by means of the senses are the means that most obviously reflect his fallen nature.

The long poem "Home" (1633, pp. 99–101) emphasizes more than does "Deniall" a connection between sickness and perceptual error. The poet calls on God (again recalling the language of the Psalms) from a state in which "my head doth burn, my heart is sick" (1). Release is presented as a choice between two alternatives; these are summed up in the refrain:

O shew thy self to me,
Or take me up to thee!

The first alternative is dismissed after five stanzas. God's delay does not make sense in terms of traditional beliefs. Yet these are invoked through an analogy as distortedly perverse as that we have already noticed in "Deniall": in his appeal to the iconography of Christ's passion, what the speaker seems most inclined to notice is the "pace" or "haste" with which the blood flows. This suggests that whatever else the passion of Christ signifies to the speaker of "Home," it can offer little consolation in the present mood:

> How canst thou stay, considering the pace
> The bloud did make, which thou didst waste?
> When I behold it trickling down thy face,
> I never saw thing make such haste. (7–10)

Indeed, God's tardiness also seems at odds with the almost unnatural eagerness of the Redeemer leaving "that nest, / That hive of sweetnesse" (19–20). If God is reluctant to reveal himself, then the poet can have nothing to lose by springing up from his sickbed, the earth:

> hence all ye clouds, away,
> Away; I must get up and see. (33–34)

Yet this alternative fails, too; Herbert's speaker is still "chained" to the world and can only hold it in contempt, by "blasting" its pleasures or by conceiving of pleasure simply in terms of its being an immediate precursor of release from the world by death or Judgment:

> Some may dream merrily, but when they wake,
> They dresse themselves and come to thee. (51–52)

> There is no fruitfull yeare, but that which brings
> The last and lov'd, though dreadfull day. (57–58)

Like "Deniall," "Home" is resolved (although less spectacularly) in sonorous terms. A. Alvarez is one of those who has noticed an apparent departure from the rhyme scheme of the other twelve stanzas in the last line of the last stanza:

> And ev'n my verse, when by the ryme and reason
> The word is, *Stay*, sayes ever, *Come*. (75–76)

The departure may be regarded as appropriate because in seventeenth-century pronunciation the last word almost certainly rhymed with the title, "Home," although the rhyme is probably best thought of as "visual."[19] Herbert has here admitted that neither of the refrain's two alternatives is possible within the existing discourse of the poem. A third alternative will be to change the form of discourse, thereby apparently destroying the poem. But this destruction *is* only apparent; closer, and arguably better, more patient, reading of the sign of poetic destruction may suggest a more profound sense of resolution. Such resolution will explicate the title of the poem in a manner impossible without the destruction and may suggest that the alternatives of the refrain have been, as it were, wrongly posed in all but the last stanza; the poet may not have been perceiving in the right way. The notion of "ryme and reason" needs serious reconsideration by a spiritually healthy mind enriched by clarity of perception.

There is further correspondence in *The Temple* between sickness and complexity: in "H. Baptisme" [II] (1633, pp. 36–37), Herbert declares that "The growth of flesh is but a blister; / Childhood is health" (14–15), and such remarks have discouraged some readers;[20] there seems to be insistence here that only in a childlike state of mind are reasonably clear perceptions possible. The mood at moments of revelation such as those in "Dialogue" (1633, p. 107), or more particularly "Love" [III] (1633, p. 183), might be said to support this view. In "Home," the structure of the poem is straightforwardly rejected in the last stanza. In this way the manner in which the refrain's alternatives have been posed is seriously questioned. In other words, Herbert's contrasts between a reluctant God *now* and an eager Redeemer *then*, however wittily expressed, are tacitly undermined by the poem's ending. Similarly, the way the stanzas in the second half of the poem embroider the prayer "O . . . take me up to thee!"—that is, in terms of con-

19. A. Alvarez, *The School of Donne*, p. 76.

20. Especially Wilbur Sanders; see Sanders, "'Childhood is Health': The Divine Poetry of George Herbert" and "Herbert and the Scholars." J. Max Patrick, "Critical Problems in Editing George Herbert's *The Temple*," pp. 19–23, considers that the stanzas of "H. Baptisme" [II] reflect its content, although this is not usually reckoned among Herbert's shaped poems.

tempt of the world—may be questioned. Herbert expresses mortality in terms of the "frame" or "knot" cluttering an otherwise free soul and draws on an emblematic language of correspondence between the "cage" of mortality and freed birds:

Oh loose this frame, this knot of man untie!
    That my free soul may use her wing,
Which now is pinion'd with mortalitie,
    As an intangled, hamper'd thing. (61–64)

In conceiving of mortality in this way, Herbert enables his speaker to endure the suffering brought about by God's apparent unresponsiveness. He claims that, however painful the sufferings are, they do not matter very much, since:

    The most of me to heav'n is fled:
My thoughts and joyes are all packt up and gone. (68–69)

The paradox here is that witty though this kind of argumentation may be, it is expressed in a way that reflects a Herbertian strategy that from this point on I shall term "figurative perversity." Figurative language is used, in the instances at issue, not just to reveal something by means of comparison, but also to reveal the limitations of comparison. Thus Fowler writes, about "Affliction" [I] and [IV], of Herbert's ability to "demonstrate . . . the tendency of a disturbed imagination to see deep correspondences that to normal consciousness appear absurd."[21] This strategy is inherent in the idea that dependence on sensory perceptions complicates the prelapsarian ideal intuition of knowledge. In its very complexity, in Herbert's poetic, such dependence is seen as unwholesome; it is complicated further by a process of perceptual error that results from a state of spiritual inadequacy. The strategy that Herbert's expressiveness reflects may therefore be regarded as both reenacting and rejecting the realizations with which poems such as these are concerned. Herbert can only articulate his relation to God by means of the senses; to realize this is to concede his spiritual inadequacy. Moreover, he enacts in his poetry a process of learning how to articulate. This process is

21. Fowler, "'With Care and Courage,'" p. 138.

analogous to learning how to read and express the opaque signs that lie about him. The signs are opaque, and the experience often seems painful and damaging because Herbert is frequently unable to get his senses to "work" and does not know what he should do to rectify the situation.

It seems to me that a notion of figurative perversity may help to account for the clear differences between traditional medieval treatments of the *contemptus mundi,* which attack the apparent source of the difficulty (the world), and Herbert's approach, in "Home" and in poems such as "Miserie" (1633, pp. 92–94) and "Giddinesse" (1633, pp. 119–20), which is often one of considerable puzzlement. At its most characteristic, this puzzlement may be seen in terms of gentle mockery directed at man:

O what a sight were Man, if his attires
    Did alter with his minde;
And like a Dolphins skinne, his clothes combin'd
    With his desires! ("Giddinesse," 17–20)

Here the element of figurative perversity is stressed because the comparison is speculative, not "seen." Characteristically man's folly is expressed, as in "Miserie," as a personal attribute, realized at the end of a long *contemptus mundi* meditation: "My God, I mean my self" (78). Perhaps even the address to God is double-edged. Rosemond Tuve, discussing "The Jews" (1633, p. 146), found this aspect of Herbert particularly attractive.[22] It has been suggested that the realization in "Man" (1633, pp. 83–85) becomes more personal as the poem proceeds.[23] The existence of the world presents man, for whom it was created, with a serious problem; its joys manifestly do not last, and even when they are fleetingly present, the means by which man can make the most of them are unsatisfactory. A concession such as this depends on the implications of the Bonaventurine doctrine of the Fall of Man.

The sickness, burnings, and gaspings of "Home" are commuted in "Dulnesse" (1633, p. 108) for a general feeling of torpor:

22. Tuve, *A Reading of George Herbert,* p. 124.
23. See Mary E. Rickey, *Utmost Art: Complexity in the Verse of George Herbert,* pp. 143–44.

Why do I languish thus, drooping and dull,
As if I were all earth?
O give me quicknesse. . . . (1–3)

The complaint, which is especially familiar from the often-anthologized "Jordan" poems, is of the relative fecundity of "wanton" poets. To rival the descriptions of their "fairest fair," Herbert finds that he cannot say anything of the "beauties" and "perfections" of the Divine. Again, his mortality is connected with this clouding of his abilities; he is so "lost in flesh" that he desires first of all the ability to "*Look* onely" toward the Divine. The very emphatic trochaic stress in these words seems finally to jolt the reader out of the lethargy that the poem's subject matter and the metrics of the majority of its stanzas have induced.[24] The line represents another request for a clearing of Herbert's perceptions. The reader must decide whether these clouded perceptions are themselves responsible for Herbert's feeling of God's absence, deafness, and seeming refusal to communicate.

Herbert's celebrated poem "The Collar" (1633, p. 147) is perhaps only tenuously included as a poem of "suffering," but it does contain one very interesting comment about perceptions. As its rebellion culminates, Herbert is scrupulously careful about how his speaker records the events:

Me thoughts I heard one calling, *Childe*:
And I reply'd, *My Lord*. (35–36)

This comment on his own perceptions, its very carefulness indicative of some clarity of vision, does not tell his reader that he actually heard anything, only that he thought he did, says so, and responds accordingly. His perception seems to have been cleared, and Herbert intimates that the agency is divine Grace; but the clearing of perception occurs at a point when both thematically, according to the narrative "line," and formally, in terms of the fevered, breathless prosody, it is least expected. This suggests that divine revelations are quite arbitrary when considered in human terms and therefore allows for the possibility of an ironic

24. But compare Arnold Stein's analysis in *George Herbert's Lyrics*, pp. 97–101.

treatment of these revelations from the poet's viewpoint. Thus the scrupulous accuracy of the ending of "The Collar" is important, because it documents a response to what the poet thought he perceived; that he may not in fact have heard what he reports is an ironic comment on the way in which submission to God has been unpredictable in terms of the human perspective of the poem's dramatic monologue.

In "The Glimpse" (1633, p. 148), which immediately follows "The Collar," Herbert again presents his perceptions of a particular moment; here that moment has to do with the glimpse of Delight he has just been offered. Delight is pictured at the point of departing, like a guest leaving too early, and the explicitness of the moment is so hard to seize that we may mistakenly be tempted to deduce that we can also trust the assertions with which he tries to persuade Delight to stay. Yet what Herbert is doing, in contrasting the "many weeks of lingring pain and smart" for which he must wait for just "one half houre" of the divine presence of Delight, is recapturing *how things seemed to him at the time.* It is important not to be so impressed with Herbert's dramatic accuracy that we mistake his description of the mood in this poem for the terms of the assertions with which he recaptures that mood. While we may appreciate that these assertions make ironic use of figurative perversity, the effect is at times so subtle that it can best be suggested by example. Henry King writes:

But heark! My Pulse like a soft Drum
Beats my approch, tells *Thee* I come;
And slow howere my marches be,
I shall at last sit down by Thee.[25]

The figure of the beating pulse as drum illuminates the state of mind of the poet who celebrates the memory of his beloved in "The Exequy" (1633, pp. 52–57). The reader may be sympathetic with this state of mind; there is the sense of numinous terror that T. S. Eliot noticed, and there is also intellectual assent. Though the pulse is only likened to a drum, we assent to the sense in which the simile is both decorous and functional, since once the pulse/

25. Henry King, "The Exequy," *Poems, Elegies, Paradoxes, and Sonnets,* p. 57.

drum stops beating, the announcement of approach will have been made: the poet, like the beloved, will be dead, actually, not figuratively. It is not really possible to feel the same intellectual assent for a similar figure in "The Glimpse"; the figure is perverse because the reader's sympathies are distanced:

> Yet if the heart that wept
> Must let thee go, return when it doth knock. (21–22)

Here Delight is being asked to return on the poet's very next heartbeat—in other words, never to absent itself. This would be unexceptionable if we did not have the dramatic context of the poem to guide our responses; seen in this dramatic context, so that the words are uttered to a departing guest in the full knowledge that the guest will depart, the utterance reflects a kind of foolish courtesy on the part of the speaker. The figurative perversity here tells the reader much more about the speaker, and does so in a much more detached manner, than do King's lines.[26]

Awareness of the ironic potential of Herbert's expression of assurance guides our response to other poems, such as "The Flower" (1633, pp. 160–61). This has been well analyzed by Helen Vendler, who points out that one effect of Herbert's strategy is to have made the poem appear repetitive to readers who do not sense that all but its last stanza consist of retellings of the experiencing of the moment of assurance, each progressively more accurate and each in a different mode.[27] The first is an impersonal generalization ("How fresh, O Lord, how sweet and clean / Are thy returns"); the second account, "almost as rosy" according to Vendler, is more personal; and subsequent retellings increasingly stress both the feeling that grief is perhaps almost intolerable after all and the knowledge that it persistently returns. In the first half of the poem the figurative perversity is notable: the behavior of God is presented as inherently unsearchable and arbitrary in itself, yet perceived by Herbert's heart as seasonal or cyclical; there

26. My reading of "The Glimpse" is perhaps harsher than Vendler's (*The Poetry of George Herbert,* p. 258), for whom the speaker is courteous but probably not foolish.

27. Vendler, *The Poetry of George Herbert,* pp. 48–54.

are "returns" (2) that are like "flowers in spring." In such a season grief inevitably "melts away," (5) and periods of divine absence are conceived of as winter, in which plants in the form of bulbs "All the hard weather, / Dead to the world, keep house unknown" (13–14). Such expression suggests that God's returns can almost be timed in their seasonal inevitability. The fourth stanza records a plea for escape from this state of affairs:

> O that I once past changing were,
> Fast in thy Paradise, where no flower can wither! (22–23)

Herbert's wishes to become a plant (as in, for instance, "Affliction" [I]: "I reade, and sigh, and wish I were a tree"; and "Employment" [II] (1633, pp. 70–71): "Oh that I were an Orenge-tree, / That busie plant!") characteristically carry a curious and problematic combination of spiritual fervor and withdrawal. The lines in "The Flower" are no exception; plant life represents effortless praise and signals a desire to escape from a troublesome spiritual existence. In the fifth stanza the cyclical figure is questioned as its perverseness or inadequacy becomes apparent. Here the antonym for God's "returns" is not "absence" but "anger," and it can strike with all the incomprehensible force of a cataclysm:

> But while I grow in a straight line,
> Still upwards bent, as if heav'n were mine own,
> Thy anger comes, and I decline:
> What frost to that? what pole is not the zone,
> Where all things burn,
> When thou dost turn,
> And the least frown of thine is shown? (29–35)

The sixth stanza leads us to feel that the terms of God's anger ("tempests") and the effect on Herbert ("deaths") are figuratively the least perverse, the most accurate, because the experience of trying to find and express them has been recorded in what has gone before. In submitting to God's unpredictable actions, Herbert has realized the cyclical figure to be inadequate and has in this way unexpectedly been able to come to terms with the conflict in this poem.

So far, the stress has been on poems in which Herbert's documentation of a particular moment takes the form of constant reevaluation, such that the terms of that documentation are scrutinized in a process that assists in the recapture of the momentary. It would be wrong, however, to suggest that all of Herbert's poems of suffering take this form. Some, while asserting that moments of assurance are fleeting when compared with the more prevailing nature of grief, do not revalue the assertion; a poem such as "Repentance" (1633, pp. 40–41) instead presents the assertion in terms that we might still consider erroneous, this time because of the slightly histrionic confessional mode:

> Mans age is two houres work, or three:
> Each day doth round about us see.
> Thus are we to delights: but we are all
> To sorrows old. (7–10)

Other poems, such as "The Discharge" (1633, pp. 138–139), show rather greater stability of mood. "The Discharge" concedes that recalling the past is inevitably tainted with subjectivity and that it is pointless fearfully to imagine the future, since it will come whatever happens; addressing his heart, Herbert says "Onely the present is thy part" (21). And the ending may be felt to be refreshingly commonsense:

> Either grief will not come: or if it must,
> Do not forecast.
> And while it cometh, it is almost past. (51–53)

Yet it should not be assumed that this commonsense voice represents any more final kind of statement than we find elsewhere in *The Temple*. One of the paradoxes of Herbert's achievement is that his dramatic gifts render the poems in which he revalues and reexpresses an experience at once more provisional *and* more satisfyingly complete than poems such as "The Discharge," which insist on the limitations of discoursing about experience. "The Discharge" appears more assured and resigned to what it insists is the pointlessness of moving imaginatively outside the present; yet this very insistence betrays a complacency that a poem such as "The Flower," with its more provisional quality, does not. This is not, of course, necessarily to suggest that "The Discharge" is a less "successful" poem: its range is less, to be sure, but one would need to show that that limited range was not part of the mimetic effect of the experience of this particular speaking voice in order to maintain that the poem had failed.

A poem of suffering, then, may be dramatically effective without necessarily showing the provisional quality; the more plangent instances, such as "Complaining" (1633, pp. 137–38), "Longing" (1633, pp. 142–45) and "The Search" (1633, pp. 156–57), may be felt to be more static in mood. But even in poems such as these, we still question Herbert's empirical sensory perceptions; they do not seem consistent with each other in *The Temple* as a whole, and frequently, as we have seen, even a single poem displays a lack of consistency. There is clearly great uncertainty in the mind of the many-faceted speaker who relates all this suffering, and we should now devote some consideration to traditional expressions of the notion of the "hidden" or "absent" God *(Deus absconditus)* that Herbert may have drawn on, in an attempt to assess exactly how it is that God can be felt to spend considerable periods of time hiding himself from his creature. The problem is acute to Herbert; although both "herbs below" and "starres above" are part of God's creation, they, unlike him, seem to have no difficulty in asserting the existence of their Creator and their apparent pleasure in this assertion. Unlike Herbert in the times when the Divine is hidden, they do not "pine" or "decay" ("The Search," 9–16). Most disturbing to Herbert is the acuteness of the feeling of epistemological uncertainty that the paradox of the absent God represents:

> Where is my God? what hidden place
> Conceals thee still?
> What covert dare eclipse thy face?
> Is it thy will? ("The Search," 29–32)

* * *

The phenomenon under discussion has been described by Stanley Fish as "God's fitful presence";[28] it is not unique to Her-

28. Stanley E. Fish, *Self-Consuming Artifacts: The Experience of Seventeenth Century Literature*, p. 160.

bert; indeed, it characterizes most of the Psalms, where it takes the form of a movement that is an oscillation between extremes of lament and praise.[29] Herbert reviews this movement succinctly in a complete poem, "Bitter-sweet" (1633, pp. 165–66):

> Ah my deare angrie Lord,
> Since thou dost love, yet strike;
> Cast down, yet help afford;
> Sure I will do the like.
>
> I will complain, yet praise;
> I will bewail, approve:
> And all my sowre-sweet dayes
> I will lament, and love.

This is a poem that alludes to a form of spiritual experience that is more than once documented by Hugh of St. Victor. Hugh's most expository statement occurs in the *De arca Noë morali* 4. God's absence, insofar as he is permanently veiled from man's eyes, is a consequence of man's Fall; if this were not the case, there would be no call for faith and no cause for lack of it. God therefore makes himself known in order to nourish human faith, yet he is permanently hidden lest the faithful be convinced and their faith thereby rendered superfluous. He hides himself permanently in order to test the faithful, but he makes himself known in order to condemn the unfaithful.[30] Hugh adopts a more devotional tone in other writings; although God is permanently veiled from human eyes, he does sometimes approach close to man:

> Sometimes he withdraws, at other times he disappears, so that by making himself missed when he is not there, he is valued still more when he is.[31]

The sensuous writing of the Song of Songs—particularly Chapter 5—is an obvious influence behind a passage such as this:

29. Cf. Coburn Freer, *Music for a King: George Herbert's Style and the Metrical Psalms*, pp. 35–40.

30. Hugh of St. Victor, *De arca Noë morali* 4, iii; *PL* 176, col. 668.

31. Aliquando se subtrahit, aliquando ad tempus recedit, ut dum requiratur absens, strictius teneatur praesens. Hugh of St. Victor, *De amore sponsi ad sponsam*; *PL* 176, col. 987.

6 I opened to my beloved; but my beloved had withdrawn himself, and was gone: my soul failed when he spake: I sought him, but I could not find him; I called him, but he gave me no answer.

8 I charge you, O daughters of Jerusalem, if ye find my beloved, that ye tell him, that I am sick of love.

The echoes from the Song of Songs are stronger still in Hugh's *De arrha animae.* Towards its end, Hugh rapturously describes the soul's response to God's presences, regarding them as rare and treasured visits. In both of these devotional treatises, as in their scriptural source, Hugh's writing is erotic in the extreme; the soul of man is the bride, and the divine lover the bridegroom:

> For suddenly I am renewed and am completely changed, and I begin to feel better than I am capable of putting into words. My consciousness is exhilarated, forgetting all past sorrow my soul exults, my understanding is illuminated, my heart glows, my longings are now filled with joy, and now I see that I have a place, though I do not know where, and I have a feeling of love inside me as though I were being embraced, which I cannot exactly explain, and yet I put all my efforts into keeping this feeling always and never losing it. My soul is involved in a pleasurable struggle lest it should let go the feeling, which it longs always to embrace, and it rejoices immeasurably, having as it were found its end in this summit of all desires, seeking nothing further, wanting nothing more, wishing always to be in such a state. Now is not this my beloved?[32]

The withdrawings and approaches recall the exquisite hesitances of "Love" [III].

Hugh's mystical writing provides an interesting example of the way in which, despite apparent disconfirmations of the divine

32. Subito enim innovor et tota immutor, et bene mihi esse incipit ultra quam dicere sufficiam. Exhilaratur conscientia, in oblivionem venit omnis praeteritorum dolorum miseria, exsultat animus, clarescit intellectus, cor illuminatur, desideria jucundantur, jamque alibi (nescio ubi) me esse video, et quasi quiddam amplexibus amoris intus teneo, et nescio quid illud sit, et tamen illud semper retinere, et nunquam perdere toto adnisu laboro. Luctatur quodammodo delectabiliter animus, ne recedit ab eo, quod semper amplecti desiderat, et quasi in illo omnium desideriorum finem invenerit summe et ineffabiliter exsultat, nihil amplius quaerens, nihil ultra appetens, semper sic esse volens. Nunquid ille est dilectus meus? Hugh of St. Victor, *De arrha animae*; *PL* 176, col. 970. In *N&Q* (1969), pp. 368–70, Heather Asals suggests that this devotional treatise may have influenced Herbert's poem "Dialogue."

presence and apparent inconsistencies in divine behavior, their initially disturbing nature can eventually be interpreted in terms of a positive divine significance: they are in the soul's best interests. The effect on the soul is profound, and Herbert records it most lyrically in arriving, by "reinvention," at his most accurate statement in "The Flower":

> And now in age I bud again,
> After so many deaths I live and write;
> I once more smell the dew and rain,
> And relish versing: O my onely light,
> It cannot be
> That I am he
> On whom thy tempests fell all night. (36–42)

God's presence, as in a poem such as "The Collar," appears actually to heighten Herbert's own perceptions, so that any unreliability that Herbert's reader may have discerned in the speaker's previous perceptions of God's absence is placed in a new context by an affirmation such as Hugh's: *"clarescit intellectus, cor illuminatur."*

Reinvention is characteristic of poems whose mood remains plangent throughout, and we may assume that the assertions that Herbert does scrutinize should be considered more reliable, since the unquestioned, unexamined assertions allow their reader to see them as ironically presented functions of Herbert's perceptual inabilities in a time of spiritual crisis. In at least tacitly admitting that his documentation of spiritual affairs is more to be relied on when his conception of God is the least static and complacent, Herbert accommodates the notion of the absent or hidden God to his fallen understanding. It does not take much effort to see that Herbert's mode of expression differs from Hugh's mystic, exalted treatment of the *Deus absconditus* in being characteristically more down to earth; what is particularly suggestive is that Herbert adopts an expressiveness that depends on the ironic potential of the lyric form he uses. In this way, epistemological discovery is revealed through the possibilities for restatement that the lyric form, in Herbert's hands, offers its reader. Among the possibilities offered by writing in Herbert's mode, we may therefore number his documenting of the experience of the arbitrariness of divine behavior, such that caprice or unresponsiveness can actually be attributed to God. The examples so far discussed suggest that God can be revealed in Herbert's very restatement of a simple and at times complacent assertion, whether this assertion be of divine presence or absence. The sudden beginnings of many of Herbert's poems characteristically reflect the possibilities of this mode of expression.[33]

The example of "Deniall" suggests that when Herbert expresses unresponsiveness and attributes it to God, he uses the figure of deafness. Other poems, such as "Longing" (1633, pp. 142–45), suggest that this is a central notion and that it can be supplemented by the idea of an immobility or even death, which is somehow worse than that shown in the iconography of the crucifixion of Christ:

> Lord Jesu, thou didst bow
> Thy dying head upon the tree:
> O be not now
> More dead to me!
> Lord heare! *Shall he that made the eare,*
> *Not heare?* (31–36)

As Hutchinson remarks (*Works*, p. 529), the allusion is to Ps. 94:9. Herbert offers, seemingly unavailingly, "cries," "grones," "teares," and "sighs." There is no response from God. Among the possibilities we must entertain here is that there is no means available of conceiving of divine response in the very plangency of this poem, which does not seem to reinvent. It has been argued that we trust Herbert's assertions more when they are in some way scrutinized or restated; perhaps one means of restatement would be to think less in terms of God's deafness to Herbert's entreaties than in terms of our realization that Herbert is blind to God's response. In this way, his apparent lack of response might nev-

33. Robert Ellrodt, *L'Inspiration personnelle et l'esprit du temps chez les poètes métaphysiques anglais* 1, p. 271, notes that Herbert's sudden beginnings are distinguished from Donne's by the "contraste de l'instant présent et du temps qui l'a précédé." Among many other cases in point one would have to include "The Temper" [II].

ertheless come to be seen as communication, since some significant content is conveyed to the perceiver. Certainly Hugh of St. Victor perceives the significant dimension of lack of response, and we need now to consider the extent to which such signification illuminates our reading of Herbert's poetry.

The distinction between divine deafness and Herbert's blindness is summarized in the opening lines of "Prayer" [II] (1633, pp. 95–96), the assured mood of which seems utterly at variance with the mood of "Longing." "Prayer" [II] is not a poem for which the notion of restatement seems appropriate, since despite its addressive tone it is a meditation rather than a poem whose mood itself comes under scrutiny; though it may seem less personal because of this, the language is nonetheless revealing of the documentation of spiritual perceptions:

> Of what an easie quick accesse,
> My blessed Lord, art thou! how suddenly
> May our requests thine eare invade!
> To shew that state dislikes not easinesse.
> If I but lift mine eyes, my suit is made:
> Thou canst no more not heare, then thou canst die. (1–6)

The distinction that emerges from a reading of these lines is reinforced by Valerie Carnes's persuasive suggestion that in *The Temple* the divine Logos descends and is apprehensible to man's soul in the form of images visually perceptible by man, and that it reascends in verbal form as Herbert's own song of praise.[34] It is true that when Herbert is capable of communicating with God, he tends to perceive such communication as a silent, visible word: a sign. We are now in a position to suggest that even what initially encourages reproachful conceptualization in terms of "absence" or "unreceptiveness" can be interpreted as a divine signification. God seems rarely actually to speak in *The Temple*, with the exception of "Love" [III] and certain ecstatic points en route such as "Dialogue." In view of this, it might be most accurate to say that

34. See Valerie Carnes, "The Unity of George Herbert's *The Temple*: A Reconsideration," pp. 509–510. Compare Ernest B. Gilman in "Word and Image in Quarles' *Emblems*," p. 389.

when Herbert is at his most lucidly receptive, he is capable of interpreting everything, even God's absence, in terms of silent significance; this would be entirely consistent with Augustinian sign theory. When Herbert does interpret the hidden God in terms of divine unresponsiveness, he tends to express dissatisfaction with God's deafness; when he interprets the phenomenon as a significant response in itself, coming to perceive the essence of this response and consequently coming to interpret his feelings in terms of divine presence, what Herbert has actually been repining over is his own blindness. It is common to find that Herbert intimates divine response (and the clearing of his own perception) in the *form* of a poem, and "Deniall" again provides a good instance of this. The sign that signifies divine response is presented here sonorously rather than visually, probably because it is still being sued for in the words:

> O cheer and tune my heartlesse breast,
> Deferre no time;
> That so thy favours granting my request,
> They and my mind may chime,
> And mend my ryme. (26–30)

* * *

These significant properties of acts of interpretation in *The Temple* should be illustrated from other poems than those of suffering. There is a straightforward expression of the possibility of the clearing of man's perceptual error in "[Love] II" (1633, p. 46):

> All knees shall bow to thee; all wits shall rise,
> And praise him who did make and mend our eies. (13–14)

But perhaps it is more interesting to note the extent to which an ability to see perceptual error as itself having a significant dimension characterizes poems of "quest." There are several of these in *The Temple*. Discussion of two of Herbert's allegorical quest poems "Peace" (1633, pp. 117–18) and "The Pilgrimage" (1633, pp. 135–36) illustrate other aspects of interpretative "illiteracy," an inability or disinclination to read God's visible words, than those so far considered; each poem reveals a rather different strategy from the other. "Peace" falls into two parts, both consisting of an allegorical narrative. The first part belongs to the narrator of the poem, and this is abandoned for the second, that of the "rev'rend good old man" (19), whom the narrator, having failed to make sense out of his own experience, eventually meets. In the first half of "Peace," the narrator in effect relates the failure of various kinds of emblematic portrayal to offer the kind of significance he thinks ought to belong to Peace. A "secret cave" (3) seems an appropriate place to seek, yet "A hollow winde did seem to answer, No: / Go seek elsewhere" (5–6). We are faced here with a comment on the difficulty of reading signs in general and on the perceptions of this narrator in particular; it is reminiscent of the self-conscious ironies of a poem such as "Love-joy" (1633, p. 109). Since the wind has no articulate voice, any sound it makes can only approximate human speech. The truth is a general one, and a universal phenomenon (the human tendency to hear articulate speech in inarticulate sounds) is being described in the poem. But the deftly presented characteristics of the narrator of "Peace" particularize the act. Such particularization has been endured by the time we reach the second stanza, where the narrator, seeking elsewhere, notices a rainbow ("Surely, thought I . . ."), and we find that his confident interpretative assertion ("This is the lace of Peaces coat") has been dispersed by the passage of natural events:

> But while I lookt, the clouds immediately
> Did break and scatter. (11–12)

In the third stanza, the interpretative confidence is stronger still, and to a careful reader, less apparently reasonable than before. The narrator shows himself to have been deceived by appearances, the root of the "gallant flower" is worm-eaten, and there is now a note of real disappointment. Impatient, the narrator moves on, meets the sage "At length," and "demands" Peace. The second narration, that of the old man, is continuous and not "reinvented," as are the first narrative's interpretative assertions; indeed, the reinvention in the first narration may be considered satirically retrogressive, since the narrator becomes more ignorant and less reasonable. The old man, instead, relates a thinly disguised allegory, whose significances, in being rather more public, are easier for the reader to share *in themselves*; in this second narration the reader for the most part follows the narrative exclusively, whereas in the first account he has been simultaneously following both the narrative and the narrator's strategies for making sense of it. In a fine account of the poem, Barbara Harman shows how in its first part "meaning is regularly suspended on [the narrator's] journey."[35] Once the second narrative is over (the allegorical account of Christ's life and passion is characteristically truncated: "He sweetly liv'd, yet sweetnesse did not save / His life from foes" [25–26]), the interpretation is offered with total assurance: the quester is invited to make bread of the grain dispersed from the "twelve stalks of wheat" that have grown out of Christ's grave. The answer satisfies the narrator; the old man's story, not looked for and impatiently demanded, has brought about what it has set out to signify, as none of the narrator's previous efforts could do. We may notice the way in which revelation is once again unexpectedly and spontaneously made available.

The signs in "Peace" have been opaque, but the narrator's interpretative powers are endorsed by the old man's story; terms for clarity of vision are offered and accepted, and we can speak of a "resolution" in this poem. We cannot, however, do so quite as straightforwardly in the case of "The Pilgrimage"; here, it might be said, the signs become, on the contrary, increasingly opaque. But while this baffling process is taking place, the allegorical narrative is being rejected in favor of what Helen Vendler calls the "lyric impulse" of this poem.[36] As the poem proceeds, its particular mode of emblematic discourse is found not to be adequate to the experience being conveyed, so that, unlike "Peace," "The Pilgrimage" can be said to "dispute its form" (Vendler, p. 97). Vendler rightly draws attention to the perfunctory allegory of the first half of the poem, and this quality indicates the extent of the derivative experience described in the first half. The "cave of Desperation,"

35. Barbara Harman, *Costly Monuments: Representations of the Self in George Herbert's Poetry,* p. 142.
36. Vendler's account of this poem (*The Poetry of George Herbert,* pp. 92–98) can scarcely be bettered.

"the rock of Pride," and the other labeled points on the way are not felt nor even described in any but the most attributive way; they are simply named. For Vendler they are indications of the secondhand nature of the pilgrimage up to the point where the narrator "got unto the gladsome hill, / Where lay my hope" (19–20); it is from this point on that the labels are abandoned. Instead, the narration now relates a series of surprises for which labels are inadequate; at times interpretations are offered, but they are questionable. Apparently climbing the hill that he considers the end point of his quest, the narrator finds what turns out not, after all, to be a summit, only "A lake of brackish waters on the ground" (23); there is no secondhand allegorical language for this, and the experience now becomes real, not already charted by others. The narrator finds at the "summit" not the expected peak, but a hollow depression; the significance becomes more opaque, and it is here that allegory is abandoned for the "lyric impulse":

I fell, and cry'd, Alas my King;
Can both the way and end be tears? (27–28)

Only by seeing the goal of the journey as being as traumatic as the journey itself can the narrator make any sense of his experience. But even this histrionic conclusion is denied him; experience is not to be reduced to the formulaic even in this way. He has climbed the wrong hill; yet as he impetuously sets about to right this state of affairs, he hears the words "*None goes that way / And lives*" (33–34). However the tone in which these words are uttered is to be interpreted, they can only lead to the conclusion that, compared to a journey such as the narrator has undergone, death is "fair," so that nothing will really be lost by completing the quest. "The Pilgrimage" turns out to be a poem of suffering in which the pain increases; it ends having rejected one form of discourse in favor of something both less satisfactory and more resistant to interpretation. That something, however, carries a sense of having been experienced firsthand. The narrative ending is "open" in the sense that a reader is left guessing as to whether the journey will or will not be completed.

Elsewhere in *The Temple* allegorical narrative and suffering come together, notably in "Love unknown" (1633, pp. 121–23), which, as Ira Clark has suggested, may be seen as Herbert's version of Psalms 51.[37] At one point it employs the pre-Freudian slip (also used in "The Rose") to suggest something of the narrator's hesitant garrulousness:

> I found that some had stuff'd the bed with thoughts,
> I would say *thorns.* (51–52)

The urbanity of the reply of the "Deare Friend" (61–70) to whom the narration has been addressed contrasts with the persistent inability of the narrator to speak straight:

> A Lord I had,
> And have, of whom some grounds which may improve,
> I hold for two lives, and both lives in me.
> To him I brought a dish of fruit one day,
> And in the middle plac'd my heart. But he
> (I sigh to say)
> Lookt on a servant, who did know his eye
> Better then you know me, or (which is one)
> Then I my self. (3–11)

Yet not only does the narrator speak awry; he also seems to be incapable of comprehending the friend's interlocutions, apparently replying to them at cross-purposes. Each of the friend's remarks (except the last, which seems to silence the narrator) is politely but impetuously brushed aside as commonplace knowledge ("Indeed . . .") [19, 38, 57]). In one sense, all these *indeed*s concede the validity of what they are replying to: what the friend says *is* true. Yet in a manner that the reader is encouraged to realize as the poem proceeds, they give away much about the narrator's preconceptions. As we saw to be the case with "Love-joy," we may account for the comments of the friend in "Love unknown" by suggesting that the narrator is somehow, though giving the "right" answer, responding to the wrong question, or in the wrong way, to visible signs that are open to other interpretations than those he seems inclined to give them. The friend serves as an interpreter of events, even if, during the flow of narrative, a

37. Ira Clark, " 'Lord, in Thee the *Beauty* Lies in the *Discovery*': 'Love Unknown' and Reading Herbert," pp. 583–84.

reluctant one ("*I fear*"). But his final reply indicates that the narrator *has* misread the signs; what the narrator has interpreted as refusal of his gifts and ungrateful behavior on God's part can be read differently. The interpretation offered by the friend suggests, in its assured precision, that all these divine responses to the narrator's gifts can be read as the means to spiritual renewal. The hiddenness of the Divine is conveyed in this poem by means of behavior that the narrator reads as capricious until another interpretation is offered by someone other than the narrator of the events described, and the poem's reader participates by observing the process of debate and deciding which of the rival interpretations to accept.

Brief invocation of Herbert's "Vanitie" poems (1633, pp. 77–78, 104) may help to summarize the discussion so far. Like "Dotage" (1633, pp. 161–62), "Vanitie" [II] opposes true and false readings of the cosmos; but whereas the contrast in "Dotage" is between the way man takes "griefs in earnest [and] joyes in jest" (14), the terms of reference in "Vanitie" [II] are extended to more general aspects of "misreading": what should aspire is defeated, and instead "flat delights . . . do creep and grow" (2). The tone of "Vanitie" [II] is unusually impersonal, even though "Dotage" and "Vanitie" [I] share something of it. The easy feminine rhymes in lines 5 and 6 also cause us to question, as so often with Herbert's poetry when it exhibits this kind of mood, how deliberately ironic the sermonizing note is supposed to be:

> Heark and beware, lest what you now do measure
> And write for sweet, prove a most sowre displeasure.
>
> ("Vanitie" [II], 5–6)

The note of these lines is somewhat mitigated in "Vanitie" [I], a poem that ends by showing how man's forensic wisdom and understanding can nevertheless signify folly if unattended by spiritual health. The statement that man is himself incapable of reading his own wisdom as spiritual health remains, however, an unusually general one for Herbert. What is more, it is distinctly reminiscent of the Augustinian idea cited at the beginning of the previous chapter (*Video enim quae fecerit Deus meus, non autem video ipsum Deum meum qui fecit haec*):

What hath not man sought out and found,
But his deare God? who yet his glorious law
Embosomes in us, mellowing the ground
With showres and frosts, with love & aw,
So that we need not say, Where's this command?
Poore man, thou searchest round
To find out *death*, but missest *life* at hand. (22–28)

* * *

Characteristic of the phenomenon of the silent or absent Divine, then, is that its strategic treatment by Herbert may be regarded as a highly accommodative tactic. In learning to perceive a significant dimension to his experience of divine caprice, he presents himself as revising and revaluing many of his initial assessments of and responses to his experience. God's presence is conceptualized as fitful, so that Herbert's lyric expression of his experience is seen to be symptomatic of an attitude discernible also in the utterances of the Psalmist and of Job. But the experience that Herbert portrays is susceptible to restatement in terms of a clearing of spiritual "sight," and when this occurs Herbert can express it in terms of the exploitation, through the formal properties of the lyric mode, of various strategic devices (such as that of "Love unknown") for distancing himself or his narrative persona from his experience sufficiently for his reader to see what the experience truly represents. For central to Herbert's strategy is the reader's unfolding realization that it typifies what is scripturally the sole occasion of utter desertion by God. This occasion is formally meditated on by means of the spiritual technique of imaginative recall in "The Sacrifice" (1633, pp. 19–26):

But, *O my God, my God*! why leav'st thou me,
The sonne, in whom thou dost delight to be?
My God, my God—
Never was grief like mine. (213–16)

The occasion is remembered in "Obedience" (1633, pp. 96–98):

thy death and bloud
Show'd a strange love to all our good:
Thy sorrows were in earnest; no faint proffer,
Or superficiall offer. (26–29)

These lines indicate the uniqueness of the desertion of Christ during the Passion; to invoke them here is to remind ourselves that every other conviction of desertion by God is delusory. The plangency of a poem such as "Longing" is thus in more than one respect an expression of ineffectuality; not only does it represent a feeling of abandonment, but it also enacts the process of arriving at the knowledge that this feeling, although irresistible, should not be submitted to, since it is delusory and mocks the one genuine experience that it typifies. The humiliating consequence, of which Herbert's reader becomes aware, is that perceptions that reflect and enact abandonment by God cannot be trusted.

We may now appreciate something of the extent to which, in Herbert's hands, the properties of the lyric are exploited so as to allow us to experience his realization of the various ways that communication from God can be accommodated to man's understanding. Man as *homo significans* can only communicate by means of what has significant potential. One of Herbert's preoccupations in *The Temple* is with the need to learn the divinely given language of visible words, and consequently to move from a state of illiteracy toward learning how to address God. A great many falterings, hesitancies, and outright mistakes are involved; Herbert's errors in his attempts to interpret the divine language are supplemented by those he introduces in his attempts to communicate with God, even to the extent of his not getting the words right. We shall see later that such "errors" in Herbert's approach to divine signs are not confined to his use of words but can extend more generally to his use of things.

There is, however, a more positive side to the realization that apprehending significances frequently implies perceptual error; indeed, a note of considerable optimism emerges from the exalted writing of Hugh of St. Victor, who stresses that, in addition to being rewards for faith and punishments for infidelity, the phenomena open to interpretation as the "returns" of the Divine are actually a pledge of future bliss. The note of optimism strongly implied in the *De amore sponsi ad sponsam* is still more rapturously realized at the end of the *De arrha animae*. Divine absences are interpreted by the mystically assured soul in terms of God hiding himself for a while but returning from time to time to comfort the soul, allowing it a foretaste of what is to come. As before, the terms of expression are "sensory": here, however, there is great emphasis on tasting, and we are reminded of the concise yet lucid relationship that involves the beginning and the end of "The Church." The "Superliminare" (1633, p. 17) exhorts the purified reader to "approach, and taste / The churches mysticall repast" (3–4), and one of the more ecstatic poems late in the sequence of *The Temple* treats with "olfactory" ardour the name "My Master": the words impart "a sweet content, / An orientall fragrancie" (4–5). Indeed, "The Odour" (1633, pp. 169–70) may almost be seen as an "earnest" of the bliss offered at the end of "The Church," where Love says "You must sit down . . . and taste my meat," and where the vision is at last fully realized: "So I did sit and eat" ("Love" [III], 17–18). In a state of bliss—we are strongly invited to believe—the soul no longer "tastes" or "scents" but will eat. In the more assured moments throughout *The Temple,* Herbert is aware of God's "earnest." The Bible, for example, is, as he puts it in "The H. Scriptures. I." (1633, p. 50), "joyes handsell" (13). It is true that "The Glance" (1633, p. 166) expresses the idea using the sense of sight rather than of taste, but this is a little unusual, both for Herbert and in what may be called a more general "handsell tradition":

If thy first glance so powerfull be,
A mirth but open'd and seal'd up again;
What wonders shall we feel, when we shall see
Thy full-ey'd love!
When thou shalt look us out of pain,
And one aspect of thine spend in delight
More then a thousand sunnes disburse in light,
In heav'n above. (17–24)

The expression here is arresting because it paradoxically posits a sensory confusion that seems to accompany extreme and assured familiarity with God's significant language of visible words. There is an analogous example in "Josephs Coat" (1633, p. 153), whose tone is as resigned as anything to be found in *The Temple*:

such is his will,
Who changeth all things, as him pleaseth best. (3–4)

It is this poem that ends:

I live to shew his power, who once did bring
My *joyes* to *weep,* and now my *griefs* to *sing*.

These may be seen as examples of the kind of reticent opacity of expressiveness that is distinctive to Herbert's lyric mode in *The Temple.* They seem to assert that in moments of greatest clarity and understanding, experience cannot, paradoxically, be conveyed in its essence; instead it must be signified by the climactic nature of sensory confusion.

However, before any such state of assurance is reached, Herbert has documented his experience of suffering fully. At its worst, it seems that, as he puts it in "Affliction" [IV] (1633, pp. 82–83), "Nothing performs the task of life" (16). Two conclusions may be indicated here, since they suggest directions that our inquiry should now pursue. We are first made aware of a feeling with which Herbert must come to terms, namely that incomprehension of his "griefs" is tied to a perceptual inadequacy and is interpreted accordingly. The tone takes on a stridency that suggests that the suffering persona whom Herbert is portraying has become physically distorted by grief. "Complaining" offers a striking and so far unremarked instance of this stridency:

Art thou all justice, Lord?
Shows not thy word
More attributes? Am I all throat or eye,
To weep or crie?
Have I no parts but those of grief? (11–15)

Second, Herbert's poetic attempts to state the phenomena that he perceives show a tendency, in extreme suffering, to progress towards an enactment of the inadequacy of poetic language to express grief; an example can be found in the last lines of the poem entitled "Grief" (1633, p. 158):

Verses, ye are too fine a thing, too wise
For my rough sorrows: cease, be dumbe and mute,
Give up your feet and running to mine eyes,
And keep your measures for some lovers lute,
Whose grief allows him musick and a ryme:

> For mine excludes both measure, tune, and time.
> Alas, my God! (13–19)

The first of these two aspects of Herbert's expressiveness is related to the concept of human "illiteracy" and to the need to learn how to read divine signs. Acceptance of this need in relation to the traditional dichotomy displayed in conceptualization of God's two books, Nature and Scripture, provides a convenient way of structuring the discussion in the next two chapters. The second aspect of Herbert's expressiveness, alluded to in the lines from "Grief," is inherent in the expression in verse of what God's signs are considered to signify once they have been perceived.

Among Herbert's own contemporaries, the apposition of Nature and Scripture—one we have traced in its development from Augustinian sign theory through the Middle Ages—becomes commonplace and often formulaic. The apposition is expressed in terms of a twofold book by writers such as Donne, Browne, and perhaps most interestingly, Joseph Hall (1574–1626), successively bishop of Exeter and Norwich.[38] Hall's elegant formulation not only provides further evidence of the weight of tradition that underlies conceptions of God's acts of creation and redemption; it also offers a convenient terminology for their discussion in the context of Herbert's *The Temple.* According to Hall:

> There are but two Bookes wherin we can reade God; The one is his Word, his Workes the other; This is the bigger Volume, that the more exquisite. The Characters of this are more large, but dim; of that smaller, but clearer. Philosophers have turned over this, and erred, That, Divines and studious Christians, not without full and certaine information. In the Workes of God we see the shadow, or footsteps of the Creator, in his Word we see the face of God in a glasse.[39]

Although the very form of this summary seems to have been made possible by Bonaventura's memorable restatement of Hugh,

38. See citation in note 39 below. See, e.g., John Donne, *Sermons*, ed. Evelyn M. Simpson and George Potter, vol. 8, p. 94, and Sir Thomas Browne, *Religio Medici*, I, xvi (vol. 1, p. 25 in *Works*, ed. Geoffrey Keynes). See also Thomas Taylor, *Meditations from the Creatures*, p. 5 (sig. B3^{r}).

39. Joseph Hall, *Contemplations* 15 (introductory letter to Lord Burleigh), in *Works*, pp. 1125–26 (sig. Ccccc^{r-v}). There is a similar view in Joshua Sylvester's *Bartas: His Devine Weekes and Workes*, and it is copied by Francis Quarles, *Emblemes*.

Hall gives particular prominence to a sense of man's inadequacy when faced with the divine language of the Book of Nature. Here Hall shares what seems in fact a traditional sense of unease as to whether or not man's illiteracy is a permanent state of affairs; man sees the letters of the book, yet he cannot say what they mean:

> Thou idle Truant, doest thou learne nothing of so many masters? hast thou so long read these capitall letters of Gods great booke, and canst thou not yet spell one word of them?[40]

The mixture, between certainty relating to man's illiteracy and epistemological unease relating to the inadequacy of man's perceptions, remains paradoxical; man's Fall requires that he interpret the original prelapsarian sense of the universe, seeing the Book of Nature once more as written by the finger of the Divine, yet there is a sense of hopeless urgency in this need to interpret. It is captured in Hall's words, and perhaps appropriately summarizes the nature of the Augustinian inheritance of Hugh and Bonaventura.

* * *

So far we have been assuming the centrality of the Fall of Man to the attitudes to divine signs that I have surveyed in this chapter. The assumption is sound, but it is now time to prepare for a more systematic discussion of Herbert's reading of the Book of Nature by reminding ourselves not only of the intellectual precision that Bonaventurine formulations of man's Fall reveal, but also, more particularly, of the various ways in which such formulations demonstrate a conception of man's illiteracy in the natural world. How did Herbert's contemporaries view man's Fall? It has been justly remarked that Renaissance commentators of the Book of Genesis

> devote rather little attention to the intellectual consequences of the fall. . . . Much more . . . space goes to the loss of domination over brute creation which resulted from Adam's sin. In Paradise all the animals served man, none were ferocious or noxious. After the fall, the animals in some measure rebelled. Man could still use them to a degree, and

40. Joseph Hall, *The Arte of Divine Meditation*, p. 22 (sig. B8v).

> after the deluge he received permission to kill and eat them. Their submission after the fall was no longer voluntary or innate.[41]

There is never any doubt that, in Hall's words:

> Man is placed in this Stage of the world to viewe the severall natures and actions of the creature; to viewe them not idly, without his use, as they doe him.[42]

As the influential sixteenth-century Franciscan François de Sales puts it:

> As S. Augustin sayth . . . all things in this world speak unto us with a kind of language, which though dumbe, in that it is not expressed in words, yet intelligiblie enough in regard of their love: for all things provoke us and give us occasion of good and godlie thoughts.[43]

The creatures are mute though eloquent ciphers in the Book of Nature, and the interpretative onus placed on man, who must read them, is a result of his Fall. The creatures are capable, as are words, of arousing thoughts of a "good and godlie" kind. The meaning of the creatures, insofar as this is what they *represent,* is accessible to whomever will take the trouble to read them. For the seventeenth century, one of the principal ways in which the creatures were understood to "speak unto us with a kind of language" was founded in the contrast between Adam's prelapsarian naming of the animals (Gen. 2:19–20 and paraphrased by Milton in *Paradise Lost* 8, 338–54) and the efforts of postlapsarian man to comprehend them and his relation to them. This subject had held a fascination for Ambrose, and we are fortunate in having a lucid paraphrase, by Donne, of part of Ambrose's *Hexaemeron* (6: [vi] 36):

> In this consists the power, which every man hath over the creature, that man understands the nature of every creature, For so *Adam* did, when he named every creature according to the nature thereof. And by this advantage of our understanding them, we master them, and so, *Obliviscuntur quod nata sunt,* says Saint *Ambrose;* the Lion, the Beare, the Ele-

41. Arnold Williams, *The Common Expositor: An Account of the commentaries on Genesis, 1527–1633,* p. 133.
42. Hall, *The Arte of Divine Meditation,* p. 11 (sig. B3r).
43. François de Sales, *Introduction to a Devoute Life,* trans. I. Y., p. 156 (sig. G6v).

phant have forgot what they were borne to. *Induuntur quod jubentur;* they invest and put on such a disposition, and such a nature, as we enjoine them, and appoint to them. *Serviant ut famuli;* (as that Father pursues it elegantly) and *verberantur ut timidi*: they waite upon us as servants; who, if they understood us as well, as we understand them, might be our Masters: and they receive correction from us, as though they were afraid of us; when, if they understood us, they would know, that we were not able to stand in the teeth of the Lion, in the horne of the Bull, in the heels of the Horse. And *adjuvantur ut infirmi*; they counterfeit a weakenesse, that they might be beholden unto us for help: and they are content to thanke us, if we affoord them any rest, or any food; who, if they understood us, as well, as we doe them, might teare our meate out of our throates; nay teare out our throates for their meat.[44]

The theme recurs in the *Holy Sonnets*:

Why brook'st thou, ignorant horse, subjection?
Why dost thou bull, and bore so seelily
Dissemble weaknesse, and by'one mans stroke die,
Whose whole kind, you might swallow and feed upon?[45]

Ambrose and Donne are not alone in seeing man's naming of the creatures as a significant act: Hall shares the belief and expresses it in terms of the Victorine dichotomy:

God gives the nature to his creatures: Man must give the name; that hee might see they were made for him, they shall be to him, what he will. Instead of their first homage, they are presented to their new Lord, and must see of whom they hold. He that was so carefull of mans soveraignte in his innocence, how can hee be careless of his safety in his renovation?

If God had given them their names, it had not bin so great a praise of *Adams* memory to recall them, as it was now of his judgement (at first sight) to impose them: he saw the inside of all the creatures at first; (his Posteritie sees but their skins ever since;) and by this knowledge he fitted their names to their dispositions. All that he saw, were fit to be his servants, none to be his companions. The same God that findes the want, supplyes it.[46]

Hall's last sentence offers a suggestion that must be pursued in the next chapter: that there exists, informing the created order, a

44. Donne, *Sermons,* vol. 9, pp. 83–84. Cf. *PL* 14, col. 255 for Ambrose's account.
45. John Donne, *Holy Sonnets 8,* in *The Divine Poems,* ed. Helen Gardner, p. 10.
46. Hall, *Contemplations* 1, in *Works,* p. 814 (sig. Zzz5^{v}).

divinely providential supplying of "want," and that this phenomenon is one of the gracious consequences of the Fall of Man. In Paradise before the Fall, man understood the creatures perfectly, and this understanding was reflected in Adam's naming of them; he needed to do no more, yet the permission granted him to do this signified that he was lord of creation. Postlapsarian man, in contrast, needs to exercise a great deal more effort before he can comprehend the Book of Nature, and sometimes he can scarcely read it at all. Yet man's mediatory role as lord of creation does equip him to read the book by conferring upon him the unique ability to understand his place in it. No other sentient or nonsentient creature possesses even the potential for reading the silent book of which it is a "page" or "word." In a fallen world, man needs to discover once more what has been forgotten since the Fall—that the naming of the creatures by Adam signified the perfect understanding he possessed of their divinely ordained natures. Fallen man needs to assimilate to himself the significance of this apparently unsignificant act of Adam's. Such rediscovery is one practical example of the way that partial recovery of man's original nature, according to Bonaventura, can be attained by means of the Book of Scripture. But man will never regain the full comprehension that existed in paradise before the Fall:

> Man could no sooner see, then hee saw himself happy: His eye sight and reason were both perfect at once, and the objects of both were able to make him as happy as he would. When hee first opened his eyes, hee saw heaven above him, earth under him, the creatures about him, God before him, hee knew what all these things meant, as if he had beene long acquainted with them all.[47]

Applying what we have so far been discussing to *The Temple,* we can conclude that acts of interpretation, when undertaken by Herbert in a state in which his perceptions are not dulled, may accurately be described as "prayer," if by this may be indicated some of the assured expressiveness discernible in the poems of that title. The assured tone of "Prayer" [II] has already been noted: it seems to suggest that Herbert's perceptions have been cleared and that

47. Ibid., p. 815.

the silent words of God are once more visible and able to be read. "Prayer" [I] (1633, p. 43) has been described as a *catena*;[48] the analogues for prayer linked together in this sonnet are nothing less than visible words whose significance is now available to Herbert as their reader. "Prayer" [I] suggests that these visible words can constitute "something understood," but the placement of that phrase as the poem's last, and the absence of any more explicit indication of its status or essence, invests what seems to be an assurance with qualities that are, to say the least, enigmatic. In order to assess whether our engagement with Herbert's lyric expressiveness can indeed ever confer on us the sense of "something understood" or whether it must, in view of the fallen nature of language, perpetually evade doing so, we need to consider how Herbert perceives the providential qualities that he regards as flowing from its author, how man's response may be said to figure spiritual "illiteracy," and how the clarity of perception that eventually accompanies Herbert's reading of God's signs in the Book of Scripture may be figured in terms of Grace.

48. E. B. Greenwood, "George Herbert's Sonnet 'Prayer': A Stylistic Study," pp. 32, etc.

4. "Providence"

Reading the Book of Nature

It is essential to grasp at the outset that, for Herbert, the act of reading the Book of Nature is implicit in the act of learning to see the hand of God's Providence at work. Conceptions of divine Providence had in fact found a central place in the thought of the period. Renaissance statements of divine Providence seem to derive chiefly from the formulations of Aquinas.[1] Where Renaissance apologists deal with the theme, however, they invariably show a tendency to insist on the sovereignty of God over the created order, even to the exclusion of chance, which Aquinas himself had conceded could be reconciled with his conception of providential governance.[2] As far as the English Renaissance is concerned, Richard Hooker was able to assert that "Nature . . . is nothing else but Gods instrument,"[3] and the sixteenth and seventeenth centuries in England are characterized by a conviction that all natural processes and occurrences are answerable in terms of God's having ordained, purposed, and permitted them to take place. Providence as conceived of during this period might best be thought of as a Christianization of pagan notions of a fortune or destiny that is inscrutable and capricious. Providence had come to be seen as God's maintenance of the natural order after the disastrous consequences of man's Fall, when the earth became plagued

1. See Thomas Aquinas, *Summa contra Gentiles*, 3, 64 and 70; and *Summae Theologicae Ia*, 22, 2. See Etienne Gilson, *The Spirit of Medieval Philosophy*, trans. Downes, pp. 156ff.

2. Keith Thomas, *Religion and the Decline of Magic*, pp. 78ff. See Peter Martyr Vermigli, *The Common Places . . . Translated and partly gathered by Anthonie Marten*, 1, xvi, 1 and 4, and Philippe de Mornay, *A Woorke concerning the trewnesse of the Christian Religion*, trans. Sir Philip Sidney and Arthur Golding, pp. 174ff. See also D. P. Walker, *The Ancient Theology: Studies in Christian Platonism from the Fifteenth to the Eighteenth Century*, pp. 132–35, etc.

3. Richard Hooker, *Of the Lawes of Ecclesiastical Politie* [Books 1–4], p. 54 (sig. E3v). Cf. Aquinas, *Summae Theologicae Ia IIae*, 91, 2; 93, 4; 94, 2. See Peter Munz, *The Place of Hooker in the History of Thought*, pp. 46ff., 178.

by infertility at worst, and weeds, pests, and the decline of domesticity at best. The position of man in this prevalently hostile environment was stabilized after the Flood, when God enjoined man's ascendancy over the natural order and sanctioned carnivorousness under the restrictions familiar to us from the Old Testament.[4] By the seventeenth century it had become commonplace to assume not simply that there was a purpose underlying God's maintenance of his creation, but that it was a purpose that man could—and should—learn to decipher. Related to this commonplace is the notion of man's ascendancy over the natural order of creation. Keith Thomas has written of "the breathtakingly anthropocentric spirit in which Tudor and Stuart preachers interpreted the Biblical story"[5] and has argued that this confident way of thinking reached a peak in the seventeenth century, gradually after this point losing ground to "an altogether more confused state of mind" by the beginning of the nineteenth. By this time, as Thomas puts it, "The world could no longer be regarded as having been made for man alone, and the rigid barriers between humanity and other forms of life had been much weakened."[6]

Herbert's attitude toward the doctrine of divine Providence, then, is entirely conventional. Yet while it is not my purpose to claim that his use of figurative language to express the workings of Providence is without precedent, it is important to emphasize the particular forms that this figurative expressiveness takes. For Herbert, interpretation of the Book of Nature is clearly related to domestic figures having to do with housekeeping. In "Man," for instance (1633, pp. 83–85), the Creation is accommodatively figured as a cupboard or a cabinet, and in "Ungratefulnesse" (1633, p. 74), the entirety of what has been significantly revealed by God is presented as "two rare cabinets full of treasure."[7] One of these

4. Gen. 3:17–19; 9:1–4.

5. Keith Thomas, *Man and the Natural World: Changing Attitudes in England 1500–1800,* p. 18.

6. Ibid., p. 301.

7. In this latter poem, man's "poore cabinet of bone" (18) recalls the figure of the heart in "Confession" (1633, pp. 118–19) as a nest of boxes. Robert Ellrodt, *L'Inspiration personelle et l'esprit du temps chez les poètes métaphysiques anglais,* 1, pp. 281–90, has some interesting reflections on the attitudes which this kind of writing

is celestial and only dimly apprehensible, the other earthly and fully available to man's understanding. Related to this conception is the idea of *husbandry* (thrift or economy); this, as we shall see, turns out to be the mode of operation of divine Providence. In "Ungratefulnesse" man and God are both seen as housekeepers; Herbert is scrupulously clear, however, that *thrift* does not necessarily imply *meanness,* though in man's fallen case it inevitably does:

> But man is close, reserv'd, and dark to thee:
> When thou demandest but a heart,
> He cavils instantly. (25–27)

There is a clear contrast between man's attitude and God's liberal bestowal of his mercies. Man defrauds God in keeping a box of his own "apart" in "his poore cabinet of bone," refusing, in other words, to open it, so that he spurns divine generosity at the same time that he undermines a tacit agreement made with God, "who gavest two for one." God, on the other hand, has "unlockt" both of his cabinets, which Herbert sees in this poem as

> jewels to betroth
> The work of thy creation
> Unto thy self in everlasting pleasure. (10–12)

God therefore makes the contents of his earthly cabinet fully available to man in a process of movement and *flow*: man refuses to disclose the contents of his cabinet, so that the "box" that it contains remains static, hard, and compressed. In the next chapter I show how, for Herbert, this unresponsiveness and reluctance on man's part can be overcome; the emphasis here must be on that unrestrained flow of divine generosity by which Herbert figures the operation of Providence.

---

represents. Richard Strier, in *Love Known: Theology and Experience in George Herbert's Poetry,* pp. 23–27, offers a fine reading of "Ungratefulnesse," but his stress on the poem's appositions is related primarily to the poem's theology, rather than to the divine bounty portrayed in, say, "Providence," a poem Strier sadly underrates (pp. 168–70). See also Chana Bloch, *Spelling the Word: George Herbert and the Bible,* pp. 214–30.

As Herbert expresses matters in "Ungratefulnesse," God's liberal husbandry renders his cabinets potentially accessible to man, so that they could be of interpretative use in man's approach to the cosmos as the creation of the Divine. This availability recalls the "handsell" notion to which I previously referred. The cabinets allow a better destiny for man, and it is in this way that they testify to divine generosity. That of the "Trinitie," however (analogous perhaps to the inner book of the Victorine scheme), is at the moment not accessible to man, since it reflects the nature of the Divine and is only perceptible by means of the curative properties of death that will blow dust into man's eyes.[8] But the other cabinet, the Incarnation, analogous to the outer book, *is* open to interpretation by man. For Herbert, the Trinity is austere and even frightening in nature; the Incarnation, on the other hand, "allures" man with "delights" (22). The Trinity is something of which man knows only the existence but not the details. The Incarnation allows him to attain a fuller knowledge: the contents of the latter are seen as "sweets," "mercies," and "delights." It is by means of the operation of the poet's wit that Herbert's reader can see how the contents of God's cabinet can come to be regarded *as* "sweets," "mercies," and "delights." The cabinet of the Incarnation ought to be especially appealing to man because he seems to be in possession of it in a double sense: first, as it exists in relation to the whole of fallen mankind, and second, as it exists in relation to each soul personally. Yet given this possession, man's response to divine munificence is to be "close, reserv'd, and dark"; he is, in short, unwilling to respond. This is not a permanent state of affairs, since in the very next poem, "Sighs and Grones" (1633, p. 75), Herbert's terms have changed. He is suffering here, but in this poem he expresses his sheer unwillingness and inability as a matter of the past, using a figure (central to his interpretative activity) of "consumer" response:

8. F. E. Hutchinson's note (*The Works of George Herbert*, p. 504) on the seventeenth-century treatment of horses or dogs with bad eyes by blowing powder into them is interesting; the dust of death also cures in "The Church-floore" (1633, p. 58). John R. Mulder in "George Herbert's *The Temple*: Design and Methodology," p. 38, refers to death in this poem as being "God's way of keeping a clean house."

For what account can thy ill steward make?
I have abus'd thy stock, destroy'd thy woods,
Suckt all thy magazens: my head did ake,
Till it found out how to consume thy goods. (8–11)

These lines indicate an attitude toward the Book of Nature that needs to be considered. It seems that interpretation of the book comes to involve its reader in the business of learning how to consume its resources, or to make use of them, finding that at first there is difficulty and reluctance in doing so. In fact, to the response that is implied, man "cavils instantly." The initial reaction can, however, be overcome; Herbert indicates in "Sighs and Grones" that inability "to consume thy goods" does not always trouble him, and consequently his health can be restored ("my head did ake / Till it found out how to . . ."). The title of this poem is recalled in "Gratefulnesse" (1633, pp. 116–17), where a curious change has taken place from the sense of sheer inability of "Ungratefulnesse" and the suffering of "Sighs and Grones":

thou hast made a sigh and grone
Thy joyes. (19–20)

Sighs and groans seem for Herbert capable of assuming significance: they can be seen as something whose achievement pleases the Divine, as "Gratefulnesse" shows. As evidence of cleared perceptions, they are presumably not incongruous in a poem of praise. They seem to signify remorse rather than merely suffering on the part of the poet and allow him to begin to write praise.[9]

It is useful to see poems such as these in the general context of Herbert's belief that the act of praise is somehow implicit in the act of writing; "Praise" [I] (1633, p. 53) begins:

To write a verse or two, is all the praise,
That I can raise (1–2)

and "Praise" [III] (1633, pp. 151–53) combines the notion of the

9. There is another example in "Dulnesse" (1633, p. 108).

offering of praise with the significance of sighs and groans, which has already been noted in "Gratefulnesse":

> Lord, I will mean and speak thy praise,
> Thy praise alone.
> My busie heart shall spin it all my dayes:
> And when it stops for want of store,
> Then will I wring it with a sigh or grone,
> That thou mayst yet have more. (1–6)

In a poem such as "Ungratefulnesse" we should notice how interpreting the Book of Nature seems actually to lead to the writing down of praise. This is made possible by clear perceptions, to the extent that Herbert is able to see the working of the providential aspect of the Divine in the world of created things.

These matters may serve as introduction to a consideration of Herbert's longer poem "Providence" (1633, pp. 109–14). This poem makes apparent how the figure of "consuming" divinely provided "goods" or resources may in fact be a way of expressing a sacramental truth. This consuming is sacramentalized in the Eucharist, and it is this that man has been required to learn how to carry out as a result of his Fall. In addition, man must learn his role in Creation: he is nothing less than "lord" of it. All these issues are raised in the opening lines of "Providence," where Herbert is concerned with finding an appropriately reciprocal manner in which to respond to the providential flow of divine bounty:

> O Sacred Providence, who from end to end
> Strongly and sweetly movest! shall I write,
> And not of thee, through whom my fingers bend
> To hold my quill? shall they not do thee right?
>
> Of all the creatures both in sea and land
> Onely to Man thou hast made known thy wayes,
> And put the penne alone into his hand,
> And made him Secretarie of thy praise. (1–8)

Herbert's reading of the silent words of the Book of Nature will involve him in discerning their interactions with each other, as well as their mutual interaction with him. He documents his cognition of these interactions very fully in "Providence," and we may assume that coming to realize the interrelatedness of the interacting constituents of both divine books, Nature *and* Scripture, form different aspects of the same activity. As Herbert writes in "[The H. Scriptures] II." (1633, p. 50), the interpreting of interacting constituents is both inevitable and pleasurable:

Oh that I knew how all thy lights combine,
And the configurations of their glorie!
Seeing not onely how each verse doth shine,
But all the constellations of the storie.

This verse marks that, and both do make a motion
Unto a third, that ten leaves off doth lie. (1–6)

Reading the Book of Scripture will lead Herbert to praise God through seeing the interactions of its words and things; reading the Book of Nature will lead him to praise God by seeing the interaction of its silent words under God's providential aspect, both with each other and with him.

We should realize that Herbert, by no means uniquely, regards the act of reading the silent words of the Book of Nature not as a luxury that he can choose to perform or not, as he pleases, but as something that carries a sense of urgency, inevitability, and reciprocity. The words of Joseph Hall suggest this with particular clarity; reading the silent words of Nature is

> not onely lawfull, but so behoovefull, that we cannot omit them, without neglect of God, his creatures, our selves. The creatures are halfe lost if we onely imploy them, not learne something of them: God is wronged if his creatures bee unregarded; our selves most of all, if we reade this great volume of the creatures, and take out no lesson for our instruction.[10]

The terms of Hall's distinction between employing the creatures and learning from them is central to Herbert's understanding of man's place in Creation. We have seen that Adam's naming of the creatures signified that he understood their natures perfectly. Fallen man's initial inability to attain this clear understanding means that he needs to learn from them, in addition to employing

10. Joseph Hall, *The Arte of Divine Meditation,* pp. 15–16 (sigs. $B5^{r-v}$).

the creatures as God enjoined Adam before the Fall.[11] Before the Fall, Adam had a perfect intuitive understanding of the place of the creatures in relation to himself, and he was able to signify this intuition by naming them. His role was that of lord of Creation. Fallen man can aspire to this role, but his clouded understanding needs more laboriously to attain a knowledge of the relation of the creatures to himself. Where Adam before the Fall employed the creatures and in so doing knew his place in relation to them and to God, mankind after the Fall employs the creatures and in so doing learns from them about these relations. This does place emphasis on the interactions of the various parts of the Creation.

The reader of the Book of Nature, then, learns about the book by employing it. This conviction was able to be maintained throughout the medieval and Renaissance periods in terms of man's place in Creation; he was characteristically seen as being served by nature. Here is a passage from Hugh of St. Victor's *De arrha animae*:

> Look at the whole world, and consider whether there is anything in it which does not wait upon you. All nature directs her course to this end, to provide for your desires and to serve your requirements, and in all your wishes and needs, equally, to meet your deficiencies with her own abundance. This heaven, this world, this sky, this sea—they never cease to fill the creatures that are in them with all these things; in this yearly cycle, which is perpetually renewed, what is old is renovated in redistributed parts, what is decayed is rebuilt, what has been consumed is restored, and nourishment is continually being provided. Who then do you think brought this about? Who instructed nature to serve you so single-mindedly?[12]

The realization that man is "lord of all" (this is what he learns from

11. Gen. 1:26.

12. Respice universum mundum istum, et considera si aliquid in eo sit, quod tibi non serviat. Omnis natura ad hunc finem cursum suum dirigit, ut obsequiis tuis famuletur, et utilitati deserviat, tuisque oblectamentis pariter et necessitatibus secundum affluentiam indeficientem occurrat. Hoc coelum, hoc terra, hoc aer, hoc maria, cum iis, quae in eis sunt, universis, explere non cessant; in hoc circuitus temporum annuis innovationibus, et redivivis partubus [sic] antiqua innovans, dilapsa reformans, consumpta restaurans, pastu perpetuo subministrat. Quis ergo putas hoc instituit? quis istud naturae praecepit ut sic uno consensu tibi serviat? Hugh of St. Victor, *Soliloquium de arrha animae*; *PL* 176, col. 955. There is an interesting echo of this in Robert Parsons's *A Booke of Christian Exercise, appertaining to Resolution. . . . Perused . . . by Edm. Bunny,* pp. 76–77 (sigs. F6^{v}-7^{r}).

the creatures from employing them) confers a particular obligation of duty upon the reader of the Book of Nature. The reason for this lies in a distinction fundamental to Augustinian Christianity; on it depends Hall's distinction between "employing" and "learning from." This is the distinction between "use" and "enjoyment," and it corresponds to a distinction between the creature and the Creator. A thing is "used" for a purpose other than itself and "enjoyed" *for* itself alone. The creature is, and should be, used for a purpose other than itself, and in the context of interpreting the Book of Nature this purpose may be expressed in terms of revealing or laying open the actions of that divine Providence who informs all the interactions of the creatures. As a result, the Creator alone is enjoyed. The thought of Herbert's "Providence" is consistent with these realizations, but the poem achieves its purpose in a characteristically Herbertian manner.

According to Augustine, it is an error to use God in order to enjoy the world; the good man uses the world in order to enjoy God. Rosemond Tuve draws attention to a further distinction in Augustine's conception, which ought to be made here: "The distinction is not . . . the one we should have in mind if we spoke of God as end and creatures as means; our usual use of such terms (e.g. to 'use' one's friends) points to something Augustine calls not 'use' at all but 'abuse'. . . . We 'enjoy' the human beings whom we love . . . but enjoy them 'in the Lord.'"[13]

This distinction throws some useful light both on Herbert's argument in "Man" (1633, pp. 83–85) and on the figurative language of "Ungratefulnesse." *Use* as Herbert understands it seems to be summarized neatly and clearly in "Man":

> Nothing we see, but means our good,
> As our *delight,* or as our *treasure:*

13. Rosemond Tuve, *Essays by Rosemond Tuve,* ed. Thomas P. Roche, Jr., pp. 201–202. See Augustine, *De Doctrina Christiana,* 1, iv (4); *PL* 34, cols. 20–21; *De Civitate Dei* 15, vii (*PL* 41, col. 444) and *De Trinitate* 9, xii (*PL* 42, cols. 970–72). See also John Burnaby, *Amor Dei: A Study of the Religion of St Augustine,* p. 12, and the *New Catholic Encyclopedia,* vol. 1, p. 1056. Heather Asals, *Equivocal Predication: George Herbert's Way to God,* pp. 57ff., relates the distinction between "use" and "enjoyment," as Tuve herself does not, to "The Quidditie" (1633, p. 61), and, further, to the writing of poetry itself.

The whole is, either our cupboard of *food,*
Or cabinet of *pleasure.* (27–30)

There are two ways in which the creatures are used by man: both as a "cupboard of food" for the purposes of physical sustenance (corresponding to Hall's "employing"), and as a "cabinet of *pleasure*" for the purpose of leading the mind from creature to Creator (corresponding to Hall's "learning from"). It is this "cabinet of pleasure" that God makes available to man with such easy, flowing openhandedness in "Ungratefulnesse" and whose operations Herbert details in "Providence." Herbert's response is in effect a reading of the Book of Nature. The response implies writing praise; both activities are figurative for using Creation "as referred to God," and they lead to realizations that cannot be derived in any other way. If the Book of Nature were to be read in any other way than "as referred to God," the creatures would be abused because they would be made use of solely as a "cupboard of *food*." Though God enjoined Adam to use the Creation in this sense, it was before man's Fall, when he understood the Creation perfectly. Herbert elsewhere sums up the role of fallen man in terms that clearly rely on the Augustinian distinction but particularize it:

Indeed mans whole estate
Amounts (and richly) to serve thee:
He did not heav'n and earth create,
Yet studies them, not him by whom they be.

Teach me thy love to know;
That this new light, which now I see,
May both the work and workman show:
Then by a sunne-beam I will climbe to thee.
("Mattens" [1633, p. 54, 13–20])

It is hard to decide what the poet's attitude is in the first of these stanzas; is man's action in "studying" being commended here, or regarded simply as what he does in default, being unable to study "him by whom they be"? In the light of what has been gathered from Hugh and Bonaventura, it would seem that Herbert's statement is to be read as quite neutral; man can only see the creature, not the Creator. This would be in keeping with Augustine's remarks in the *Confessions* 10. Augustine's discovery seems not to have the same revelatory impact for Herbert, who is more concerned to "climbe" to God by means of such an arresting particular as a "sunne-beam."

Fallen man, then, studies the Creation and must strive towards his prelapsarian state by learning from it at least something of divine love; he does not simply use the Creation for the purpose of physical sustenance alone. It would be more accurate to say that he aspires toward learning what his consuming of natural resources, provided by God, could signify. As I have indicated, this implies the uniqueness of man's place in Creation. Herbert argues these very fully in "Providence," where he asks how it is possible to write without writing the praise of divine Providence, since it is through this agency that the physical act of writing is possible in the first instance. The answer to the rhetorical question is therefore given in terms of the poet's wit. God has not only created his image in man but has also allowed him the possibility of interpretative response, so that it is impossible for the poet to write without revealing the providential operation of the "sacred Spirit" (25) of whom he writes. Since man is the only one of God's creatures who has this interpretative ability, he must act as "secretary" on behalf of the other creatures. This is presumably to be taken as Herbert's poetically realized expression of the belief that to fallen man the Book of Nature is meaningless unless referred to God. Herbert expresses this belief in terms of his own witty response to the divine wit that he sees about him: his doing so in this way is crucial to the argument of "Providence." None of the creatures can offer praise to God in words, though they may seem to want to do so. Yet even this assertion is made in terms of a witty apprehension of what the poet sees:

> Beasts fain would sing; birds dittie to their notes;
> Trees would be tuning on their native lute
> To thy renown. (9–11)

We may recall François de Sales's assertion, which owes much to Augustinian sign theory, that "all things in this world speak unto us with a kind of language"; we have so far been considering only that "language" that is inherent in the creatures by virtue of their being signs of their Creator. We ought, however, to distinguish this sense of "silent language" from the noises the creatures make. Man occupies a mediatory role, as we have seen, and it is possible for him to realize that these creaturely noises do in fact constitute a "language" addressed to the divine Creator. In his fallen state man is unable to interpret this. From man's point of view, indeed, the creatures may only be "dumb" insofar as they are incomprehensible; it is possible that they speak to the Divine in a language that man cannot understand because his perception of the books that were once clear and representative has clouded. This sense of creaturely "language" ought probably to be kept distinct from the sense in which François uses it, but Herbert is sympathetic with both senses. He is certainly not alone in conceiving a language of the creatures, but he makes it a crucial argument of "Providence" that it is given to man to realize the mute and mutual interdependence of the creatures with each other and with him. Since this is a realization uniquely granted to man, he becomes a focal point for the dumb praises of the creatures. Having previously extended the idea of the creatures' inarticulacy into one of lameness, so that in addition to needing man as their voice, the creatures need him as their hands (11–12), Herbert expresses man's response to the Book of Nature in terms of priesthood:

> Man is the worlds high Priest: he doth present
> The sacrifice for all; while they below
> Unto the service mutter an assent,
> Such as springs use that fall, and windes that blow. (13–16)

The hieratic figure contains sacramental implications of such centrality to Herbert's whole aesthetic that they must be considered here, albeit briefly. In "Providence," Herbert's emphasis is on man as "the worlds high Priest" (13) and on the ways in which this role implies the mediatory offering of praise. Elsewhere in *The Temple,* the role of priest is less figurative, and in poems such as "The Priesthood" (1633, pp. 154–55) and "Aaron" (1633, pp. 168–69), Herbert emphasizes the need for purity and the problem of man's very presumption in daring to contemplate assuming the robes of priestly office.[14] As Herbert poignantly expresses it in *The Countrey Parson,* it is the priest's highest duty "to break, and administer" God.[15]

"The Priesthood" begins with a direct address to the office itself. This is seen as being so powerful that it excels even earthly, temporal power, which can promote to fame or degrade to obscurity. The priesthood can actually raise to heaven or cast down to hell; its power is so inscrutable that, unlike providential power, its movements seem arbitrary enough that we can say that what we have in the opening lines of this poem is actually an unillustrated emblem of Fortune's wheel. This is a bold conceit in the light of Herbert's need elsewhere to conceive of divinely providential movement as something implying meaningful interpretation. Is the inscrutable power of the priestly office then arbitrarily evenhanded and not susceptible of meaningful interpretation?

> Blest Order, which in power dost so excell,
> That with th'one hand thou liftest to the sky,
> And with the other throwest down to hell
> In thy just censures; fain would I draw nigh. (1–4)

Herbert is, however, held back and withdraws from assuming the desired robes of office. The reason for this is expressed figuratively: the office is seen as "sacred and hallow'd fire" (7) and the aspiring priest "but earth and clay" (8). This realization of the potency of the priestly robes with respect to the person of the priest recalls, as Hutchinson saw, the familiar scriptural figure of the divine potter and human clay.[16] Here the contrast between the inexplicable movement (that of fire) that characterizes the supernatural office, and the static quality of the man on whom this office can act, is a significant one. Whatever Herbert may have intended, the movement certainly parallels the natural easy flow

14. Neither poem is in the Williams MS (which also does not contain "Providence"). Amy M. Charles (*A Life of George Herbert,* p. 141) tentatively assigns "The Priesthood" to 1628 and such a date can be postulated for "Aaron" also.

15. George Herbert, *The Countrey Parson,* 23 (*Works,* p. 257).

16. See Herbert, *Works,* pp. 533–34, where Hutchinson cites Isa. 44:8, Jer. 18:6 and Rom. 9:21–23.

of Providence, and the stationary hardness with which the human vessel is conceived of parallels the frequent allusions in *The Temple* to man's static, compressed unwillingness and lack of generosity. The sense of movement and stasis come together in the fear that is voiced by Herbert's priest; not only does he feel himself to be sinful, but, as in the manner of fired clay containing an air bubble, he would actually be dangerous ("brittle" [11]) with the transforming fire of the priestly office upon him. Since they would destroy him and he is "foul," he is doubly unfit for the office.

Herbert takes consolation in observing that fire may, given a skillful potter, be the means of catalytically transforming clay and earth into "curious things" (14); as a result, the muddy earth where he characteristically "once . . . scorn'd to stand" (15) can be transformed by those with the necessary skill into tableware fine enough to suit even those who keep the finest tables. By implication, the finest table of all is God's, but that is held for a while. At this point, Herbert perversely pursues the implication of his poetic figure rather than the implications of what the figure signifies. Those mortals who keep the finest tables are themselves made of mud and clay; they, their tableware, and their food are all of the same origin. In the light of this, man's affinity for mud and clay is unsurprising and more naturally excusable than his fastidiousness. Even God submits to a degrading transformation in being "broken" eucharistically; yet someone must serve this divine fare. The paradox with which this notion is invested is finely caught in a single line:

> Their hands convey him, who conveys their hands. (28)

Herbert still does not dare "put forth my hand / To hold the Ark"—the figure recalls, as C. A. Patrides notes, the story of Uzzah attempting to steady the Ark when it was in danger of falling, and being struck dead[17] —but at the same time, the sense of crisis that has led to its apparent shaking "through th'old sinnes and new doctrines of our land" (33) now demands response. The introduc-

17. The reference is to 2 Sam. 6:6–7. See C. A. Patrides, ed., *The English Poems of George Herbert*, p. 168.

tion of the figure of the Ark and the scriptural reference recalling God's providential command of history (however perplexing individual episodes such as the death of Uzzah may appear) combine to move Herbert into action. He must relinquish his fastidiousness, burn his fingers on the fire of priestly office, and abandon himself to divine craftsmanship in a completely trusting attitude. Paradoxically, the poem's last figure suggests that this dynamic act of prostration must finally be understood in terms of passivity and waiting. Herbert here gives significance to power and freedom:

There will I lie, untill my Maker seek
For some mean stuffe whereon to show his skill:
Then is my time. The distance of the meek
Doth flatter power. Lest good come short of ill
In praising might, the poore do by submission
What pride by opposition. (37–42)

When, runs the argument, is Herbert more powerful and free than when his "time" of assuming priestly office is seen to coincide with the divine "time" of bestowing grace to enable him to assume that office? Herbert reveals why it is that when he subjects his own will to God's, he is at his most powerful and free. This is a dramatization of the findings of Aquinas, corroborated by Martyr and Hooker, on man's cooperation with the Divine. Man, thus cooperating, is paradoxically most free to act. Perhaps in this last stanza there is a hint of divine and human wills in contest, where the movement of the sentences momentarily cuts across the lineation of the verse. But in accordance with the poem's argument, this contrary movement is stilled in the final lines.

In "Aaron," Herbert considers the significance of Aaron's robes, arriving at a definition of them as something he can assume once they are seen to signify a divine Grace. There is a long history of divergent patristic and scholastic opinion over the exact nature of the typological relationship between Aaron and Christ. Herbert's poem can be seen as an attempt to come to terms with divine Grace in the action of submission to the consequences of the Incarnation. The associations in the poem are less with a belief that Aaron's priesthood typifies Christ's mediation between man and

God[18] than with Paul's injunctions to "put on" Christ.[19] Herbert sees himself as fallen man, unable to regain Grace. The work of restoration is a central concern to the poem insofar as Herbert's attempts to regain Grace inform his chief worries in it: he is, at first, totally unable to exist or communicate "harmonically" as a priest, to see and read the silent words of the Divine, and to offer a shared reading with the rest of the Church. The reason for this inability lies in his own sinful nature; he expresses this by conceiving of himself as being out of tune, sounding as "a noise of passions ringing me for dead" (8).[20] The perfections of Aaron are described:

> Holinesse on the head,
> Light and perfections on the breast,
> Harmonious bells below, raising the dead
> To lead them unto life and rest.
> Thus are true Aarons drest. (1–5)

Herbert characteristically contrasts his own imperfections with close reference to this standard ("Poore priest thus am I drest"). The only way for Herbert to resolve the difficulty of his impurity and tunelessness in the face of the exacting requirements of the office of priest is to dress himself in the "garments" that the Incar-

18. See 1 Tim. 2:1–2; Rom. 15:30; Heb. 8:18.

19. See Col. 3:10ff. and Eph. 4:24ff. See also Asals, *Equivocal Predication*, pp. 38ff.

20. Despite the disrepute into which allegorical scriptural exegesis later fell, and to some extent still remained in the seventeenth century, the association of Aaron with harmony is a very old one, going back at least as far as the Alexandrian Jewish allegorical exegete Philo Judaeus (ca. 20 BC – ca. AD 50). There is an extensive commentary on Aaron in Philo's treatment of the Exodus (*De Migratione*, vol. 4 in the Loeb edition). Philo's works were available to the seventeenth century, though the *STC* lists only *Omnia opera quae extant* (1691), of which there is a copy in the library of Balliol College, Oxford. But the British Library also catalogues editions produced at Paris in 1552, Geneva in 1613, and Paris in 1640, of which the last two claim to be complete works. According to H. M. Adams, *Catalogue of books printed on the Continent of Europe, 1501–1600, in Cambridge libraries*, vol. 2, p. 74, there is in more than one Cambridge library, though not Trinity's, a copy of the 1552 work; Trinity, however, possesses an edition (Basle, 1527) of a commentary of Philo's on Genesis. Most of these works are bilingual (Greek/Latin) editions. Yet despite the availability of works such as these, some skepticism persisted; the Scotch divine John Weemse (or Wemyss) remarks that "Philo-Judaeus was a great affecter of these Allegories. . . . The Fathers have beene too great followers of this Allegorical exposition" (Weemse, *The Workes . . . in Three Volumes*, vol. 1, p. 235 [sig. Q6^r]).

nation has made it possible for him to wear: the divine Grace that "tunes" his doctrine. The surrender to Christ is a humiliating act insofar as he has been given a duty both to the Divine and to the Church. As priest he strives to meet the perfection of Aaron but finds he has no hope of being properly equipped at all for the role of priest on his own. Christ, however, "tunes" his doctrine and lives in him: he is Herbert the priest but effective only when dressed with Christ, harmonious and no longer at variance within himself.

Herbert's priestly figure in "Providence," concerned as it is with the necessity of interpreting the Book of Nature and thus with the act of learning how to consume providentially supplied goods, is entirely consistent with the thought in the chapter in *The Countrey Parson* devoted to "The Parson's Consideration of Providence." In this chapter Herbert stresses the role of observation in coming to conclusions about the workings of Providence.[21] What Herbert is doing in his poem "Providence" may become clearer if it is briefly set beside "Mans medley" (1633, pp. 123–24), where he follows traditional ideas in considering that the noises the creatures make foreshadow future bliss:[22]

> Heark, how the birds do sing,
> And woods do ring.
> All creatures have their joy: and man hath his.
> Yet if we rightly measure,
> Mans joy and pleasure
> Rather hereafter, then in present, is. (1–6)

The poem expresses man's uniqueness as a double privilege; he is able to use temporary pleasures in order to enjoy lasting ones. On earth, he shares pleasures with the creatures, but he is unique among them in claiming also those pleasures that the angels

21. Herbert, *Works*, pp. 270–72.

22. See the *Imitatio Christi* 3, xxxi, and Lorenzo Scupoli, *Spiritual Combat*, 23. Louis L. Martz's arguments for the influence on Herbert of the *Imitatio* are well established; see *The Poetry of Meditation: A Study in English Religious Literature of the Seventeenth Century*, pp. 285ff. More recently, A. L. Clements, "Theme, Tone, and Tradition in George Herbert's Poetry," pp. 264–83, has suggested not only familiarity on Herbert's part with Scupoli, but parody of the *Combat* in Herbert's "Artillerie" (1633, pp. 132–33).

enjoy. The temporal and the eternal are therefore joined uniquely by man:

> Man ties them both alone,
> And makes them one,
> With th'one hand touching heav'n, with th'other earth. (10–12)

In "Mans medley" Herbert explores man's uniqueness in terms of the theologically traditional double realization upon which my reading of *The Temple* is based. The poem pursues the idea of man's mediation between the "inner" and the "outer" in terms of "double joys" and "double pains"—that is, in terms of man's spiritual and physical makeup. Herbert realizes that the result of his theological insight is the result of writing the poem itself, seeing the response elicited by a reading of the divine book as something he is privileged to be able to record:

> Yet ev'n the greatest griefs
> May be reliefs,
> Could he but take them right, and in their wayes.
> Happie is he, whose heart
> Hath found the art
> To turn his double pains to double praise. (31–36)

In "Providence," "art" of this kind is also unique to man. Herbert uses the secretarial and priestly figure to set down his realization not only that it is man's duty to offer the praises of the creatures to God (to "present / The sacrifice for all") but that, in performing this duty, man in effect interprets and thereby makes sense of the Book of Nature. In other words, Herbert gives the "mutterings" of the creatures sense by offering them to God, and the reader here as elsewhere in *The Temple* sees the process of sacramental offering up at work. Again, poetically realized wit reflects—or, better, responds to—the divine wit it interprets. Surely there are clear relations to be seen here with Bonaventura's formulation of God's significant revelation. The reader of the "outer book" can make sense of it by interpreting it, where "interpretation" is to be conceived of, in terms of Augustine's theology of love, as referral to God: this is the lesson that above all others is gained from a reading of the substitute for the "inner book," that is, the Book of Scripture. The implications of divine love and the potential for man's response that emerge from a reading of the Book of Scripture not only apply to a reading of the Book of Nature as well, but actually assist the reader in making sense of this outer book. Making sense of the Book of Nature corresponds to offering praise to divine Providence. This sense is something the poet as reader of the Book of Nature may express in terms of poetic wit, and in this way the whole argument of "Providence" can well be seen as the consequence of an action whose self-conscious presentation to God confers sense on the action as well as the praise. Put another way, Herbert's poem both expresses and reflects Providence in action. Man is an interpreter of the creatures insofar as he will now, having presented it to the Divine, understand that what the creatures are "muttering" *is* praise; he does not necessarily understand the praise in terms of words he himself could or would use. This conception is wholly consistent with Augustinian sign theory.

It follows from this that the man who declines to praise God debars not only himself but thousands of other, incapable, creatures from this act. This adds great responsibility to man's act of praise of God:

> He that to praise and laud thee doth refrain,
> Doth not refrain unto himself alone,
> But robs a thousand who would praise thee fain,
> And doth commit a world of sinne in one. (16–20)

This responsibility is a result of God's commandment to Adam before the Fall, and of how, in a fallen world, that commandment is to be understood. Man must constantly remember that, in his quite legitimate use of Creation for his own sustenance, he is using those means by which Creation, through man's secretaryship, praises God. Man's duty is to be constantly aware of this, lest his use of Creation should, through his forgetting its purpose, be referred away from the Divine and thus become abuse.

> The beasts say, Eat me: but, if beasts must teach,
> The tongue is yours to eat, but mine to praise.
> The trees say, Pull me: but the hand you stretch,
> Is mine to write, as it is yours to raise.

> Wherefore, most sacred Spirit, I here present
> For me and all my fellows praise to thee. (21–26)

We may explicate these lines in terms of man's complete interaction with nature. Man's tongue praises God, as do those of the beasts whose tongues may form part of man's diet: trees may "use" man's hand to write, just as man may use that hand to uproot them. The chiasmus not only draws attention to what Creation is mutely *saying* but also enacts mimetically the fiction of Providence's abundant and resourceful flow. The unit of the half-line takes on importance as the reader is constantly being "wrong-footed" and pleasurably surprised by the inventiveness of expression, which is referred to the working of Providence. The only attribute given to Providence, apart from "skill and art" (40), is the quality of its *movement*; this is twice (2 and 31) described as "strong and sweet." Providence is in fact accommodatively personified entirely in terms of action. One of these actions invokes the figure of Providence as a divine tuner, adjusting all Creation to its pitch (38–39). In addition to recalling the unavailing wishes of the trees (10–11), this figure recalls the stretching and contracting of "The Temper" poems (1633, pp. 46–48) and of "Easter" (1633, p. 33); it recalls, too, Hooker's assertion that "Nature . . . is nothing else but Gods instrument." To understand Providence in this way is yet again to accept and come to terms with the correctiveness of the divine perspective, in which Creation is a means to its end, and man must learn how to use it in order to enjoy the Divine. This perspective is summarized in "The Pulley" (1633, pp. 153–54), where God remarks that if he had bestowed the gift of rest on man, man would quickly have become complacent:

> He would adore my gifts in stead of me,
> And rest in Nature, not the God of Nature:
> So both should losers be. (13–15)

It should now be clear that although Hutchinson suggested a source for "Providence" in Psalms 104 (*Works*, p. 518), it is a source that accounts for the "many echoes" of the psalm in the poem only and not for the overall tone and effect, which differ from the following verses from "a meditation upon the mighty power and wonderful providence of God," where Providence is seen as an expression of God's power, unsearchable and unknowable by man:

> 24 O LORD, how manifold are thy works! in wisdom hast thou made them all: the earth is full of thy riches. . . .
> 27 These [creatures] wait all upon thee; that thou mayest give them their meat in due season.
> 28 That thou givest them they gather: thou openest thine hand, they are filled with good.
> 29 Thou hidest thy face, they are troubled: thou takest away their breath, they die, and return to their dust.
> 30 Thou sendest forth thy spirit, they are created: and thou renewest the face of the earth.

We may appreciate how the stress that Herbert's poem places on the interaction of the creatures with each other and on man's interaction with them is not an emphasis in the psalm. The way that both Herbert and God participate in an accommodatively expressed relationship is a matter for concern here insofar as the figure of Providence is itself seen as an accommodative personification of the total interdependence of the created order, animate and inanimate, so that even the noises that springs and winds make are offered to God (16).

* * *

It may be easier for twentieth-century readers to appreciate Herbert's achievement in "Providence" if some space is devoted to contrasting Herbert's accommodative personification of divine Providence with another seventeenth-century attempt to praise God's ways to his Creation. Joshua Sylvester's translation of du Bartas's *Les Semaines* first appeared in 1605, though the French original dates from 1578. In the section of the poem that treats the sixth day of Creation (the creation of man), there occur passages dealing with God's providential power. Sylvester writes, for instance, of God's protection of man in the face of the creatures that are hostile to him:

> O gracious Father! th'hast not only lent
> Prudence to man, the Perils to prevent,

Whearwith these foes threaten his feeble life:
But (for his sake) hast set at mutuall strife
Serpents with Serpents, and hast rais'd them foes
Which unprovoked, fellie them oppose.[23]

Sylvester's words show an anthropocentric view of the cosmos that does not, however, draw on any sense of mutual interaction of man and Creation, such as may be deduced from the writing of Hugh and Bonaventura and is to be found in *The Temple.* Although for Sylvester it is actually for man's sake that serpents attack each other, his attempt to solve the problem of how man is protected by his Creator immediately raises further questions: would protection be necessary if God had simply not created serpents and their like, all of which are at least potentially harmful to man? With reference to man, what sort of omnipotence is this? Sylvester seems to express it as somewhat hasty tactics in which, most importantly, there seems little place for the consequences of man's Fall. Herbert conveys a subtler strategic inherence, more leisured and planned, less myopic; this seems a direct result of the implications of the particular view of the cosmos as God's Creation that Herbert wittily accepts from the formulations of Hugh and Bonaventura and expresses in terms of the "strong and sweet" movement of Providence. Herbert's anthropocentric treatment of these formulations is such that he accommodates Providence to the human mind, and he manages to show that accommodating divine omnipotence by no means undermines his conception of it. For Sylvester, however, man's enemies manage to injure each other so that they dissipate the harmful energies that they might otherwise unleash on man himself; thus serpents are "set at mutuall strife," and the weasel and serpent kill each other. Divine tactics for Sylvester do include symbiosis: the ichneumon (a small mongoose-like creature) dispatches the "aspick" but cannot so easily overcome the crocodile, and here the wren assists, picking the crocodile's teeth so that, "charm'd with pleasure," the crocodile yawns more widely still, upon which the ichneumon "instantly / Into the

23. Joshua Sylvester, *Bartas: His Devine Weekes and Workes,* sig. 08^r. The pagination is erroneous here (p. 169 for p. 199).

Tirants greedie gorge doth flie, / And feeds upon that Glutton" (p. 21). Yet all Sylvester concludes from this is:

> Nay more (good Lord) th'hast taught Mankind a Reason
> To draw life out of Death, and Health from Poyson:
> So that in equall Ballance ballancing
> The good and evill which these Creatures bring
> Unto mans life, we shall perceive, the first
> By many graines to over-waigh the worst. (p. 201)

Here Sylvester seems to be making sense of the cosmos as God's Creation—that is to say, reading God's Book of Nature—in such a way as to turn (at times rather desperately) every hostile and harmful element in it to the use of man. Sylvester's marginalia at this point read: "God hath taught us to make great use of them," yet his concession of this is utterly different from Herbert's. Herbert's treatment of Providence enables him, for example, to praise the Divine by actually attributing, through Providence, a significance to symbiosis—it is part of a general interaction of the Creation with itself and with its Creator. *Use* for Sylvester does indeed seem to mean little more than *employment* of the creatures; if man learns from them, it is to the effect that he is lord of Creation. For Herbert, man learns more than this: he is lord of Creation, and this does not simply demand but actually *implies* a response that is expressed in terms of praise.

One of the most dramatic discoveries of Herbert's poem occurs at line 53, where we see that even the more unsavory forms of symbiosis are actually to be interpreted as expressions of praise because they are frank responses to God's liberal husbandry:

> Nothing ingendred doth prevent his meat:
> Flies have their table spread, ere they appeare.
> Some creatures have in winter what to eat;
> Others do sleep, and envie not their cheer. (53–56)

In fact, this offers a very good example of the kind of thing that is both traditional and innovatory in Herbert's poem. Keith Thomas provides a number of examples of seventeenth-century anthropocentrism but none, surely, that quite manage to convey the sense embodied here that natural phenomena could be depicted in terms of refinements of human behavior. Flies have the good manners not to turn up for meals before the table has been laid. By proceeding immediately to the phenomenon of hibernation, the roving eye of Herbert's secretary not only lights on the traditional conviction that hibernation was a providential means of ensuring that those creatures who remained active in winter had enough to eat, but also links the phenomenon to that of unsavory symbiosis. He wittily draws attention to the interpretative potential offered by observation of hibernating animals, in terms of a repeated suggestion of ordered social behavior as evidenced in good table manners. The pleasure taken by the active creatures in winter will not be spoiled by complaints from those who are necessarily going without.

The most extreme conclusion that Herbert's secretary draws from observed phenomena does perhaps recall Sylvester:

> Ev'n poysons praise thee. Should a thing be lost?
> Should creatures want for want of heed their due?
> Since where are poysons, antidots are most:
> The help stands close, and keeps the fear in view. (85–88)

The assertion that "poysons praise thee" is probably unexpected, but there is an explanation. This is teleological, as it is in Sylvester, but is more robustly expressed. Whereas Sylvester implies that man learns from the very existence of poisons that health is stronger, Herbert attributes what we may call "creative wit" to divine Providence by giving antidotes, as well as poisons, sense in the general scheme of things. Once again this is expressed in terms of God's thrifty husbandry ("Should a thing be lost?"). Sylvester shows less sense of any providential relationship between cause and effect than does Herbert and is consequently unable to relate his observation of natural phenomena to implicit conclusions about the interpretation of those phenomena. For Herbert it is the actions of divine Providence that are of such importance: his portrayal of those actions enables him to assert that God's creative wit can be apprehended by man as he reads the Book of Nature. This portrayal may indeed involve recourse to extremely accommodative expression, and it is this upon which

Herbert's teleology, so characteristically exploitative in its general strategy of the notion of chiasmus, is based:

> To show thou art not bound, as if thy lot
> Were worse then ours; sometimes thou shiftest hands.
> Most things move th'under-jaw; the Crocodile not.
> Most things sleep lying; th'Elephant leans or stands. (137–40)

What can we conclude from Herbert's demonstration of creative wit in this poem? It is characterized by remarkable naiveté as the catalogue of Providence's "strong and sweet" movement is unfolded. The teleological, accommodative expression both draws attention to Herbert's curious talent for disingenuous, self-aware discovery of man's smallness and celebrates the wit exemplified by God's providential aspect. In effect, the poetic fiction mimetically conveyed in "Providence" is that divine creative wit is "discovered" by the poet, who does not take credit for the discovery but refers it to God in terms of a gracious insight divinely bestowed. Both Herbert and his reader come to see that the very ability to write is itself a result of man's privileged mediatory role in the divinely appointed order of Creation. It is as though the poet has been given the wit both to apprehend his own role and to express the Providence through which the former insight has been made possible. Consequently, Herbert's poetically realized and poetically expressed act of interpretative understanding leads him to offer praise to God, and it can be seen that this understanding is something that, once it has broken in upon him, Herbert hands back to God. The act itself resounds with praise.

As readers reading this poem, however, we can only appreciate such an understanding as long as we are prepared to accept the poem's mimetic fiction. Although this is part of a general issue that will be reserved for the final chapter of this book, I will briefly anticipate some of that discussion here. We know that the poem "Providence" is Herbert's invention and that the poetic strategies employed, including the informing device of chiasmus, are Herbert's own, however traditional the notion it apostrophizes. Is Herbert, then, drawing attention to his own ingenuity? This is presumably related to the question of who is supposed to be reading this poem.[24] The terms of the fiction suggest God: the realities and pragmatics of the poem's status as a disseminated publication urge us to say that once a human reader reads "Providence," that fiction has been exploded. There is no indication in Herbert's documentation to suggest that he is in any way displeased with his own poetic achievement in drawing attention to a witty association of the multifariousness of the creative wit of divine Providence by means of a double conclusion.

The double doxology that ends the poem was thought by Herbert's early twentieth-century editor Palmer to be erroneous, in that one of the two final stanzas represented an uncancelled version of the other. Hutchinson, the Oxford editor, agreed and read "twice" (148) as "in his own person and as the spokesman of priest of all creation."[25] Patrides, a much more recent editor, understands the joke but nevertheless follows Hutchinson's view of "twice." If what has been urged in this reading of the poem is at least substantially correct, such a view of the double doxology is surely unnecessarily defensive. Herbert's role as poet in "Providence" and his role as secretary-priest are shown to be aspects of one another. The "twice" represents his inadequate response to the "many wayes" (150) of the creatures as providentially revealed. The last two stanzas are, in any case, not strictly parallel but stand in the kind of chiasmus-like relation to each other that we have seen to be characteristic of the poem's expressive mode. "Many" flows into and out of "one," and "one" into and out of "many." The penultimate stanza asserts by means of its structure the plurality of Creation's purpose, and its "one advise," mediated through man, to "honour" Providence. Herbert's response, elsewhere in *The Temple* single, must here be plural. The last stanza asserts through its structure the singularity of Creation's "use and name" and its abundance of revealed purpose: each "way" of honoring Providence in effect signifies a "hymne" not of Herbert's making. The final twist is that Herbert, himself wrong-footed and

24. This question is of course central to the thesis advanced by A. D. Nuttall in *Overheard by God: Fiction and Prayer in Herbert, Milton, Dante and St John*.
25. Herbert, *Works*, pp. 519–20.

responding to this abundant plurality by offering "yet this one more," has now tacitly admitted the superfluousness of his entire poem. It is a gesture of humility that, from the point of view of the human reader, the strategy of the entire poem belies:

All things that are, though they have sev'rall wayes,
Yet in their being joyn with one advise
To honour thee: and so I give thee praise
In all my other hymnes, but in this twice.

Each thing that is, although in use and name
It go for one, hath many wayes in store
To honour thee; and so each hymne thy fame
Extolleth many wayes, yet this one more. (145–52)

* * *

In this chapter I have shown some of the ways in which Herbert's expressiveness makes clear certain aspects of man's approach to a reading of the Book of Nature. Its characters can be used or abused. The response that Herbert's secretary records may be seen, in terms of the Victorine and Bonaventurine synthesis of Augustinian sign theory, as the praise that is implicit in a clear perception, and consequently an inevitable reading, of God's silent words. Even if, as in the case of some of the creatures, the "silent words" are themselves capable of "mutterings," these inarticulate responses are given sense only by their referral to God: Herbert in fact dramatizes the Augustinian distinction between use as referred to man and use as referred to the Divine. He deploys original modes of expression, in addition to traditional ones, in order to express again God's silent words. In the rich context supplied by Victorine and Bonaventurine formulations of man's relation to the cosmos, Herbert allows the relation between man, God, and Creation to take on great freshness. In contrast, a statement such as that by John Williams (1582–1650), bishop of Lincoln from 1621 and archbishop of York from 1640, says nothing very new, however attractively expressed:

To meete . . . with this curiositie of humane nature; Almightie God, hath filled all places with pleasing *objects,* which we may most safely behold and *see.* We have the flowrie Carpet of the Earth beneath us, the spangled Canopie of the Heavens above us, the wavie Curtaines of the Ayre about us, the whole hoast of the Creatures before us, all which we may (with profit) behold and *see*. . . . This world is a schoole, men are the schollers, the creatures are the Characters, by which we spell and put together the greatnesse of the Creator; whom thus, to our happinesse, we learne to *see*.[26]

In "Providence," Herbert actually shows that conditioned responses in the creatures come to seem surprising in the new context engendered by an interpretative recording of the working of Providence; thus he details how he learns to see:

Each creature hath a wisdome for his good.
The pigeons feed their tender off-spring, crying,
When they are callow; but withdraw their food
When they are fledge, that need may teach them flying. (61–64)

Here the instinctual behavior of pigeons is traditionally figured in terms of the rational. Perhaps what is most remarkable in this stanza is the prosodic control whereby the *abab* rhyme scheme is offset by the repeated clauses in consecutive lines (63 and 64). Thematically, Herbert's adaptation of animate creaturely behavior to the conditions and laws of the rational and human is extended, both in this poem and elsewhere, to aspects of the inanimate and cosmic: diurnal phenomena such as sunset and sunrise are expressed in terms of their benefit to man, as in the poem "Man":

The starres have us to bed;
Night drawes the curtain, which the sunne withdraws;
Musick and light attend our head. (31–33)

These household figures are reductive enough when applied to the cosmos; when applied to its divine Creator they are so much so that they seem to Herbert's reader to grant pleasure and excitement for him in a revelation of easily apprehensible relationships on every side. This culminates in a sense that everything is capable of being expressed in terms of the intensely familiar, as in these lines from "Providence," which, falling as they do between the stanza relating the activities of flies and hibernating creatures and the one that relates the activities of pigeons, plunge us into the

26. John Williams, *A Sermon of Apparell*, pp. 5–6 (sigs. B3^{r-v}).

inanimate world as though Herbert's catalogue were expressly designed to obscure the distinction between animate and inanimate by asserting that both worlds are equally subject to providential guidance:

> How finely dost thou times and seasons spin,
> And make a twist checker'd with night and day!
> Which as it lengthens windes, and windes us in,
> As bouls go on, but turning all the way. (57–60)

The figure in this stanza recalls the "silk twist" of "The Pearl" (1633, pp. 81–82). C. A. Patrides has shown how it participates in a rich allegorical tradition of explication that goes back to the episode of Jacob's ladder in the Bible.[27] By the seventeenth century it had become a traditional figure for God's Providence.[28] Here Herbert's "twist checker'd with night and day" is characteristically savored for the pleasure provided both by its visual apprehension and by the evidence it offers of divine craftsmanship. Another utterly domesticated example of cosmic accommodation may be found in "Even-song" (1633, pp. 55–56):

> Thus in thy Ebony box
> Thou dost inclose us, till the day
> Put our amendment in our way,
> And give new wheels to our disorder'd clocks. (21–24)

Figuring night as an "Ebony box," this extract reminds us of Herbert's fondness for notions of enclosure. More than this, it may also provide further evidence of the contrast between divine and human behavior in the context of the figure of enclosure and prepare us for the main argument of the next chapter. God's action in putting man away for the night not only alludes to the healing properties of the dark but also suggests a restorative generosity in shrinking his creation into a container that is in stark contrast to man's own sterilely reductive behavior in remaining "close, reserv'd, and dark" in response to this generosity. In the next chapter I explore this paradoxical contrast in the context of Herbert's

27. Gen. 28:10–15.
28. George Herbert, *The English Poems of George Herbert*, ed. C. A. Patrides, p. 104.

reading of the Book of Scripture, especially insofar as this reading treats the episodes surrounding scriptural portrayal of Christ's passion.

5. "Grace"

Reading the Book of Scripture

To learn to read the Book of Nature is, as we have seen, to overcome "illiteracy" in the face of God's signs by learning how to consume divinely provided resources. This act presupposes that we arrive at a particular understanding of man's place in the entire created order; only when such understanding is reached can the Creation speak to Herbert in its powerfully discernible mode of existence as a universe of consistent and divinely ordained relationships. To learn to read the Book of Scripture is also to overcome illiteracy, or disinclination to "read" God's signs, through apprehension of relationship. What makes the situation rather different in the case of the Scriptures, however, is that their reader is faced with the expression of those signs in terms of a historical movement from "law" to "grace," in which the former is transcended by the latter. Since this movement involves the superseding of the old dispensation by the new, it is not surprising to find that Herbert's approach to the Book of Scripture is pervaded with a typological sensibility.

The reader of the entire Book of Scripture is confronted with a sense of providential design, too. Here, however, providential design informs not the natural world so much as the workings of history. A reading of the Book of Scripture that is able to overcome illiteracy and disinclination is a reading that makes sense of history. History must be conceived here both in terms of its status as the public history of Old and New Testaments and their interrelationships as they were understood by the Reformation and inherited from patristic thought and reading, as well as in terms of the characteristically private and personal application of that history by Herbert's poetic voices throughout *The Temple*. In her recent study of Herbert and the Bible, Chana Bloch has shown the variety of ways in which Herbert moves backwards and forwards from Old to New, from what she calls a "nostalgia" for "tribal memories" to the "applied typology" that she usefully appropriates from A. C. Charity. In what follows it will be helpful once more to have in mind Charity's comprehensive definition of Christian typology as "the science of history's relations to its fulfillment in Christ."[1] Throughout her chapter on typology, we see Bloch's conception, articulated at another point in her book, of Herbert's believer "confronting, assimilating, and speaking the Word of God in his human and fallible existence."[2] She draws attention to the way in which we may discern a twofold exercise of authority in the process: there is first the authority of the Scriptures themselves, and second the authority conferred on the man who reads, interprets, and responds to them. Since it is not my purpose to duplicate the thrust of Bloch's inquiry, I intend to complement Herbert's application of Christian typology with what seems to me his clear apprehension of Bonaventura's view of the Scriptures as "the whole universe, contained as it were in a kind of *summa*."[3] Acceptance of a sense of concentration such as that expressed by Bonaventura would allow us to suggest that Herbert's poetic voices confront a rich distillation in the culminating events of Christ's Incarnation. The reading of these events is paradigmatic of Herbert's reading of the entire Book of Scripture. In concentrating on a small but pivotal area of Herbert's encounter with the Book of Scripture, I hope to remain faithful to the intellectual framework of this book by bringing out Herbert's strategy of response to divine Grace as the fulfillment adumbrated in typological readings of the entire Book of Scripture.

Accordingly, in this chapter I center on one of the more clearly defined sequences of poems in *The Temple*. Although I concentrate on Herbert's poems on the Passion ("The Sacrifice" through "Sepulchre" [1633, pp. 19–32]), these are not the only poems I

1. Chana Bloch, *Spelling the Word: George Herbert and the Bible*, pp. 113–69; cf. A. C. Charity, *Events and Their Afterlife: The Dialectics of Christian Typology in the Bible and Dante*, p. 1.

2. Bloch, *Spelling the Word*, p. 45.

3. *totius universi continentiam quasi in quadam summa. . .* , Bonaventura, *Breviloquium*, prol.; *Opera Omnia*, vol. 5, p. 201.

treat. The language of Herbert's poems on the distilling events of Christ's Passion is enlightened by reference to contemporary associated literature of meditation on the Passion, as I show; and as is now generally accepted, Herbert's language speaks to its readers with yet more of its characteristic individuality when it is placed beside the flourishing emblem literature of the period.

Of particular relevance to any discussion of Herbert's Passion poems is the emblematic subgenre known as *schola cordis* (the "school of the heart"). In collections of emblems that exemplify the theme, the heart is depicted as going through a particular form of spiritual progress, in such a way that emblem literature of this kind can be seen as noteworthy for its versatile treatment of the figure of the heart. My reasons for referring to this literature, even though others have done so before in the context of Herbert's poetry, are at least twofold. From a purely practical point of view, deployment of *schola cordis* literature may usefully complement Bloch's suggestive discussion of what she terms "the rhetoric of allusion," that is, Herbert's associative treatment of the range of biblical language in poems such as those in his Passion sequence. But again, I am not concerned simply with avoiding the same ground that Bloch treats. In accordance with the larger argument of this book, I want to suggest, with the help of contemporary *schola cordis* literature, that Herbert's treatment of the heart, as an expression of response to the signs he reads, actually enables him simultaneously to connect yet distinguish between the two modes of communication between himself and God for the establishment of which he prays in "The Sinner" (1633, p. 30):

> Lord restore thine image, heare my call. (12)

Herbert's emblematic treatment of the heart enables it to carry a great weight of expressiveness, both as the vehicle of a mode of significant divine communication (as in "Love unknown" [1633, pp. 121–23]) as well as that of a human response to this significance (as in "A true Hymne" [1633, pp. 162–63]). The distinction we are faced with here, between the divinely visual and the humanly aural, represents a development from the distinction between divine deafness and human blindness familiar from the discussion in earlier chapters. Here we will be concerned with the restorative implications for the heart that are prominent in *The Temple* as a whole and in the Passion poems in particular. It will be seen that Herbert's reader is invited to observe him exploring the allusive connections between events and "images"[4] or signs of the Passion, the idea of the work of restoration, his own heart, and the agency of divine Grace. This chapter ends with a consideration of Herbert's response to these associations—connections that can be seen as clearly and implicitly deriving from his reading of the Book of Scripture.

"Beholding" and "considering"

Iconographical depiction of the Incarnation of Christ is disturbing to its perceiver insofar as it implies events of extreme paradox. The justly celebrated studies of Erich Auerbach suggest that its perceived mixture of the sublime and the humble has had permanent repercussions on the representation of reality in Western literature.[5] The paradox of sublime humility is disturbing to the reader of the Scriptures, and Herbert's reader can observe him making sense of, or coming to terms with, his experience of the divine behavior that prompts the paradox.

The cross, which for the Church represents and summarizes the Incarnation and Passion of Christ, signifies extreme degradation. The undignified death it represents does, however, coexist with a sense of beauty. Iconographically, this coexistence tends to emerge in later medieval representations, together with a sense of compassion. Indeed, the relationship between beauty and com-

4. Throughout this chapter I shall try to use "image" judiciously, in light of P. N. Furbank, *Reflections on the Word "Image."* Where "sign" serves as well or better, I use that word; but it is worth remarking that the line quoted from Herbert's "The Sinner" employs the word "image" in what I take to be the obsolete sense of "concrete" "visible appearance; figure" (*NED* 3b; cf. 3a: "Aspect, appearance, form; semblance, likeness" [now, according to the *NED*, used only in allusion to or derived from biblical language, chiefly Gen. 1:26–27]).

5. See, for example, Erich Auerbach, *Mimesis: The Representation of Reality in Western Literature*, trans. Willard R. Trask, pp. 40ff., etc.

passion begins to suggest a palpable response from the perceiver to what is apprehended. As the fourteenth century progresses in England, there is a clear development in the direction of an increasingly full realization of the paradox of extreme suffering that coexists with sweetness.[6] The influence of the pseudo-Bonaventurine *Meditationes vitae Christi* is a major one in this context; the description of the Passion by its writer (probably a Franciscan monk of the early fourteenth century, one "Friar John") is full of requests to the reader to "see" and "behold" and thereby imagine himself to be at the scene of the Passion. Though there is no evidence one way or the other as to whether Herbert actually read the *Meditationes,* Patrick Grant has convincingly argued his familiarity with the Franciscan devotional tradition of which they are a part.[7] Herbert's own treatments of the Passion share the capacity of the most sensitive medieval ones for conveying the coexistence of beauty and degradation within an imaginative "seeing" of its details.[8] Thus Rosemond Tuve stresses that the ironies of "The Sacrifice" (1633, pp. 19–26) stem from the idea of man's blindness to the images of divine Incarnation:

> *Oh all ye,* who passe by, whose eyes and minde
> To worldly things are sharp, but to me blinde;
> To me, who took eyes that I might you finde:
> Was ever grief like mine? (1–4)

In "The Agonie" (1633, p. 29) the image of compassion is to be observed ("there shall he see"), and the speaker's final observation is crucial to "Redemption" (1633, pp. 31–32) ("there I him espied"). We might in fact argue that "The Sacrifice" is a pro-

6. See Rosemary Woolf, *The English Religious Lyric in the Middle Ages,* esp. pp. 19ff. and 183ff.; and Douglas Gray, *Themes and Images in the Medieval Religious Lyric,* esp. pp. 122ff. Primary texts are contained in Carleton Brown (ed.), *English Lyrics of the XIIIth Century; Religious Lyrics of the XIVth Century,* 2nd ed.; *Religious Lyrics of the XVth Century.*

7. See Patrick M. Grant, *The Transformation of Sin: Studies in Donne, Herbert, Vaughan, and Traherne,* pp. 81ff.

8. Rosemond Tuve, *A Reading of George Herbert,* pp. 19–99. This remains a pioneer study of Herbert and typology. In his "Critical Problems in Editing George Herbert's *The Temple,*" Patrick suggests that several poems in *The Temple* than are customarily so considered are patterned, and adduces as examples of cruciform poems "The Reprisall" and the first part of "Good Friday" (Patrick, pp. 15–16, 18).

longed or at least reiterated request by Christ for the clearing of man's perceptions; what is more, Christ's appeals for regard at lines 33, 45, 109, 133, 201, and 205, for example, are based on scriptural texts such as Lam. 1:12:

> Is it nothing to you, all ye that pass by? behold, and see if there be any sorrow like unto my sorrow, which is done unto me, wherewith the Lord hath afflicted me in the day of his fierce anger.

This text not only adumbrates its typological fulfillment in the events of Christ's Passion but is also a source for the liturgical *Improperia* tradition, the tradition of Christ's reproaches that, as Rosemond Tuve so famously showed, informs the structure of "The Sacrifice."

Yet Herbert's use of this wealth of tradition is by no means unique to his period. Lancelot Andrewes (1555–1626) bases the second of his three magnificent Passion sermons upon the text from Lamentations, which he expounds as follows:

> Here is a *Complaint,* and here is a *Request.* A *complaint,* that we have not: A *Request,* that we would have the Paines and Passions of our Saviour CHRIST in some *Regard.* For first he complaineth (and not without cause) *Have ye no regard*? And then (as willing to forget their former neglect, so they will yet doe it) he falleth to entreat, *O consider and behold!*[9]

Andrewes gives considerable space to this twofold approach to the events of the Passion. The reader of Scripture should be prepared, in approaching the Passion, both to "looke upon, with the eye of the body . . . and looke into, with the eye of the mind" (sig. Ii3v). Herbert makes a similar distinction in "The Sacrifice" ("*all ye* . . . whose eyes and minde").

The text *Respicient in Me, quem transfixerunt* (Zech. 12:10) prompts the first Passion sermon in Andrewes's 1629 folio and again offers a starting point for consideration by the reader:

> We that *looke upon,* it is we that *pierced Him*: and it is we that *pierced Him,* that are willed *to looke upon Him.* Which bringeth it home to us; to me my selfe that speake, and to you your selves that heare; and applieth it

9. Lancelot Andrewes, *XCVI Sermons,* sig. Ii3r. There are many errors of pagination in this folio, and in citations from it I use the signatures alone throughout.

most effectually to every one of us, who evidently seeing, that we were the cause of this his *piercing,* if our hearts be not too too hard, ought to have remorse, to be pierced with it. . . . The Act followeth in these words: *Respicient in Eum.* A request most reasonable, to *looke upon Him;* but *to looke upon Him;* to bestow but a *looke* and nothing els; which even of common humanitie we cannot denie, *Quia non aspicere, despicere est.* It argueth great *contempt,* not to vouchsafe it the cast of our *eye;* as if it were an *Object* utterly unworthy the looking toward. Truely, if we marke it well, nature it selfe, of it selfe enclineth to this act. . . . Yea CHRIST himselfe, *pierced* as he is, inviteth us to it. For, in the *Prophet* heere, it is not *In Eum;* but *In me:* not, *on Him;* but, *on Me, whom they have pierced.* But more fully in *Jeremy:* for to CHRIST himselfe do all the ancient Writers apply (and that, most properly) those words of the *Lamentation: Have ye no regard all ye that passe by this way? Behold and see, if there be any sorrow like my sorrow, which is done unto me, wherewith the LORD hath afflicted me, in the day of His fierce wrath.* (Andrewes, sig.Hh^{r-v})

The reader calls on his soul to "regard" the scene, discovering in himself a curious reluctance to do so. Andrewes very movingly details this reluctance:

For lo, of all the sharpe paines he endureth, he complaineth not, but of this he complaineth, of *No regard:* That which grieveth him most, that which most he moaneth, is this. It is strange, he should be in paines, such paines as never any was, and not complaine himselfe of them; But of want of *regard* only. Strange, he should not make request, *O deliver me,* or *Relieve me:* But only, *O consider and regard me.* In effect, as if he said; None, no *deliverance,* no *reliefe* do I seeke: *Regard* I seeke. And all that I suffer, I am content with it: I regard it not: I suffer most willingly, if this I may finde at your hands, *Regard.*

Truly, This so passionate a *Complaint* may move us; it moved all but us: For most strange of all it is, that all the *Creatures* in heaven and earth, seemed to heare this his mournfull *Complaint,* and in their kind, to show their *regard* of it: The *Sunne* in heaven shrinking in his light; the earth *trembling* under it; the very stones *cleaving* in sunder, as if they had sense and Sympathy of it: and sinfull men only, not moved with it. And yet, it was not for the *Creatures,* this was done to Him; to them it pertaineth not: But for us, it was, and to us it doth; and shall we not yet *regard* it? Shall the *Creature,* and not we? Shall we not? (Andrewes, sig.Kk4^{v})

From these passages it is evident that, for the seventeenth-century reader of the Scriptures, God is believed to request no more than a "beholding" of the culminating sign of the Incarnation, while man is incapable of supplying even this. We are here confronted with an aspect of man's blindness to divine communication. Herbert, however, differs from his earlier contemporary Andrewes in iconographically extending the notion of man's inability to see Christ's Passion with the eyes of the mind in such a way that it includes the events of the Agony in the Garden. In his poem "The Agonie," Herbert asserts that "few there are that sound" the "two vast, spacious things," sin and love; the last two stanzas present scenes to be regarded or read. His request for regard is uttered in conditional, and negative, terms ("Who would know Sinne"; "Who knows not Love"). The signs for regard are presented as remedies for inadequate knowledge, yet the reader seems disinclined or unable to regard them. The Agony is not much treated in extant Middle English lyrics, but finds its way into some of the prose. The writer of the *Meditationes vitae Christi* exhorts his reader as follows:

> Sothely here is grete mater of sorwe and compassioun / that ought to stere the hardest herte that is in this world to haue ynward compassioun of that grete and souerayne angwisshe that oure lorde Jesu suffrede in that tyme and for oure sake; for by the godhede he sawe the hardest and souerayn paynes that were to come in his body; and therfore after the manhode his tendre body for fere and anguyssh brak out violently of blode.[10]

The divinity of Christ enables him to foresee and discern in advance the pains of the crucifixion and prompts his "swetyng blood" (ed. Powell, p. 220). When the passage from the *Meditations* is set beside "The Agonie," the reader sees how Herbert can achieve in his poem a striking effect that is a conflation between the language he uses to describe the Agony and that of traditional descriptions of the Crucifixion. In this way it becomes difficult to see the language of Herbert's poem as referring exclusively to the Agony. Though in one sense the context is restricted, the poem's language has the effect of drawing attention to, without stating, a

10. *Meditationes vitae Christi*, trans. Nicholas Love, ed. L. F. Powell, p. 222. (Here "u" and "v" have not been normalized, but the long "s" is shortened, and the "yogh" rendered as "gh.")

wider context. The scriptural record notes that Christ's sweat "was as it were great drops of blood falling down to the ground" (Luke 22:44). Herbert's rendering in "The Agonie" intensifies this:

> Who would know Sinne, let him repair
> Unto mount Olivet; there shall he see
> A man so wrung with pains, that all his hair,
> His skinne, his garments bloudie be. (7–10)

The description of the Crucifixion in the *Meditationes* includes the abundant shedding of blood:

> Than rennen oute of his blessid body stremes of that holyest blood on all sides habundantly fro tho grete woundes. (ed. Powell, p. 239)

Indeed, it is not uncommon to find, in the medieval lyrics and in other literature cited by Tuve, a sense of gruesomeness, of blood abundantly shed. Andrewes's description is highly vivid, but it applies exclusively to the Crucifixion:

> When *blood* is shed, it would be no more than needs: *shed* it would be, not *poured out*. Or if so, at one part (the *necke* or *throat*:) not at all parts at once. But, heer was *fundetur*, havock made at all parts. *His Passion* (as he termeth it) a *second Baptisme*, a *River of blood*; and he even hable to have been *baptized* in it, as he was in *Jordan*. And where it would be *Summa parsimonia etiam vilissimi sanguinis*, no waste, no not of the basest *blood* that is; waste was made heer. And of what *blood*? *Sanguis* JESU, the *blood* of JESUS: and who was He? Sure, by vertue of the *union Personall*, GOD; and so, this *blood*, *blood* of GOD's *owne bleeding*; every *dropp* whereof was *precious*, more *precious* then (that, whereof it was the *price*) the world it selfe: Nay, more *worth* then *many worlds*; yea, if they were *ten thousand*. Yet this was *blood wastefully spilt, as water upon the ground*. The *fundetur* and the *qui* heere, will come into consideration, both. This is *sanguis Crucis*: and yet, this is not all neither; there is more yet. (Andrewes, sig. L16^{r-v})

Hutchinson cites another passage from the same sermon of Andrewes,[11] and we may be struck by the similarity with "The Agonie":

> Great were those paines, and this time too little to show, how great; but, so great, that in all the former, he never shrunk, nor once com-

11. George Herbert, *The Works of George Herbert*, ed. F. E. Hutchinson, p. 488.

> plained, but was, as if he scarce felt them. . . . In all those, no *blood* came, but where passages were made for it to come out by: but in this, it strained out all over, even at all places at once. This was the *paine* of the *Presse* (so the *Prophet* calleth it, *Torcular*:) wherewith, as if he had been in the *wine presse*, all his *garments* were *stained* and *goared* with *blood*. (Andrewes, sig. Mm[r])

Yet in none of the lyrics, and in neither passage from Andrewes, is the "fundetur" language made to refer to anything other than the Crucifixion. On the contrary, Andrewes explicitly distinguishes "all the former" pains by saying that "no blood came, but where passages were made for it to come out by," reserving the "havock" of the sight of the blood, which "strained out all over, even at all places at once" for the Crucifixion itself.

It would be misleading, however, to suggest that the extreme intensity of Herbert's treatment of Christ's Passion, an intensity that involves the transference of the "fundetur" language to the Agony and provides his treatment of the episode with its powerfully conflative quality, is unique, even though it is uncharacteristic of Andrewes or of earlier lyric writing. For it is in this conflative respect—among many others—that Herbert can be seen to show close affinities with the theological and aesthetic assumptions of the emblem writers of the period. The kind of reading of the Bible that Herbert endorses in "[The H. Scriptures] II" (1633, p. 50) assumes the necessity for seeking sense in "constellations" of verses that, as the poem puts it, "mark" each other. The readings that his poetic voices undertake thus provide justification, because of their pictorially conflative strategies, for considering Herbert's Passion poems in the light of the flourishing emblem literature of the period, more specifically the emblem literature of the *schola cordis* tradition.

No reader of *The Temple* will need to be told that to assert that Herbert's poetic is related to that of the emblem writers is to propose something of a critical commonplace. However, there is still room for innovative comment or suggestion, as Chana Bloch's recent original approach shows. She has located Herbert's emblematic language in his appropriation of the prophetic tradition and argues that an emblematic approach to the prophetic books can serve a twofold purpose in our understanding of Herbert's poetry. Not only is the reader of the Bible enabled to explain, in terms of their visual apprehension of God's word, what Bloch calls the "curious" and "bizarre" nature of symbolic acts that scriptural prophets are frequently called upon to perform; but our understanding of Herbert's attachment to emblematic language also helps us to account for his impulse to enact before his own reader the truth that he has discovered in such explanations.[12] Bloch's aim in advancing the view she does of Herbert's relation to the emblematic tradition is partly to fill in what she perceives as a lacuna in Barbara Lewalski's approach to Herbert's Protestant poetics, an approach with which Bloch is on the whole sympathetic; more generally, Bloch is concerned about what she sees as a failure on the part of the many commentators who have tried, in various ways, to link Herbert's verse with aspects of the emblematic tradition. As Bloch sees it, this failure can best be regarded as a failure to reconcile a stiffness or lifelessness in the emblem tradition with the flexibility and suppleness of Herbert's verse. Bloch's concern incorporates a tradition of commentary that runs from Lewalski back through Rosalie Colie and Rosemary Freeman and would include Mario Praz's comments on the "mute" emblems of *The Temple* and his view that "the poet succeeded not in spite of the emblematical method, but with its help."[13] Free-

12. Bloch, *Spelling the Word,* pp. 197–204.

13. Bloch, ibid., p. 198, mentions Colie, *The Resources of Kind: Genre Theory in the Renaissance,* and Rosemary Freeman, *English Emblem Books,* as well as Barbara K. Lewalski, *Protestant Poetics and the Seventeenth Century.* For Mario Praz's mention of "mute" emblems, see *Studies in Seventeenth-Century Imagery,* vol. 1, pp. 163 and 226; see also pp. 226–27. In addition to items mentioned below, see also the emblem collections in Daniel Heinsius, *Emblemata Aliquot Amatoria,* and Otho Vaenius, *Amorum Emblemata.* Although Lewalski's discussion (*Protestant Poetics and the Seventeenth Century,* pp. 179–212, esp. pp. 193–96) is characteristically thorough, it will be evident from my comments in my first chapter above that I cannot wholly subscribe to her thesis. Herbert seems to have read and consulted emblem books that were not only European but uncompromisingly jesuitical. Some of these were "protestantized," it is true; reorderings such as those of Daniel Cramer and Christopher Harvey are of course significant, but Harvey could still find it possible to use Benedictus van Haeften's plates. It seems to me that the case for a Protestant emblematics is a considerably subtler one than Lewalski maintains. Such a view, it may be added, is implicit in Albert C. Labriola's discussion of the *schola cordis* tradition ("Herbert, Crashaw, and the *Schola Cordis* Tradition," pp. 13–23). I share many of Labriola's assumptions and conclusions but am at the same time urging consideration of Herbert's assimilation into this tradition in the context of an intellectual framework not germane to Labriola's enquiry.

man has reminded us of the derivative and inferior quality of much English emblem writing before Quarles (1635), and it is customary for discussions of emblems and Herbert to assume that the European collections are likely to have been his major influences.

I find it hard to maintain that the *schola cordis* emblems have the stiffness that Bloch, following Freeman, imputes to much emblematic writing in contrast to Herbert's poetic mode, but I do not wish to become locked into an inconclusive debate as to the merit of emblem writing as a whole. Instead, I want to suggest that what Herbert found in the *schola cordis* literature was a language for characterizing the heart's response to the events of Christ's Passion, a response that interestingly complements his conceptions, in the context of reading the Book of Nature, of a hard, static, "enclosed" reader who has to learn "how to" respond to the abundant bountiful providential flow that he finally comes to discern around him. Herbert's poems on the Passion of Christ repeatedly and variously show him using the figure of the heart, whose hardness emblematizes both a general and—characteristically—a personalized response of illiteracy and disinclination. In short, Herbert relates the hardened heart to his apprehension of the events of Christ's Passion, and I will show that learning how to read these distilling events of the Book of Scripture involves coming to terms with the efficacy of what Herbert calls "suppling grace." That act of reconciliation, analogous to learning how to consume God's providentially provided resources, must be prefaced for Herbert by an understanding of how "beholding" and "considering" Christ's Passion can be achieved. I argue that the *schola cordis* literature provides an indispensable key to this aspect of Herbert's act of interpretation, an act that constitutes his reading of these typologically distilled elements of the Book of Scripture, the events of Christ's Passion.

Let us pause to remind ourselves of Herbert's extension to the Agony of the "fundetur" language that Lancelot Andrewes reserves exclusively for the Crucifixion itself. I have been suggesting that Herbert's strategy is part of a wider tendency in his treatment of scriptural language toward a pictorially conflative treatment of Christ's Incarnation. It is characteristic of Herbert to conflate and thereby give great immediacy to narrative treatment of the Incarnation, as we saw in an earlier chapter in the case of "The Bag" (1633, pp. 145–46). A glance at "The Bag" in its position in the order of *The Temple* suggests that it is unusual in following one of the rare poems, "Longing" (1633, pp. 142–45), that actually ends on a cadence of despair. Like "Grief" (1633, p. 158) and "The Crosse" (1633, p. 159), we are presented, in fact, with a pair of poems in which the second offers a "looking on" that compensates for, and consoles, the note of plangent, unresolved grief that has been the note on which the first has ended. Within the Passion sequence with which I am primarily concerned in this chapter, it would seem that "Redemption" is a poem that seems similarly to solicit a looking on. I characterize the experience that poem offers by showing how in the seventeenth century the *schola cordis* tradition was seen to facilitate an understanding of what Herbert, in "[The H. Scriptures] II," calls the "configurations" of the Bible.

The fortieth emblem in Benedictus van Haeften's *Schola Cordis* (1629) is entitled "Balneum cordis ex sudore sanguineo" (Fig. 1) and depicts the human heart, held by Anima, being bathed in the bloody sweat.[14] Certain of the more vividly Counter-Reformation emblems in this Flemish collection seem to have proved unpalatable to Christopher Harvey, to whom the anonymous 1647 translation of the *Schola Cordis* is attributed. It can be assumed, however, that the "Balneum cordis" emblem was acceptable to English Protestantism, since Harvey reproduces it as his forty-first emblem.[15]

14. Benedictus van Haeften, *Schola Cordis, sive aversi a Deo cordis, ad eumdem reductio, et instructio*, p. 512 (sig. Ii8^{v}).

15. Van Haeften's fifty-five emblems are reduced to forty-seven and their order altered in this rare English edition (*Schola Cordis, or the Heart of it selfe gone away from God . . .* [London, 1647]), which was later (1808, 1812, 1823, 1866) "erroneously ascribed to Quarles" (Praz, *Studies in Seventeenth-Century Imagery*, p. 362); however, Harvey's name appears on the title page of a later seventeenth-century edition (London, 1664). The verse is clearly imitative of Herbert: Freeman notes the borrowing from "Easter-wings" in Harvey's shaped "Ode 38" ("The flying of the Heart"), and cites "Ode 8," which begins: "What have we here? An heart?" but does not comment on its resemblance to "An Offering" (Freeman, pp. 135, 137). Christopher Harvey's *The Synagogue, or, Shadow of the Temple*, compiled in admiring imitation of Herbert, usually attracts critical censure; it is worth maintaining that the verse of his *Schola Cordis* is, if not actually outstanding, of an appreciably higher quality than that of his earlier volume.

Harvey attaches to it, as he does to every other emblem, an "Ode," which in this case begins:

All this thy God hath done for thee:
And now mine heart
It is high time that thou should'st be
Acting thy part, And meditating on his blessed Passion,
Till thou hast made it thine by imitation. (p. 165)

The verse suggests here that meditation on the Passion or, in other words, reading its signs with the eyes of the mind, can lead to a form of appropriation of its events that is tantamount to an imitation of Christ. Such a conception complements John R. Mulder's surely correct belief that Herbert's five "Affliction" poems incorporate an imitation of Christ by corresponding to the tradition of meditation on the five wounds,[16] an exercise that is characteristic of the Franciscan meditative tradition.[17] In "The Agonie," however, in stark contrast to Harvey's reading of the "Balneum cordis" emblem, the presentation in conditional and negative terms of the request for regard suggests, as does the evocative monotony of "The Sacrifice," that, though signs of the Passion are offered as remedies for inadequate knowledge, their reader either cannot, or will not, appropriate them.

Let us now place "The Agonie" in the context of the manner in which Herbert conveys inadequacy of perception in "Redemption." By the standards of mortal logic, that is, "accordingly" (10), the Lord is not found where he was expected, and Herbert's speaker makes a discovery that shows that his original method of proceeding was insufficient, however much it was made in good faith. Stanley Fish accounts for the "peculiar force" of such a poem as "Redemption"; it "often depends on our awareness that the terms in which we are being encouraged to formulate a concept are inadequate to it."[18]

Although Bloch's objections to Fish's "picture of Herbert, mar-

16. John R. Mulder, "George Herbert's *The Temple*: Design and Methodology," p. 44.
17. See the *New Catholic Encyclopedia*, vol. 13, pp. 711–13.
18. Stanley E. Fish, *Self-Consuming Artifacts: The Experience of Seventeenth-Century Literature*, p. 159.

tyrlike, building his poetry into a pyre of self-immolation" deserve serious attention,[19] it nonetheless remains the case that the reader of *The Temple* is constantly made to participate in discoveries that Herbert portrays himself as making. The ending of "Redemption" is peculiarly forceful. There is a tremendous acceleration in pace in the last lines. The venues in which the Lord is sought are actually listed at first (10–11), then the listing is reduced to essentials: to two characteristics ("ragged noise and mirth" [12]), and to two kinds of company ("theeves and murderers" [13]). From the second half of the penultimate line until the end, the compactness is intense. The tortuous word order throws attention forward to the last word ("died"), where extreme stress accumulates, and the effect is retroactive, contributing to the already considerable feeling of rapidity:

> there I him espied,
> Who straight, *Your suit is granted*, said, & died. (13–14)

There is little time to envisage any possible physical context, and in any case "place" is not described except negatively (it is *not* a city or a theater, for instance). It is worth recalling that in the earlier Williams manuscript this poem was entitled "Passion," since the change of title in the 1633 edition of *The Temple* seems consonant with a desire on Herbert's part to extend the poem's conflative resonance. There is little in the poem as it stands in the 1633 version to point us exclusively toward Christ's Passion, except perhaps the reference to "theeves and murderers," because so much descriptive freight is compacted or actually missing. In addition, there are many conflicting movements in the poem's ending. There is the speaker's own well-intentioned error and his eventual, apparently chance, discovery of his Lord; this discovery occurs so suddenly that the speaker seems not to have time to state his suit before the Lord's mysteriously unspecified death. Strangest of all, there is the Lord's complete awareness of what the suitor was going to say before the death that precludes reply. These disparities offer extraordinary emotive force to an

19. Bloch, *Spelling the Word*, p. 31.

Fig. 1. The fortieth emblem in Benedictus van Haeften's *Scholar Cordis* (1629).

Fig. 2. Van Haeften's thirty-fourth emblem.

Fig. 3. The forty-seventh emblem in Daniel Cramer's *Emblemata Sacra* (1624).

Fig. 4. Cramer's fourteenth emblem.

EMBLEMA XLI.

Erunt ubera tua ſicut botri vineæ, & odor oris tui ſicut odor malorum.

Cant. 7. 8.

Laß deine Brüſte ſeyn wie Trauben am Weinſtock / vnnd deiner Naſen Ruch wie Epffel.

SANOR

XLI.

Lædit me modicè, medicè me curat, ita uvæ
Sunt mihi ſtillantes ubera, Chriſte, tuæ.

M ALTA

Fig. 5. Cramer's forty-first emblem.

EMBLEMA XXIII.

Ille vocabit in nomine Iacob, & hic ſcribet manu ſua Domino.

Eſa. 44. 5.

Jener wird genennet werden mit dem Namen Jacob. Vnd dieſer wird ſich mit ſeiner Hand dem HErren zuſchreiben.

PRÆDESTINOR

XXIII.

Annumeror Chriſto, cui ſum de nomine notus,
Rubrica is vitæ eſt penna liberque meæ.

G 5 PRO-

Fig. 6. Cramer's twenty-third emblem.

EMBLEMA XXI.

Chriſtus donavit vobis omnia delicta, delens quod aduerſus nos erat chirographum decreti, quod erat contrarium nobis.

Coloſſ. 2. 14.

CHriſtus hat vns geſchenckt alle Sünde / vnd außgetilget die Handſchrifft ſo wider vns war.

ABSOLVOR

XXI.

Scripta fuit dica magna mihi: Crux aurea Chriſti
Sola ſatisfecit, ſola ſatisfaciet.

G NON

Fig. 7. Cramer's twenty-first emblem.

CORDIS TABVLA LEGIS.

Dabo legem meam in uiſceribus eorum, et in CORDE eorum ſcribam eam. *Ierem.* 31. 33.

Scribo nouam teneri nunc CORDIS in æquore legem,
Cum vetus in duris ſit mihi ſcripta petris.

23.

Fig. 8. Van Haeften's twenty-third emblem.

Fig. 9. Van Haeften's fifth emblem.

Fig. 10. Cramer's first emblem.

Fig. 11. Van Haeften's eleventh emblem.

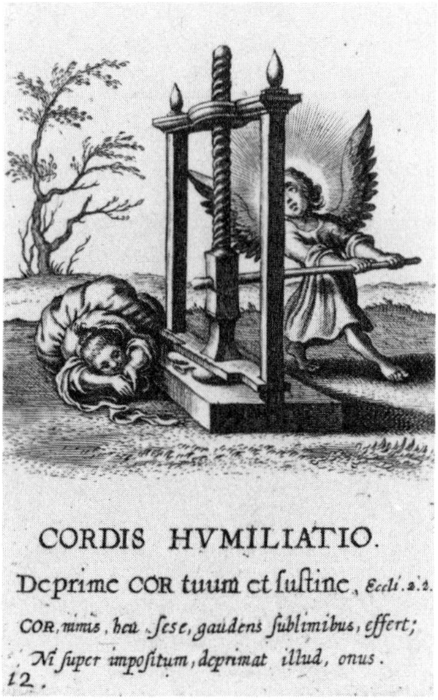

Fig. 12. Van Haeften's twelfth emblem.

Fig. 13. Van Haeften's thirteenth emblem.

Fig. 14. Van Heaften's fourteenth emblem.

Fig. 15. Van Haeften's fifty-second emblem.

ending that may be seen as having great tragic power. The ending is prefaced by a speeding-up of the action and by contrary emotions that suddenly come to a dead end: any visualization of the scene, which is made very difficult for the reader because of the absence of any but the most perfunctorily allusive description of the physical situation, is almost certain to acquire a tableau-like effect, and the kind of sign the reader will be left with will be an entirely motionless, arrested one. And of course the Crucifixion offers precisely such a sign. What in "Redemption" appears initially to be "beholding" ("there I him espied") may, by its peculiar force of presentation, jolt the reader into "considering."

Clarity of perception of the details of the Passion, then, may involve the reader of divine signs in some kind of remedial recognition. The "Balneum cordis" emblem shows the heart being bathed and forms part of a group of associations in the *schola cordis* emblem literature, with which Herbert was undoubtedly familiar. For in a number of his sequence of Passion poems, Herbert recognizes that his beholding and considering of the signs of the Passion involve expressions of inadequacy, inability, and reluctance; he dramatizes his illiteracy in the face of the theology of these signs in "The Thanksgiving" (1633, pp. 27–28) and "The Reprisall" (1633, pp. 28–29):

> Then for thy passion—I will do for that—
> Alas, my God, I know not what.
>
> ("The Thanksgiving" [49–50])

> I have consider'd it, and finde
> There is no dealing with thy mighty passion.
>
> ("The Reprisall" [1–2])

Yet to set down realizations of this sort is to begin to come to terms with them: to know that one is in error is no longer to be wholly in error. Herbert's acts of beholding and considering lead him on toward making sense of his recognition of their inadequacy by expressing a request for a clearer knowledge of the Divine. In "The Sinner," the speaker asks God to "write" an "image" in his hard heart:

> Lord restore thine image, heare my call:

And though my hard heart scarce to thee can grone,
Remember that thou once didst write in stone. (12–14)

A similar idea is expressed in "A true Hymne," where the divine "secretary" actually completes a poem, and the kind of wit exemplified by an ending of that kind may possibly detract from other appearances of the divine secretary. What is at issue here is a very widespread typology: the writing of the Commandments on the tablets of stone (Exodus 20) is held to typify the writing of a new covenant on the meditator's heart. It is a typology that is familiar from the Middle Ages onwards. Douglas Gray (p. 127) quotes the following lyric in support of it:

Jesu that hast me dere ibought,
Write thou gostly in my thoght,
That I mow with devocioun
Thynke on thy dere passioun:
For thogh my hert be hard as stone,
Yit maist thou gostly write theron
With naill and with spere kene
And so shullen the lettres be sene.

Rosemary Woolf (pp. 164–65) relates the tradition to the idea of the wound of love, referring to the divine secretary as "a slightly conceited variation." The extent to which the two ideas are associated in the seventeenth century may be indicated by their persistent presence in the *schola cordis* literature. Herbert's documentation of the way in which he learns how to overcome illiteracy in the face of the distilling events of his encounter with the Book of Scripture is illuminated by the association.

"Suppling grace"

Let us invoke the *schola cordis* tradition more closely than we have done so far. Van Haeften's thirty-fourth emblem (p. 436) depicts Christ shooting an arrow into the heart held by Anima, who looks lovingly on (Fig. 2). The text is Lam. 3:12 ("He hath bent his bow, and set me as a mark for the arrow"), and the emblem carries a sense of a remedial, curative experience. It is, in effect, Cupid's bow and arrow transmuted into witty theological paradox.[20] It may be compared with several emblems in another collection. In Daniel Cramer's forty-seventh emblem (p. 201), a divine hand shoots arrows from a bow into the heart, in which five (the number of Christ's wounds) are already embedded (Fig. 3).[21] The text is Ps. 38:2 ("For thine arrows stick fast in me, and thy hand presseth me sore"). Cramer's fourteenth emblem, CRUCIFIGOR (p. 69), depicts the heart crucified with four nails (Fig. 4). On the cross itself are inscribed the four letters I, E, S, U, and the inscription suggests, once again, imitative participation by the beholder. Cramer's forty-first emblem, SANOR (p. 177), shows the heart transfixed crosswise by two arrows (Fig. 5). An important feature of this emblem, to which I shall return, is the divine hand above the heart, squeezing over it the juice from a bunch of grapes. Comparable with SANOR in design is Cramer's twenty-third emblem (PRAEDESTINOR), in which the word IESU is written on the heart by a divine hand holding a pen and issuing from clouds at the side of the picture (p. 105; that is, sig. G5^r) (Fig. 6). Some such representation may have given Herbert the idea for his intensely pictorial poem "Jesu" (1633, p. 105), and the position of this poem midway through *The Temple* may indicate the stage already reached in the progress of the *imitatio* of which it is surely a part. Finally, Cramer's twenty-first emblem, ABSOLVOR (p. 97), depicts a parchment nailed to the cross, and a divine hand, similarly issuing from the clouds, appending a signature to the writing on the parchment (Fig. 7). The emblematic mode allows its reader to make a connection between the sacred representation of Cupid's arrows and the nails of the cross, as well as with the notion of the divine secretary.

Jesuit emblem books take the tradition of the arrows of love to ecstatic extremes,[22] but in Herbert the control of the idea, where it

20. Edgar Wind's discussion (*Pagan Mysteries in the Renaissance,* pp. 53ff. and pp. 90–91) is of particular relevance here.

21. Daniel Cramer, *Emblemata Sacra: Hoc est, decades quinque emblematum ex Sacra Scripture, de dulcissimo Nomine & Cruce Jesu Christi.*

22. In the first plate from Hermann Hugo's *Pia desideria,* the soul, languidly resting on the ground, releases arrow-like sighs, three of which approach the ears and eye of the Divine; a fourth issues from the soul's heart. Herbert's references to sighs

does appear ("Discipline," 1633, pp. 173–74),[23] is so tight that it would be inappropriate to speak, as does Rosemary Woolf in the more medieval context, of "a certain sign of the ecstatic view of love, and the violence of its effect" (Woolf, p. 165). The curative idea is certainly present, however, in "Discipline." Love is emblematically represented as God's arrow ("Love . . . can shoot, / And can hit from farre. / Who can scape his bow?" [21–25]), and we are told that "For with love / Stonie hearts will bleed" (19–20). Yet the speaker's response is conceived of not in ecstatic terms, but in far more dutiful words:

Not a word or look
I affect to own,
    But by book,
And thy book alone. (16–20)

Discipline is suggested in an unstated collocation such as "to learn to live by the book," but in the context of this discussion it is impossible to miss the idea that the speaker is abdicating all of his claims to significant communication, both verbal and nonverbal ("Not a word or look / I affect to own"), in favor of a rule that is based on the lived consequences of a reading of the Book of Scripture ("thy book alone").

Here, in "Discipline," we are faced with a sense of accomplishment that has admittedly been reached at a price. But the poem's position in *The Temple* is interesting, in that it precedes the eucharistic pair "The Invitation" and "The Banquet," the entire group occurring near the end of the collection. We need to supplement the picture we are assembling of the consequences of learning how to overcome illiteracy and disinclination in the face of the Book of Scripture by returning to the idea of the divine secretary. Lancelot Andrewes's fifth sermon on the Resurrection provides a

---

in, for example, "Sighs and Grones" and other poems of suffering, show sympathy with this idea. Hugo's thirty-first emblem goes further than anything in *The Temple,* depicting the languid soul, with an arrow in her heart, admonishing the daughters of Jerusalem: "If ye find my beloved . . . tell him, that I am sick of love" (Song of Songs 5:8). Quarles's *Emblemes* contains both of these. Herbert reserves a more subtle erotic expression for "Love" [III].

23. See J. H. Adler, "Form and Meaning in Herbert's 'Discipline,'" pp. 240–43.

suitable point of departure. Andrewes takes as his text verses from Job 19:

> 23 Oh that my words were now written! Oh that they were printed in a book!
> 24 That they were graven with an iron pen and lead in the rock for ever!

He expounds this text as follows:

> Why would not a *booke* serve for this? Why no remedy but it must be in *stone*? There want not reasons: Let me touch some few. *Moses* and *Job* are holden to have lived at one time. *Mose's law* was *graven* in *stone,* we know. This of *Job* (heer) is *Gospell,* the *substance,* the chief article of it. No reason, the *law,* in *tables of stone*; and the *Gospell,* in sheets of *paper.* Good reason, *Job,* as zealous for the *Gospell,* as *Moses,* for the *Law.* If that wrought in *stone,* this is no lesse; as firme and durable, as it, every way. And the same reason is for the *yron penne.* . . . One more: That *Job* needed this wish, in regard of those, that were to receive this doctrine. It will not well be *written,* there is such unbeleife and hardnesse of heart, yea, even in the Disciples, and so generally in our nature; as, enough to doe, to *grave* it in us: yet so necessarie withall, as where it will not be *written,* he wishes it *graven. Written,* where it may: but *graven,* where it must. But *written,* or *graven,* one of them in us all. (Andrewes, sig. Qq5$^{r\text{-}v}$)

Andrewes, presumably here remembering the famous imprecation from the pseudo-Augustinian *Meditationes* 36 ("*Scribe in tabulis cordis mei* . . ."), calls attention to man's natural intransigence and to his disinclination to accept communication from God. Herbert's speaker seems to be recalling the idea in "The Sinner" when he pleads, "Remember that thou once didst write in stone." The association of heart with stone in this poem is derived by a route that has its beginning in the speaker's meditative recall, a spiritual act in consequence of which he is reminded of the immensity of the disproportion between the "quarries of pil'd vanities" (5) and the "shreds of holinesse" (6) within. Although the latter "dare not venture" to make themselves seen, this is not the result of false modesty so much as a necessary consequence of the blasphemous inversion of the laws of God's universe, an inversion whereby the earth has come to surround the heavens. For the speaker, his "shreds of holinesse" form a heavenly distillate whose presence at the *center* of his being is paradoxically inherent in his status as a sinner ("In so much dregs the quintessence is small" [9]). With a characteristic turn of the figurative perversity that we noted in an earlier chapter, this heavenly quintessence, which is far from heavenly, is identified with the speaker's hard heart and thereby implicitly contrasted with the "quarries of pil'd vanities." All is finally seen to be hard in the speaker's being: the hardness of the heart is if anything worse than that of his "vanities," since it has been compacted into "stone" on which, as Andrewes might have said, God's word may be "*Written,* where it may: but *graven,* where it must."

Cramer's twenty-third emblem, as has been seen (Fig. 6), shows the Divine inscribing IESU on the heart. Van Haeften stresses the typology of the notion by representing in his twenty-third emblem (*Schola Cordis,* p. 328) Christ inscribing words on the heart, which Anima holds spread out so that the emblem reenacts the inscribing of the Commandments on the tablets of stone (Fig. 8). The emblem is entitled "Cordis tabula legis." Van Haeften's fifth emblem ("Cordis durities," p. 124) shows Christ about to strike the heart with a hammer. Anima looks away as a diabolic figure holds the heart on an anvil (Fig. 9). The text is Zech. 7:12 ("Yea, they made their hearts as an adamant stone, lest they should hear the law"), and we may compare Cramer's first emblem (MOLLESCO), in which a hammer strikes the heart (Cramer, p. 17) (Fig. 10). Harvey accompanies the "Cordis durities" emblem (his eighth, p. 32) with the allusion to Herbert's "An Offering" (1633, pp. 141–42) (see note 15 above). Harvey's stanzas are, it might be argued, anvil-shaped:

What have we here? An heart? It lookes like one,
      The shape, and colour speake it such:
      But having brought it to the touch
I find it is no better then a stone.
            Adamants are
            Softer by farre. (p. 33)

Van Haeften's eleventh emblem (and Harvey's fourteenth), "Cordis contritio," shows Anima about to crush the heart in a mortar: the pestle is raised and Christ looks on (Fig. 11). This is the first of a sequence of four worth mentioning (van Haeften, pp. 186–226, Harvey, pp. 56–71). The second, "Cordis humiliatio," shows Christ squeezing the heart in a vice, and the third, "Cordis emollitio," shows an icy heart melting in the heat of the sun (Figs. 12–13). In fact, the heat seems to emanate from Christ, an association that recalls Herbert's by no means unique exploration of the English pun in his sonnet "The Sonne" (1633, p. 162).[24] The text to "Cordis emollitio" is Job 23:6 ("God maketh my heart soft"). The fourth emblem in the sequence, "Cordis mundatio," depicts the heart being washed in the liquid that pours fountain-like from the side wound of Christ (Fig. 14). Harvey's poem to "Cordis emollitio" indicates the efficacy of blood, which is traditionally a virtually all-powerful solvent.[25] The world of nature—John Unrau gives other sources for the belief that diamond could be dissolved only by the blood of goats or lions—interprets the working of grace in Harvey's "Ode 16," of which I quote the second, third, and sixth stanzas:

> When the Sun shines with glitt'ring beames,
> His cold dispelling gleames
> Turne snow, and ice to wat'ry streames.
> The waxe, as soone as it hath smelt
> The warmth of fire, and felt
> The glowing heat thereof, will melt.
> Yea pearles with vinegar dissolve we may,
> And adamants in bloud of goats, they say.
>
> If nature can doe this, much more
> Lord, may thy grace restore
> Mine heart to what it was before.
> There's the same matter in it still,
> Though new inform'd with ill,
> Yet can it not resist thy will.
> The pow'r, that fram'd it at the first, as oft
> As thou wilt have it, Lord, can make it soft.

24. Cf. Hugo's Emblem 35 (*Pia desideria*, p. 306), and Quarles, *Emblemes*, sec. 5, 5 (p. 260), where the heat of Christ actually melts the soul.

25. See John Unrau, "Three Notes on George Herbert," pp. 94–95. The third note is referred to here.

. . . . . .

Yea, though my flinty heart be such,
That the Sun cannot touch,
Nor fire sometimes affect it much,
Yet thy warme reeking self-shed blood,
O Lam of God, 's so good
It cannot alwayes be withstood.
That Aqua-regia of thy love prevailes,
Ev'n where thy powers Aqua-fortis failes. (Harvey, pp. 65–67)

"Nature" (1633, p. 37) presents the heart as a stronghold that must be overcome, and in doing so reminds us of Donne's "Batter my heart"; but Herbert's poem takes a characteristically different direction in its second stanza, where the speaker threatens God that failure to intervene will bring about—by a form of obedience to natural laws—the evaporation of his soul. In order that God's "workmanship" should not be belied, the speaker pleads with God for the "graving" implicitly sued for at the end of "The Sinner" but immediately rephrases the request: his heart is incapable of being sufficiently purified to hold God, being fit for nothing but the remains of his dead body. In a poem whose logic is dictated by the laws of natural progression, this rephrasing represents the one "natural" non sequitur; up until this point there has been no room for the "or" of 15:

O smooth my rugged heart, and there
Engrave thy rev'rend law and fear;
Or make a new one, since the old
Is saplesse grown,
And a much fitter stone
To hide my dust, then thee to hold. (13–18)

The association between hard heart and monument or tombstone recurs in "Sepulchre," providing that poem with its point of departure; one is inclined to ask the extent to which both poems operate on a subliminal play on the word "grave." Addressing the body of the dead Christ, Herbert again exploits the contrast between the heart's unwillingness to offer "room" and the "store" or abundance with which the heart can "lodge transgressions" and "thousands of toyes" (5–7). This time, the contrast is developed into a claim for the purity of the rock that constitutes the sepulchre holding the crucified body, a claim that is held up against the heart's spurious generosity ("that which shews them large, shews them unfit" [9]). Similarly, the ordered quiet of the stones that constitute Christ's sepulchre is contrasted with the disorder in which stones were cast by an ungrateful and mendacious public. These contrasts, however, are set aside for the more conventional emblematic comparison of the last of the poem's three paired stanzas; here it is maintained that, despite the heart's extreme hardness, communication from God cannot be withstood:

And as of old, the law by heav'nly art
Was writ in stone; so thou, which also art
The letter of the word, find'st no fit heart
To hold thee.

Yet do we still persist as we began,
And so should perish, but that nothing can,
Though it be cold, hard, foul, from loving man
Withold thee. (17–24)[26]

In "Love unknown," Herbert conflates eucharistic associations with the notion that blood is an all-powerful solvent; taken repeatedly, it will cure the cancerous profusion of hardness in the heart:

Your heart was hard, I fear.
Indeed 'tis true. I found a callous matter
Began to spread and to expatiate there:
But with a richer drug, then scalding water,
I bath'd it often, ev'n with holy bloud.

(36–40)

There can be no doubt that Herbert alludes to this idea in "Grace" (1633, pp. 52–53). Association of dew and manna ("Drop from above") is enriched in this poem by an extraordinary confla-

26. A. D[avenport], in the last of his "Five Notes on George Herbert," p. 422, notices that *letter* in this context could very appropriately be taken as "one who lets loose." The word *let* is, of course, "primal," in the sense that it can convey its opposite. William Empson refrains from discussing this example, though he does comment on seventh-type-ambiguity uses of such words (*Seven Types of Ambiguity,* pp. 225ff.), and he notices the play on "let" in "Affliction" [I] (*Seven Types of Ambiguity,* p. 215).

tion of ideas, so that the all-powerful solvent comes to be associated with divine Grace:

Sinne is still hammering my heart
Unto a hardnesse, void of love:
Let suppling grace, to crosse his art,
Drop from above. (17–20)

The conceit of sin actually doing the hammering, hardening the heart still further in the absence of Grace, may very well have been suggested by the pictorial representations of the hardness of the heart in contemporary emblem literature. One way of portraying this hardness emblematically is simply to picture the law in terms of a hammer, thereby indicating the heart's unreceptivity to it. Herbert is able to add further effectiveness to this traditional idea in the lines from "Grace." The eucharistic associations of "holy bloud" in "Love unknown" suggest that it may be thought of as a sacramental expression for the restorative, "suppling" properties of divine Grace. In "Good Friday" (1633, pp. 30–31), Herbert asks for the actual writing of the divine secretary to be done in blood:

Since bloud is fittest, Lord, to write
Thy sorrows in, and bloudie fight;
My heart hath store, write there. (21–23)

In this poem, divine Grace is seen as what will "keep possession" on the departure of "sinne," so that Grace, in addition to suppling the heart, protects it.[27]

For Herbert, then, divine Grace is capable of restoring his heart, healing it to a point where he can ask to be made "soft and supple to thy will" ("H. Baptisme" [II] [1633, p. 36] [8]). The speaker is thus made receptive to divine communication, to such an extent that his softened heart need no longer be engraved on but may be written on, and not with ink but with a sacramental representation of it: "holy bloud." Herbert's invocation in "Grace" ("Drop from above") may therefore be compared with his invocation in "The Sinner" to the Divine to "restore thine image, heare my

27. Among many references in *The Temple* for which there is no space to treat in detail, see "The H. Communion" (1633, pp. 43–44), "Sunday" (1633, pp. 66–68), "Conscience" (1633, p. 98) and "Ephes. 4. 30" (1633, pp. 128–29).

call"; the words from "The Sinner" neatly summarize the idea of divine communication being of a visual nature and human response being audibly verbal.

Mention of "Grace" reminds us that it would be wrong to leave the impression that Herbert's use of the associative, conflative language is confined to his poems on Christ's Passion. In "The H. Scriptures. I" (1633, p. 50), the restorative effect of reading the Book of Scripture is "To cleare the breast, to mollifie all pain" (4), and the stress has so far perhaps been unduly placed in the present discussion on the second term in this description. The first may remind us, however, of the clearing of the intellect that also accompanies learning "how to," and with this in mind we may approach Herbert's ringing of one of his most exquisite variations on the idea of the hardness of the heart in "Church-lock and key" (1633, pp. 57–58):

Yet heare, O God, onely for his blouds sake
Which pleads for me:
For though sinnes plead too, yet like stones they make
His blouds sweet current much more loud to be. (9–12)

Our excitement in reading this figure lies in apprehending the way it bestows an active significance. In his poem "Sinne" [II] (1633, p. 55), Herbert describes sin as

flat opposite to th'Almighty, seeing
It wants the good of *vertue,* and of *being.* (4–5)

("Vertue," as so often, has a primary sense of "power" here.) The figure of sins as stones in the flowing stream of Christ's blood turns them to positive use; lacking "vertue" and "being," they are nonetheless forced to carry significance because of—and in terms of—the efficacy of Christ's blood, making it "much more loud to be" in suing for divine Grace.

Such an equation of the restorative actions of blood and Grace is confirmed in "An Offering":

There is a balsome, or indeed a bloud,
Dropping from heav'n, which doth both cleanse and close
All sorts of wounds; of such strange force it is. (19–21)

The state of affairs that has brought about the hardness is depicted dramatically in "Decay" (1633, pp. 91–92). Here what Bloch would term the "tribal memory" of God's former liberally dispensed appearances to Lot, Jacob, Gideon, Abraham, and Moses (1–4) is contrasted with a present reality of closeness and stasis:

> But now thou dost thy self immure and close
> In some one corner of a feeble heart. (11–12)

Human reluctance to communicate appears accommodatively to affect God's appearances to man; the result is seen in terms comparable to those of the hypothetical holocaust of "Vertue" (1633, p. 80) ("though the whole world turn to coal" [15]):

> I see the world grows old, when as the heat
> Of thy great love once spread, as in an urn
> Doth closet up it self, and still retreat,
> Cold sinne still forcing it, till it return,
> And calling Justice, all things burn. (16–20)

The terms for expression have arisen from man's conduct towards God, as Herbert makes clear. Finally, we may note a reference to the cleansing properties of blood in "Artillerie" (1633, pp. 132–33). This poem interchanges the arrows of love and sighs with stars. Herbert's response to God, "whose ministers / The starres and all things are" (11–12), is expressed as a request that he

> refuse not ev'n with bloud
> To wash away my stubborn thought. (14–15)

The *schola cordis* tradition not only provides supportive analogies for Herbert; conflative use of the Bible's language is his reading of the Book of Scripture, and in addition it casts considerable light on the close relationship between Christ's work of restoration and the sacrament of the Eucharist. The emblem "Cordis humiliatio" (van Haeften, p. 196; Harvey, p. 60), depicting Christ squeezing the heart in a vise (Fig. 12), prompts comparison with a later emblem in the *schola cordis*: "Mustum CORDIS e Torculari Crucis" (van Haeften's fifty-second [p. 598]; Harvey's forty-seventh [p.

188]). This emblem shows Christ being crushed in a wine press;[28] Anima holding the heart as a receptacle, collects blood from the five wounds (Fig. 15). The sacramentalism is clear: the blood is also wine and the heart is also the chalice, and the entire emblem provides another example—if more were needed—of how the *schola cordis* tradition encourages conflative interpretations, as does Harvey's accompanying verse. I quote the second and fourth stanzas of his "Ode 47":

> Shall he, that is thy Cluster, and thy Vine,
> Tread the winepresse alone,
> Whilst thou stand'st looking on? Shall both the wine
> And worke be all his owne?
> See how he bends, crusht with the straitned Screw
> Of that fierce wrath, that to thy sinnes was due.
>
> . . . .
>
> Thy Saviour being press'd to death, there ran
> Out of his sacred wounds
> That wine, that maketh glad the heart of man,
> And all his foes confounds.
> Yea, the full-flowing fountain's open still
> For all grace-thirsting hearts to drinke their fill. (pp. 189–90)

The emblem itself might almost have been designed to illustrate the last couplet from "The bunch of grapes" (1633, pp. 120–21), a poem in which Herbert develops his reasons for adoring the Divine:

> Who of the laws sowre juice sweet wine did make,
> Ev'n God himself, being pressed for my sake. (27–28)

In addition to illustrating its text, Ps. 104:15 ("And wine that maketh glad the heart of man"), "Mustum CORDIS e Torculari Crucis" recalls through its title Isa. 63:3 ("I have trodden the winepress alone"). Andrewes, we recall, in speaking of "the paine of the *Presse* (so the Prophet called it, *Torcular*:)," reserves his "fundetur" diction of "havock made at *all parts*" for the Crucifixion itself; here again we see how the emblem tradition associates the

28. See Wilson F. Engel III, "Christ in the Winepress: Backgrounds of a Sacred Image," for an extended discussion of the traditional sources of this idea.

"havock" also with the agony. If Patrick's suggestion is accepted, Herbert underlines this association by making the shape of the stanzas of "The Agonie" resemble the press (Patrick, pp. 17–28). It is arguably the case that those of "The bunch of grapes" and of Harvey's "Ode 47" do as well; at any rate, we are confronted here with another instance of how Herbert's conflative technique invites comparison with that of the emblem writers. The SANOR emblem of Daniel Cramer, in which the juice from the grapes is squeezed over the heart (Fig. 5), may be mentioned here, too; it demonstrates a way of representing simultaneously the suppling of the heart and the sacramentalism indicated by this gracious action of God's. It is worth noting that van Haeften's "Balneum cordis" emblem shows a chalice that can also be "read" as the cup of sorrows. It is situated in the upper corner of the picture and lit up by light from heaven (Fig. 1).[29] The reader of the emblem finds, just as Herbert's reader discovers experientially in the lyrics of *The Temple,* that an allusive approach to God's signs seems actually to be encouraged from their apprehender.[30]

Herbert's approach to the sacrament of the Eucharist itself, in his role of the priest who has come to terms with his duty of administering the elements that the Church must share, is characterized poetically by such allusiveness. The whole conception reveals a marvelous economy: it is the action of a shared consuming of the elements,[31] of lifting the chalice, that sacramentalizes interpretation of the Book of Nature, while the elements themselves, under their restorative aspect, sacramentalize interpretation of the Book of Scripture. Let us conclude this section by looking briefly at the

29. That the significance of the cup in this emblem is highly ambivalent is a suggestion I owe to Professor L. Strengholt of the Department of Dutch Language and Literature at the Vrije Universiteit, Amsterdam.

30. The group of emblems under discussion here again seems to derive from secular sources: in earlier collections (e.g. Guillaume de La Perrière, *Le Théâtre des bons engins*) Cupid is often seen weeping or blowing bellows in front of an alembic apparently distilling tears. See also Arthur Henkel and Albrecht Schöne, *Emblemata: Handbuch zur Sinnbildkunst des XVI. und XVII. Jahrhunderts.* Cf. the "large / And spacious fornace flaming" in "Love unknown" (25–26).

31. See the interesting remarks in Raymond Williams, *The Country and the City,* p. 43, who argues, with reference to Rosa Luxemburg and others, a limitedness in "the Christian tradition of charity," which he sees as "a charity of consumption only."

two eucharistic poems, "The Invitation" and "The Banquet" (1633, pp. 174–77). Helen Vendler's fine analysis of "The Invitation" shows how Herbert sees the eucharistic sacrament as supremely economical with regard to resources:

> Come ye hither all, whose taste
> Is your waste;
> Save your cost, and mend your fare. (1–3)

God is the feast, and subsumes in himself "all dainties." This realization allows for the constant play on *all* throughout the poem, a play that culminates in the last stanza:

> Lord I have invited all,
> And I shall
> Still invite, still call to thee:
> For it seems but just and right
> In my sight,
> Where is all, there all should be. (31–36)

The last *all* of the poem[32] conveys Herbert's Lord in both his human and his divine aspect. The Lord's presence simultaneously completes and gives sense to the gathering.

It is economy or "husbandry" that was seen in the previous chapter to be important to Herbert's attempts to describe his interpretation of the Book of Nature; his poem "Providence" (1633, pp. 109–14) shows that economy in action. One of the realizations bestowed by the divine Grace that informs a truly literate reading of the Book of Scripture is that economy and generosity are seen, in effect, to be aspects of one another; to "read" God's generosity in the Book of Scripture is to come to terms with what economy really means. The conflative technique that Herbert learns from the *schola cordis* tradition seems to provide one strategic means for Herbert's poetic expression of this paradox. C. A. Patrides has noted the allusion in "The Invitation" to Isa. 55:1–2: "Every one that thirsteth, come ye to the waters, and he that hath no money. . . . Wherefore do ye spend money for that which is not bread?"[33]

32. The Bodleian MS capitalizes "All" throughout except at line 31.
33. George Herbert, *The English Poems of George Herbert*, ed. C. A. Patrides, p. 184.

The lines referring to those "whom wine / Doth define" (7–8) recall the parable of the man whose guests all defaulted; drunkards would be found in the highways and byways (Matt. 22:1ff), and with the stroke of economy that Vendler notices so acutely, Herbert turns them into communicants:[34]

Weep what ye have drunk amisse,
And drink this,
Which before ye drink is bloud. (10–12)

Herbert's priest-communicant continues to bid society's undesirables ("all, whom pain / Doth arraigne" [13–14]; "all, whom joy / Doth destroy, / While ye graze without your bounds" [19–21]), before eventually turning to its presentable guests:

Come ye hither all, whose love
Is your dove,
And exalts you to the skie. (25–27)

The poem leads on to the next, "The Banquet":[35] no other consecutive pair of poems in *The Temple* possesses similar (or similarly unique) rhyme schemes. "The Banquet" celebrates the joy of the Eucharist in terms of sweetness; although this joy is incomparable, causing Herbert to ask whether "some starre [is] Melted there" (10–11) or whether some sweetness in the element of bread has actively overcome the "smell of sinne" (13–15), it is attended by bitterness; its sweetness is supplied by God, who "onely . . . gives perfumes" (22), though not without prior suffering. To convey the Passion in this paradoxical context, and to drive home the

34. Helen Vendler, *The Poetry of George Herbert*, p. 30.

35. It is tempting to take "banquet" in the sense given by *NED*, 2: "A slight repast between meals." Frank Kermode, "The Banquet of Sense," in his *Shakespeare, Spenser, Donne*, p. 87n, considers that this is the customary contemporary sense, but the *NED* gives "Eucharist or Lord's Supper" as 1(c): 1 is "A feast, a sumptuous entertainment of food and drink. . . ." Both senses, according to the *NED*, are current in the sixteenth and seventeenth centuries, though it is, I think, possible that 2 was prevalent and that 1(c) would more properly be included under it. Cf. "Prayer" [I] (1633, p. 43) where prayer is described as "the Churches banquet" (1); since this is juxtaposed with "Angels age," I think it is almost certainly proper to take "banquet" here, in keeping with the "handsell" notion, as *NED* 2. E. B. Greenwood in "George Herbert's Sonnet 'Prayer': A Stylistic Study," p. 35, takes it as such.

notion of the gracious gift of restoration, Herbert resorts to the exquisitely economic figure of the pomander:

> But as Pomanders and wood
> Still are good,
> Yet being bruis'd are better sented:
> God, to show how farre his love
> Could improve,
> Here, as broken, is presented. (25–30)

Financial accommodation

The Passion poems in *The Temple* are presented in such a way as to lead their reader to a beholding and considering of the divine signs they portray. Consideration of these signs leads in turn to an appreciation of the sacramental, restorative properties that inhere in them. A contemporary Divine, Thomas Adams (fl. 1612–53), summarizes this appreciation:

> They say, that *Balme* taken inwardly, dissolves, and breakes the stone in the reynes [kidneys]. But *Jeremie,* in Gods Physicke booke, saith, that our *Balme* is as a *Hammer to breake the stone in the heart*. The stone in the reines is dangerous, in the bladder painefull, but none so deadly as the stone in the heart. This *Balme* supples the stonie heart, and turnes it into *a heart of flesh*.[36]

Instead of "graving" on the stone heart, the Divine may write in "holy bloud" on the "suppled" heart. The typology of the writing of the law of Moses in the tablets of stone and the writing on the heart, referred to, for instance, in the last stanza of "Sepulchre," is presumably based on the words of Paul, who, speaking of the Gentiles, remarks that they "shew the work of the law written in their hearts" (Rom. 2:15) and suggests that what is written on the "suppled" heart has to do with the new covenant invoked by the Incarnation and Passion of Christ.

The new covenant is traditionally seen in Christian theology in terms of a "redemption"; Herbert's poem of this title dramatizes

36. Thomas Adams, "Physicke from Heaven" in *Workes,* p. 285 (sig. Aa5^{r}). The reference is to Jer. 23:29.

the financial notions to which the etymology of the title draws attention. The connection between writing down the new covenant and regarding it as a financial transaction leads a reader to envisage what Herbert considers God actually to have "written" on his heart; it is nothing less than a sealing of this financial bargain, conceived of in terms of a declaration of divine love. The idea is endorsed by the last lines of "Sepulchre," where Herbert stresses that "nothing can . . . from loving man, / Withold thee." His reader learns to relate this idea to an emerging desire to imitate Christ, of which—as so many commentators have noticed—*The Temple* may be read as the record. "Easter" (1633, p. 33) shows something of this desire:[37]

> Rise heart; thy Lord is risen. Sing his praise
> Without delayes,
> Who takes thee by the hand, that thou likewise
> With him mayst rise:
> That, as his death calcined thee to dust,
> His life may make thee gold, and much more just. (1–6)

"The Thanksgiving" and "The Reprisall" differ from "Easter" in running over the possibilities and implications of undertaking this imitation. It has been seen that "Sepulchre" strikingly sets together the ideas of law and loving Grace. Man's soul is regarded—as a result of Christ's Incarnation, Passion and Resurrection—as having been "bought back" (hence "Redemption") from the enemy to which his Fall "sold" it. Consequently, a new law must be inscribed on his receptive heart. The prevalence of references to business and finance in *The Temple* is therefore related to Herbert's attempt to come to terms with this conception of Christian theology, central to the Book of Scripture. It might seem odd to find the central idea of the Christian faith expressed as a financial transaction, until his reader sees what happens when Herbert tries to accept the idea behind it. The reader finds from "The Thanksgiving" that Herbert is disinclined, or even unable, to come to terms with the concept of a "gift." Throughout

37. A similar desire is seen in another "resurrection poem," "The Dawning" (1633, pp. 104–105).

the poem he stalls, only realizing finally that divine love is utterly preemptive:[38]

Oh King of wounds! how shall I grieve for thee,
    Who in all grief preventest me?
Shall I weep bloud? why thou hast wept such store
    That all thy body was one doore.
Shall I be scourged, flouted, boxed, sold?
    'Tis but to tell the tale is told. (3–8)

Expressions of sorrow and grief, even when envisaged as attempts to imitate the Passion of Christ, seem in the end to be of little use; certainly they are of no reparative use when the reader of Scripture offers them to God. Herbert turns to alternatives. If expressions of compassion are unavailing, he may be able then to gloss over the "dolefull storie" of divine sorrow and "side with thy triumphant glorie" instead (11–12). But even this does not avail, because then Herbert neither would nor could be imitating Christ in anything like a full sense (15–16). Perhaps he can act as a lover avenging his beloved by imitating that beloved, in this case referring all his gifts to divine munificence, offering them to the rest of mankind so that it will be seen to whom Herbert as lover belongs (17–28). The poet proceeds in this way for several lines before realizing that this is all very well for those gifts for which reparation is possible — but "as for thy passion. . . ." The problem is shelved for the moment. Herbert now declares himself in contempt of the world and will refer all its man-made beauties and pleasures to God (31–44). "The Thanksgiving" shows that for all divine gifts but one it is possible, after a fashion, to make imitative reparation. For the Passion, however, it is not, and this actually undercuts all man's other attempts at reparation; the "new" is seen to be useless cliché even before it has been offered. Herbert realizes this more soberly in "The Reprisall" (entitled "The Second Thanks-giving"

38. The nature of this love has been impressively discussed by Rosemond Tuve; see *Essays by Rosemond Tuve,* ed. Thomas P. Roche, Jr., pp. 167–206. Richard Strier's careful account of "The Thanksgiving" in *Love Known: Theology and Experience in George Herbert's Poetry,* pp. 49–52, draws attention to the poem's dramatization of its underlying theology, and Strier is particularly good on the way imitation (as he puts it) "falls away as an evasive and rationalizing fiction" (p. 52).

in the Williams manuscript). There is a further attempt to come to terms with divine prevenience, and it culminates here in a tone of genuinely perplexed distress:

> Ah! was it not enough that thou
> By thy eternall glorie didst outgo me?
> Couldst thou not griefs sad conquests me allow,
> But in all vic'tries overthrow me? (9–12)

Herbert remarkably succeeds here in showing something of the attractiveness of grief and of the strange pleasure to be gained from repining at God's humiliation in the Passion: the paradox of sublime humility is something he desires to share. This curious desire is hard to place but certainly seems to include elements of an unwillingness to accept the way God "prevents" Herbert "in all grief," and Herbert's reader reads it as a tactful admission of the sense of unease that gratitude provokes. It seems that the only possible reaction is one of resoluteness:

> Yet by confession will I come
> Into the conquest. Though I can do nought
> Against thee, in thee I will overcome
> The man, who once against thee fought. (13–16)

Herbert learns to forsake the impulse to strive with God for the limelight and, reluctantly at first, accepts the gift as he attempts, "in thee," to overcome a common foe. "The Crosse" (1633, pp. 158–59) indicates a similar defeat for the efforts of human love by the power of divine love, setting this great theological paradox into one astonishingly concise yet moving stanza:

> And then when after much delay,
> Much wrastling, many a combate, this deare end,
> So much desir'd, is giv'n, to take away
> My power to serve thee; to unbend
> All my abilities, my designes confound,
> And lay my threatnings bleeding on the ground. (7–12)

Coming to terms with the implications of the Passion, and attempting to imitate it, as in "Affliction" [II] (1633, pp. 53–54), indicate to Herbert and his reader a new and alternative approach to the poetry of suffering, again with a suggestion of a financial metaphor:

Thou art my grief alone,
Thou Lord conceal it not: and as thou art
All my delight, so all my smart:
Thy crosse took up in one,
By way of imprest, all my future mone. (11–15)

There are times, as in "Faith" (1633, pp. 41–42), when Herbert can accept the gift without apparent difficulty, yet here the ultimate expressive paradox is that God has imitated Herbert, and the problem resolves itself by means of the assurance figured in the use of poetic wit:

I owed thousands and much more:
I did beleeve that I did nothing owe,
And liv'd accordingly; my creditor
Beleeves so too, and lets me go. (13–16)

It seems that what is most disturbing about reading the Scriptures is, for Herbert, the complete gratuitousness of the Incarnation. As a "literate" reader of the Scriptures, he has the utmost difficulty in interpreting the concept of freedom that the signs of the Passion offer. The idea of a financially expressed "redemption" draws the attention away from this impossible concept and protects the reader of the Book of Scripture by accommodating factors that are utterly gratuitous to human experience.

The problems can, of course, only be sidestepped; they cannot be eliminated. One of the greatest problems that financial "accommodation" highlights is that of the value of the soul of the reader of the Scriptures. Traditionally Christian theology simultaneously accords great value to the soul ("What shall it profit a man") and expresses continued astonishment that God should find it at all worthy of attention. According to Rudolf Otto, conceptualization of the "holy" or "numinous" involves a realization that it alone is worthy to be praised ("*Quoniam tu solus sanctus*"), and this realization corresponds to a feeling of "unworth" or "disvalue" on the part of the creature.[39] The two attitudes clash

39. Rudolf Otto, *The Idea of the Holy* [*Das Heilige*], trans. John W. Harvey, p. 51.

fascinatingly in a reading of the Song of Songs such as Hugh of St. Victor's *Soliloquium de arrha animae,* a work whose title provides an instance of the prevalence of financial accommodation. The soul is persuaded into an appreciation of its own worth:

> You have a bridegroom, but you do not know him. He is the most beautiful of all, but you have not seen his face. He has seen you, because otherwise he could not love you. As yet he has not wished to show himself to you, but he has sent you gifts; he has given a betrothal-gift, a pledge of love, a sign of his affection. If you could know him, if you were to see his likeness, you would no longer hesitate about your beauty. You would know that one so fair, so handsome, so graceful, so unique, would not have been taken with your appearance if he had not been drawn to an attractiveness exceeding that of others.[40]

Here, at least initially, the reader is again called upon to learn not necessarily how to show gratitude, but a more elementary response: how to accept. Having resolved the crisis of the abject persona in his other poems concerned with his role as priest, Herbert is able to document his sharing of this response in "The Banquet":

> When I had forgot my birth,
> And on earth
> In delights of earth was drown'd;
> God took bloud, and needs would be
> Spilt with me,
> And so found me on the ground.
>
> Having rais'd me to look up,
> In a cup
> Sweetly he doth meet my taste. (31–39)

The use of the figure of the pomander in this poem (25–30) has prompted its reader to reflect that it expresses the great "stand

40. Sponsum habes, sed nescis. Pulcherrimus est omnium, sed faciem ejus non vidisti. Ille te vidit, quia nisi te vidisset, non te diligeret. Noluit adhuc seipsum tibi praesentare, sed munera misit, arrham dedit, pignus amoris, signum dilectionis. Si cognoscere illum posses, si speciem illius videres, non amplius de tua pulchritudine ambigeres. Scires enim quod tam pulcher, tam formosus, tam elegans, tam unicus in tuo aspectu captus non esset, si eum singularis decor et ultra caeteros admirandus non traheret. Hugh of St. Victor, *De arrha animae*; *PL* 176, col. 954.

with himself" of the country parson, who as priest has "not onely to receive God, but to break and administer him" (*The Countrey Parson,* 22). Much of the heart-searching of Herbert the priest is in fact a result of his wittily expressed realization that he must in one sense reenact the work of the crucifiers in breaking God; consolation comes with the paradoxical insight that "bruising" the pomander releases its scent. Not only, though, is the Incarnation to be seen as a sacramental prefiguring of the supreme communion with the Divine that the Eucharist allows in this life; the Eucharist is itself a prefiguring. Herbert is still mortal and "farre from court," and the communion that the banquet permits is one that can only be realized in this life in a mystical vision. He accordingly offers praise that, characteristically, is closely bound with his life not just as communicant-priest but as poet:

Let the wonder of this pitie
Be my dittie,
And take up my lines and life. (49–51)

* * *

In the final chapter of this book I consider how response to Herbert's "lines" is affected by the realizations to which his interpretation of divine phenomena has led him. For with this discussion of Herbert's reading of the books of Nature and Scripture, we conclude the first part of our investigation into acts of interpretation in *The Temple.* This has involved tracing an Augustinian theory of signs through medieval recensions into some of the various forms into which it can be seen to have branched in Renaissance thought, and arguing Herbert's essential familiarity with the broad march of this development. Although Herbert's readings of the books of Nature and Scripture have been presented as consistent with this intellectual history, I have asserted a distinctively Herbertian expression of the traditional view of the opacity of signs in his communication with God. Figured in providential and gracious terms, respectively, God's signs as discerned in the two books remain ultimately inscrutable. Man's "illiteracy" in the face of the natural world, and the hardness of his heart in the emblematic treatment of the distilling events of Scripture, are comparable responses; as such they contrast strikingly with the providential bounty and flow and with the gracious prevenience, accommodatively discerned in Herbert's readings of the two books. In this way, man's initial reluctance to respond to God's abundant communicativeness is overcome by being figured as a sacramental offering up to God.

6. The Opacity of Signs and the Lyric Form

Reading the two books, Nature and Scripture, through which God providentially and graciously reveals himself to fallen man, Herbert learns that the divinely ordained signs that constitute God's mode of communication demand interpretation in such a way as to imply expressive response. What God communicates to fallen man must be communicated "significantly": in his fallen state man can no longer conceive of communication from God that is in any way "beyond significance" and that we may imagine prevailed before the Fall. For Herbert, it is thus man's sacramental duty to make sense of what he perceives or "reads," and Herbert's unusually luminous apprehension of this insight suggests how an intellectual deciphering of signs actually motivates communication with God through a poetic expressiveness that reveals the more emotional aspect of Herbert's sensibility.

It is time in this final chapter to pay serious attention to the consequences for his readers of Herbert's poetic expression of response to God's signs. Such attention reveals the existence of a basic paradox that it is Herbert's informing and characteristic poetic strategy to exploit. Given that it is Herbert's deciphering of signs that motivates his expressive communication with God, the reader is automatically accorded the role, in terms of the fictions that Herbert's poems are constantly postulating, of eavesdropping on or, to use A. D. Nuttall's word, "overhearing," communicative acts between the poet's voices and God.[1] To appreciate fully what this situation involves, we need to remind ourselves once again of what John R. Mulder has termed "the distinction

1. A. D. Nuttall, *Overheard by God: Fiction and Prayer in Herbert, Milton, Dante and St John*, pp. 1–9, etc.

between Herbert and his speaker or persona."[2] The human readership supplies the historical dimension to the totality of the experience of engagement with Herbert's verse; while frequently standing outside their fictions, he gives them substance through his participation. Whatever Herbert may actually have intended as the destiny of the spiritual conflicts enshrined as his lyrics, they nevertheless exist as printed text and published work. This public status gives life to the striking conceit that Nuttall has explored so thoroughly and attentively, a conceit in which Herbert rhetorically presents himself to his reader as a speaker or persona in poems that God, rather than the human reader, seems to have overheard—since at crucial irruptive moments God himself participates in a lyric by completing it. Yet this conceit, stemming from the pragmatics of disseminated publication, is not fundamentally different in kind from the poetic and theological fictions that we encounter more regularly in Herbert's lyrics. The question remains: to whom *are* Herbert's poems addressed?

Address

Let us consider more closely Herbert's engaging presentation of the issues of "address" in his poem "The Windows" (1633, p. 59). Elsewhere in *The Temple,* such as in the very structure and nature of "The Church-porch" (1633, pp. 1–16) or, more interestingly, in the miniature exegesis of "Coloss. 3.3." (1633, p. 77), he posits a relationship between verse and sermon. Meditating upon its opening question ("Lord, how can man preach thy eternall word?"), "The Windows" is founded upon a witty examination of the relationship. Figuring man as "brittle crazie glasse" that can only take on meaningful shape once, in the manner of our perception of a stained glass window, the pieces are seen to be part of a whole, the poem at the same time contrives to suggest that man uses the resources of God's light for his effectiveness as preacher.

2. John R. Mulder, "*The Temple* as Picture," in *"Too Riche to Clothe the Sunne": Essays on George Herbert,* ed. Claude J. Summers and Ted-Larry Pebworth, p. 3.

In so doing, however, he alters that light as it shines through him, just as our perception of daylight is altered once it is refracted through colored glass. The figure draws attention to the paradox wherein man's unworthiness is the very quality that renders him capable of acting as God's instrument. Although "The Windows" illustrates a manifestation of divine Grace entirely of a piece with the insight arrived at in "Aaron" (1633, pp. 168–69), the poem's argument also recalls the more domestic context of one of Herbert's most memorable phrases, for it is likewise gracious conduct on God's part that allows the servant in "The Elixer" (1633, pp. 178–79) to make "drudgerie divine." In "The Windows," glass is additionally figured as offering the potential for transcendent vision; through it man may "then the heav'n espie" ("The Elixer" [12]). Yet besides drawing attention to man's unworthiness, the alteration that God's light undergoes as it passes through the glass also figures the enabling potential that the "life of Christ" pictured in stained glass brings about in the man who aims at living an imitation of Christ. Divine Grace permitting him to do this, God's "storie" is "anneal[ed] in glasse" (6): the preacher's "speech alone" requires the support of a "life" lived according to "doctrine" (11, 13). The implication seems to be that poetry written in accordance with "doctrine" is the most effectual kind: "the light and glorie . . . more doth win" (8–9). The notion of a sermon (and a poetry) that "more doth win" is consistent with the classical aim of persuasion, and although these matters have been discussed at length by Arnold Stein,[3] the structure of "The Windows" still presents scope for comment. The formal working-out of a notion of effectiveness is consistent with the poem's given structure: in addition to meditating on a paradox, the poem is itself a progression from uncertainty ("Lord, how can man preach thy eternall word?") to conviction:

speech alone
Doth vanish like a flaring thing,
And in the eare, not conscience ring. (13–15)

3. See the whole of Arnold Stein's introduction to his *George Herbert's Lyrics*; see also Dennis Quinn, "Donne's Christian Eloquence," pp. 276–97.

"The Windows" could be considered a miniature sermon in the sense that it persuades; the aim of the preacher "whose life shines with the infused life of Christ" (Stein, p. 31n) is to "win" his audience. But the poem is directly addressed to God, who cannot be thought of as succumbing to persuasion, as the human reader does, although God may be conceived of as responding to the poem. The human reader, overhearing a meditative colloquy between Herbert and God about the preaching of sermons and the fitness of man for the task, reads it in such a way that it is not simply an overheard colloquy but has the same effect as the ideal sermon; it brings about what it represents, that is, a conviction of certainty.[4] It should be stressed that this is a conclusion that is only reached in the process of reading; that is to say, the logical, progressive, structure of the poem and the effect it brings about are only apprehended *as* matching each other by the reader, who is not directly addressed. The reader finds these features, the "matter and manner" (Stein, p. xlii), intellectually satisfying when they are seen to correspond to each other, but it is difficult to see how the effect on God, directly addressed in this poem and not conceived of as in need of persuasion, could be of the same order. What is apprehended as accordance by the human overhearer is by no means necessarily apprehended in the same way by the divine hearer. If the recent history of Herbert criticism may serve as a guide, there is no doubt that many of his readers take both delight and intellectual satisfaction in a discovery of the sort of correspondence between form and content that is seen to emerge from a reading of "The Windows."

We may appreciate more fully what such discovery involves if we contrast William Empson's comments concerning Herbert's emblematic poem "Hope" (1633, p. 114). Regarding "the movement [of 'Hope' as] so impeccable as to be almost independent of the meaning of the symbols," Empson writes of "the means by which Herbert makes one accept [words] soberly, as things rich in

4. Compare the remarks of E. B. Greenwood in "George Herbert's Sonnet 'Prayer': A Stylistic Study," that "Prayer" [I] "contrives to *be* a prayer at the same time as being about prayer" (p. 29).

their interpretation rather than in their meaning."[5] Empson's insight suggests the existence of an act of interpretation on the reader's part,[6] and this view of the process of reading tends to remain implicit in Empson's criticism, except at certain moments. One example of those moments is his definition of the sixth type of ambiguity, which "occurs when a statement says nothing, by tautology, by contradiction, or by irrelevant statements; *so that the reader is forced to invent statements of his own* and they are liable to conflict with one another."[7] The point Empson makes about emblematic writing lies near the center of the debate with Rosemond Tuve and therefore to the goal of our investigation. Let us approach this goal by observing how the finding of "meanings" by a reader may be subsumed into a more general act of interpretation that does not primarily have to do with decoding words. Faced with a poem like "Hope," or "Peace," or "Love unknown," where the emblematic or allegorical language may work against its elucidation, the reader is initially forced to respond to something that does not necessarily emerge from the verbal "meaning"; he is instead drawn to other features of the verse, such as its "impeccable movement," although Empson's earlier discussion of this in *Seven Types of Ambiguity* shows him anxious to avoid "Tennyson's simple and laborious cult of onomatopoeia" (p. 29). Yet Empson, having referred to the "impeccable movement" of "Hope," does not really do much to characterize it. I suggest that the poem's curious reciprocity of gifts and gesture deserves some comment and that we notice the way in which a sense of

5. William Empson, *Seven Types of Ambiguity,* pp. 144, 146. This poem exemplifies "third-type" ambiguity, which, "considered as a verbal matter, occurs when two ideas, which are connected only by being both relevant in the context, can be given in one word simultaneously" (p. 127).

6. Stein, *George Herbert's Lyrics,* p. xxv, offers an Augustinian basis for this approach to a text.

7. Empson, *Seven Types of Ambiguity,* p. 207 (emphasis added). "Affliction" [I] provides an example of this type. Compare also p. 84, which makes the view explicit in order not to obscure "the main crux about poetry, that being an essentially suggestive act it can only take effect if the impulses (and to some extent the experiences) are already there to be called forth; that the process of getting to understand a poet is precisely that of constructing his poems in one's own mind." Compare also Empson, *The Structure of Complex Words* (London: Chatto & Windus, 1951), p. 53: "Of course I think one should always try to interpret paradoxes."

consequence or consequentiality increases interestingly up to the end of the sixth line: within the logic of its reciprocity, the movement of the poem transforms "but" (1) to "then" (3), to "and" (4) and finally to "with that" (5) before returning to the inscrutability of "but" (6). The sense of opacity persists into the last two lines, with an emotional irruption into the narrative description:

I gave to Hope a watch of mine: but he
          An anchor gave to me.
Then an old prayer-book I did present:
          And he an optick sent.
With that I gave a viall full of tears:
          But he a few green eares:
Ah Loyterer! I'le no more, no more I'le bring:
          I did expect a ring.

In this poem, then, Herbert's use of a language of significance is much more private than it is in "The Windows." Yet few of Herbert's readers have publicly objected to the inaccessibility it might be thought to proffer. The major challenge to this aspect of Herbert's achievement remains that of Wilbur Sanders,[8] but even though his objections appeared a decade or so after the publication of Tuve's work, the strength of Tuve's claims remains considerable. Her assertion that our willingness "to learn Herbert's language"[9] represents an adequate response to *The Temple* must be examined further.

Our discussion of "The Windows" and "Hope" has raised some interesting paradoxes. In "The Windows" we as readers are not addressed directly; instead we are put in the position of overhearing a colloquy between Herbert and God. Yet a reading of this poem can arouse an excitement in us, despite our knowledge that we are not central to the poem's transaction, prompting us to seek and take pleasure in our discernment of a relationship between the poem's "manner" and its "matter," between its form and its content. We may find it hard to imagine the divine hearer being so impressed; the artfulness of a poem such as "The Windows"

8. See particularly Wilbur Sanders, "Childhood is Health: The Divine Poetry of George Herbert," pp. 102–111.
9. Rosemond Tuve, *A Reading of George Herbert*, p. 203.

remains a concession to our fallen nature as human readers. The paradox that is beginning to emerge is that it is our very realization that we may somehow be excluded from a fuller knowledge of the transaction between Herbert and God in a poem such as "The Windows" that may prompt excitement at our discovery of the discerned relationship between form and content. In a poem such as "Hope," we seem as readers more central to the poem's transaction. In "Hope" the transaction is narrated, rather than being meditated upon and enacted in front of us as in "The Windows," yet the language chosen for the narration of events is such that in "Hope," too, we are faced with a form of enactment, one that has been rendered opaque by what Tuve would term "Herbert's language." Our discovery in "Hope," a lyric to whose transaction we might have seemed more central than on other occasions in *The Temple,* is precisely that something is going on outside our capacity to grasp. Instead we can only sense its essence, so that it seems that our exclusion from all but the essence of the poem renders us not merely less affected than we might be in another kind of poem by an apprehension of form-and-content correspondence, but actually less able to discern such correspondence. "Herbert's language" in a poem such as "Hope" thus tends to exclude the twentieth-century reader in a manner that cannot really be said to apply to a consideration of "The Windows." On the other hand, "The Windows" pushes the reader further to the periphery of the poem's transaction. The exclusion that a poem such as "The Windows" brings with it therefore enables the reader to seek compensation through a discernment of form-and-content correspondence; the exclusion that is part of our experience of "Hope," on the contrary, causes us to ask seriously whether it is possible to equip ourselves, as Tuve seems to demand, in such as way as to make inclusion possible. We must now examine the extent to which it is the very intimation of exclusion offered by a poem such as "The Windows" that presents us with the more realistic option of encouraging, even propelling, us toward finding correspondence between form and content.

Form and content

Research into such correspondences in *The Temple* yield rich results: there are certainly many poems whose form can be said ingeniously to match their content.[10] Some of these, in order for the correspondence to be fully appreciated, actually need to be seen on the page. "The Altar" (1633, p. 18) and "Easter wings" (1633, pp. 34–35), shaped as their titles, are obvious and celebrated examples. It has been a persistent critical assumption that there is a rather dilettante air about such poems, so that Joseph Summers, for instance, in order to defend Herbert's examples of the "hieroglyph" against those of his contemporaries, concedes that "before and after 1633 the literary quality of most of these poems was notoriously low."[11]

Following *NED* 2, Summers defines the hieroglyph as "a figure, device, or sign having some hidden meaning; a secret or enigmatical symbol; an emblem" (Summers, p. 123). Summers's sensitive analyses (pp. 140–45) of "The Altar" and "Easter wings" represent his attempts to show that their form-and-content correspondence is not as superficial a matter as it seems to have been to many of Herbert's contemporaries. Yet it is interesting that readings of these poems generally carry a defensive, even polemical air. Summers concludes his analysis of "The Altar":

> Herbert's attempt to use the shape of a classical altar as a hieroglyph of his beliefs concerning the relationships between the heart, the work of art, and the praise of God failed to communicate its meaning to a number of generations. While not one of Herbert's greatest poems, "The Altar" within its context in *The Temple* is still an effective poem if we take the pains to understand it. (Summers, p. 143)

And the second of the two poems "has been subject to fewer misinterpretations" (Summers, p. 141). Armed by more recent concepts such as Harold Bloom's "anxiety of influence," to which the creative, literary-historiographical role that misinterpretation may

10. The next few poems adduced are favorites of apologists for Herbert's wit. See, typically, M. M. Mahood, "Something Understood: The Nature of Herbert's Wit."

11. Joseph H. Summers, *George Herbert: His Religion and Art,* p. 140.

play is central, a critic writing a generation later may be inclined to attack Summers's remark as question-begging.[12] But the point to be stressed from his thoughtful reading of "The Altar" is that the very existence of a clearly apprehensible correspondence between its shape and content has seemed to influence our readings of it, even to encourage certain readings or emphases on certain readings. The reader is almost inevitably compelled to see the poem's content as needing explication in terms of a relationship to the form asserted on the page. A defensive reading such as Summers's is as often as not the result, so that the seriousness of Herbert's pattern poems is set against the frivolous efforts of his contemporaries. Readings of such poems are used to emphasize those aspects of their meanings that the words most obviously release and to support a correlation of such verbal significance with the significance that their shape bestows. Conceivably, other verbal significances in these poems may go unnoticed because they are not emphasized by correspondence with the poems' shapes.

During the last ten to fifteen years, defensive readings of this kind have begun to be challenged. In characteristically pioneering manner, Stanley Fish remarked in *Self-Consuming Artifacts* that "the first thing ['The Altar'] does, even before we take in any of its words, is call attention to itself as something quite carefully made; and at the same time attention is called also to the skill and ingenuity of the maker, who is presumably the poet."[13] Fish considered that this "indicates one path Herbert chose not to follow" and based his reading on a belief that the "central issue" of the poem, the question it forces its reader to ask, is "the question of agency." In accordance with his thesis, Fish argued that the reader shares in the claims that the poem makes. I suggest that the shaping of the poem not only offers potential for claims of poetic brilliance that are then seen to belong properly to God; in possessing the shape it does, the poem also actually restricts certain interpretative pos-

12. See Harold Bloom, *The Anxiety of Influence*, p. 30, etc.
13. Stanley E. Fish, *Self-Consuming Artifacts: The Experience of Seventeenth-Century Literature*, p. 207.

sibilities. We are not confronted simply with the puzzling syntax of the first few lines, "where a surfeit of interpretative possibilities interferes with [the reader's] leisurely completion of the foreseen pattern" (Fish, p. 208); the poem's entire shape actually bestows a given reading, inviting us as readers to read the poem in a particular way. At the most general level, as with all such shaped poems, the reader's attention is drawn from the words to the shape. In the particular instance of "The Altar," we might say that the reader is being encouraged to visualize and complete the shape of an altar. Yet an equally legitimate reading, not encouraged by attention to the poem's shape, would urge the reader to think about what is happening to the heart. In the manner in which we are encouraged to select the reading that visualizes and completes the shape of the heart, we are faced, as we may also be in the case of other shaped poems, with a form-and-content correspondence that helps to exclude, or even proscribe, a kind of reading such as the reader might otherwise afford "The Altar." The reader must confront the possibility that the expressive "rhetoric" of *The Temple,* signified by the form-and-content correspondence of such poems as "The Altar," may, like the various forms of divine signification we have already examined, possess the property of opacity. As far as the text of *The Temple* is concerned, however, rhetorical opacity would invite readings that renounce given interpretative possibilities and would direct the reader's attention away from readings that embody given truths or insights.

Something of this rhetorical opacity may be sensed at the end of "Affliction" [I] (1633, pp. 38–40), with its famous example of Empson's sixth type of ambiguity:

Yet, though thou troublest me, I must be meek;
                    In weaknesse must be stout.
Well, I will change the service, and go seek
                    Some other master out.
Ah my deare God! though I am clean forgot,
Let me not love thee, if I love thee not. (61–66)

Empson's analysis charts a number of possible senses (of varying degrees of plausibility) for the strange last couplet.[14] The point I

14. Empson, *Seven Types of Ambiguity,* pp. 214–16.

am stressing here is that the incipient irruption into the poem of virtually uncontrollable emotion (such irruption is indicated, as also in "Hope," "Dialogue," and "Love" [III], by "Ah . . .") is then met by the ambiguity that Empson detects. As a result, the energy of the reader's response is deflected away from the irruption and toward solving the puzzle presented by the last lines. Yet the human reader may well take considerable intellectual pleasure in this response. Empson has elsewhere remarked of these lines:

> I don't deny that there is a certain lack of self-consciousness about 17th Century writers even when they are writing about themselves, even when like George Herbert they treat the reader with a certain reserve. The reason why [this couplet] is not fussy in spite of its baffling ambiguity is that he thought of it as an effective appeal to the heart of God (as it might have been to a loved woman—"Give me more love or more disdain"); it is not primarily a display of his own complex state of mind to an interested reader.[15]

In drawing attention to the possibility of a difference between human and divine readers, Empson documents the effect that Herbert's couplet has on him: it is, he says, as though he is being treated "with a certain reserve." Empson refers to the "baffling ambiguity" of the last lines of "Affliction" [I], and we may be reminded of his definition of his sixth type, with its connotation of a puzzle that the reader works to resolve in an act of interpretation. It is precisely because the lines present themselves to the human reader in this way that the notion of "a certain reserve" can be entertained. We have already suggested that what the eavesdropping human reader documents as his own experience of Herbert's text (in Empson's words, in the case in point, the experience is a "baffling ambiguity") and what that reader can only imagine is presented to God are quite distinct. The "reserve" that Empson's remarks postulate is crucial to this suggestion, but Empson does not go as far as to assert, as I have done, the human reader's sense that Herbert is offering incomprehensible experience to God in an act of renunciation that the words may conceal. To the human reader, that act of offering must in itself possess significance of

15. Empson, "Donne and the Rhetorical Tradition," p. 583.

another kind of order, a significance not assimilable to the human reader's reasoned and analytical response to the poem.

Imagining that, as a result of Herbert's act of offering, God apprehends what lies behind all that the words that describe Herbert's experience attempt to represent, then, the reader is unable to do more than appreciate the possibility of a noninterpretative reception of the experience that the poem portrays. Only if he can surrender a certain order of interpretative claim to the experience portrayed in the poem, for example by admitting the implications of his being addressed indirectly or opaquely, can the reader maneuver himself into a position of proper relativity toward the text. In this way he will be in a position simultaneously to see Herbert's text as operating with "a certain reserve" and offering "baffling ambiguity" to its readers, and—in observing and accepting its presentation to God—to appreciate that it constitutes a form of significance outside his own interpretative or analytic powers. Only an omniscient God can be conceived of as outside the limits of interpretative engagement. What we are presented with is the paradoxical situation in which Herbert himself has had to interpret his sometimes painfully intolerable experience in terms of divinely given but opaque signs in order to communicate that experience in the first place, while his reader must respond with an act of interpretation that concedes that the essence of the experience is beyond him. The human reader of *The Temple* is confronted with the simultaneous acknowledgment both that he is accorded an interpretative role and that experience that is incomprehensible in human terms is being presented to the omniscient Divine. It follows that making sense of *The Temple* frequently results in the concession that given aspects of the text, offered up by Herbert to God, cannot be analytically "explicated" or "translated" by the human reader but must themselves imply the significance of inexplicability. The concession seems to be made, for example, in "Assurance" (1633, pp. 149–50):

> Wherefore if thou canst fail,
> Then can thy truth and I: but while rocks stand,
> And rivers stirre, thou canst not shrink or quail:
> Yea, when both rocks and all things shall disband,

> Then shalt thou be my rock and tower,
> And make their ruine praise thy power. (31–36)

Herbert chooses, then, to convey the idea that inexplicability of experience may itself have significance by resorting to a rhetorical opacity of expressiveness. He relies on the reader's felt need to interpret as inexplicable (for instance, by reading as "ambiguous" or as a "significance") what is not fully understood and may not even need explication at all, since it is addressed to a divine reader outside the interpretative realm and conceived of as apprehending things as they are (*res*), not what they represent (*verba*). This opacity and its possibilities seem most immediately evident in those poems that invite their readers to see correspondence between their form and content. "The Altar" and "Easter wings" are clear examples of poems whose shape invites a given interpretation of their content. Other poems invite given interpretations on the basis of particular sonorities and structural features and do so equally problematically. A traditional way of conveying the notion of the Trinity, for example, and one that probably derives from Augustine, is to employ trinities in writing about it; the habit is especially characteristic of medieval writing, permeating the *Breviloquium* and other writings of Bonaventura to what is at times, for the modern reader, an irritating extent.[16] Herbert writes "Trinitie Sunday" (1633, p. 59) in three stanzas, each of three lines. The last stanza of this poem, containing further triads, might seem to have little effect on its reader other than to drive home the celebration of the notion of trinity:

> Enrich my heart, mouth, hands in me,
> With faith, with hope, with charitie;
> That I may runne, rise, rest with thee. (7–9)

It is hard to say whether the insistent reinforcement of the triple structure of *The Temple* emphasizes or drowns the note of dedica-

16. John Donne, however, remarks that "it is a lovely and a religious thing to find out *Vestigia Trinitatis*, Impressions of the Trinity, in as many things as we can" (*Sermons*, ed. Evelyn M. Simpson and George R. Potter, vol. 3, p. 144. Quoted in Patrick M. Grant, *The Transformation of Sin: Studies in Donne, Herbert, Vaughan, and Traherne*, p. 64).

tion to a task that is actually the import of the words. "Sinnes round" (1633, p. 114) and "A Wreath" (1633, p. 179) operate by means of their use of an interlocked or repeated line or phrase about which preceding and succeeding lines or phrases pivot. The device was popular in sixteenth-century poetry. "Sinnes round" suggests by means of its structure (the identicality of the first and last lines of the poem and of succeeding stanzas) the inexorable way in which one sin follows another, and each line of "A Wreath" interlocks, wreath-like, into the next. In these two poems the form does seem to suggest their content more "impeccably" and less insistently.

The same can be maintained of "Paradise" (1633, pp. 125–26), despite what appear initially to be puzzling interpretative problems. If the reader is invited, by the curious device of the "pruning" of the last word of each line in every stanza, to see the poem as being "about" the pruning of the soul by divine wisdom so that, like a pruned tree, it will bear more fruit, the point is made explicitly in only the last two of the five stanzas:

I blesse thee, Lord, because I GROW
Among thy trees, which in a ROW
To thee both fruit and order OW.

What open force, or hidden CHARM
Can blast my fruit, or bring me HARM,
While the inclosure is thine ARM?

Inclose me still for fear I START.
Be to me rather sharp and TART,
Then let me want thy hand & ART.

When thou dost greater judgements SPARE,
And with thy knife but prune and PARE,
Ev'n fruitfull trees more fruitfull ARE.

Such sharpnes shows the sweetest FREND:
Such cuttings rather heal then REND:
And such beginnings touch their END.

Helen Vendler admits that the poem's contrived structure (iambic tetrameter triplets and the "pruning" theme) "pre-exist" it and "set the condition that lines having these endings have to be contrived so as to make sense, not to speak of making a poem."[17] Yet she defends the poem as sounding "perfectly natural" and sees the first three stanzas as indicating other courses of divine action with respect to Herbert's life—apprehensions on Herbert's part of, for instance, protection or neglect. However, she does not offer any defense against a possible charge that a stanza such as the second in itself possesses no reason for its unusual form (a reason that *can* be detected in the fourth and fifth stanzas). One interpretative strategy is to maintain that the form of the poem and its content, while nevertheless "related," exist in different realms in such a way that while the narrative content describes various courses of action, in a movement that could be seen as a survey of possibilities from enclosure through neglect to curative pruning, the form of the poem "fixes" Herbert's apprehension of God's actions in the last of these possibilities. Enclosure and neglect are then seen as past, rejected possibilities, and curative pruning in terms of a certain actuality and even, in the last stanza of all, as the action of the "sweetest FREND," "always," as Vendler (p. 221) points out, "a reconciliatory phrase for Herbert." And the final apprehension is midway between the two more extreme possibilities of enclosure and neglect.

An interpretative possibility that Vendler does not fully take into account would involve a more sustained historical and traditional perspective such as has been provided by Stanley Stewart.[18] Stewart has placed this poem within a long and complex line of *hortus conclusus* literature, in which God's actions towards the human soul are allegorized, following texts such as the Song of Songs, in terms of care bestowed by a loving Gardener on an enclosed paradisal garden. The whole conceit implies acquiescence in God's actions, and what Stewart describes as "that blessed state of passivity in which [the speaker's soul] no longer yearns to reward his Saviour for the Sacrifice" (p. 53). The struggles documented in such poems as "The Thanksgiving" come to mind here. Acquiescence in God's actions in turn implies that Her-

17. Helen Vendler, *The Poetry of George Herbert*, p. 219.
18. Stanley Stewart, *The Enclosed Garden* pp. 52–59.

bert's apprehension of curative pruning *must* represent a middle way, a settled calm between the oscillating extremes charted in the first three stanzas. One may think here of the movement of "The Pulley" (1633, pp. 153–54). Paradoxical suffering is accepted and not rebelled against in "Paradise." The pruning structure, superficially only directly relevant to the experience described in the last two stanzas, is after all seen to have a wider relevance, since what is enacted in this poem by means of form and content, it might be maintained, is the experience of *coming to understand the pattern* of God's actions. Form and content approach each other and resolve into a relationship apprehensible by the reader as the poem proceeds, though presumably—again—the divine addressee looks on the matter entirely differently.

Form-and-content correspondence, then, is of considerable rhetorical use to Herbert as poet, for it offers him a range of possibilities for exploiting his human readers' deepest hermeneutical urges. Relying on these urges in lyric verse that exhibits the kind of integral correspondence that we have been considering, Herbert may be pointing with considerable effectiveness to the distinction between human and divine reader. Let us now turn to a poem that can be considered pivotal in this regard. "Coloss. 3.3." (1633, p. 77) seems to postulate a form-and-content correspondence comparable to those discussed so far. In addition, it introduces a divine text into the poem's form and therefore raises interesting questions that have to do with the nature of the relationship between text or motto and its surrounding poetic context and with the poetic status claimed for each constituent of this relationship. These questions are not only intensely problematic, but also central to our conception of the rhetorical opacity that Herbert uses to express his relationship to God. "Coloss. 3.3." explicates a scriptural text, paraphrased as "My life is hid in Him that is my treasure," in a way that reflects its context,[19] so that it is embed-

19. Quinn's remarks (see note 3 above) are of extreme relevance here: "The text is seen not as verbal or rhetorical communication but as a likeness; it does not *mean* what [the preacher] says; it resembles what he says" (Quinn, p. 291). Quinn stresses, surely rightly, the role of memory in this Augustinian conception of exegesis. For further discussion of this poem, see Chauncey Wood, "A Reading of Herbert's 'Coloss. 3.3.,'" pp. 15–24.

ded within the explication. The whole constitutes a poem, presumably an example of the kind of verse that "may finde him, who a sermon flies" ("The Church-porch"). The text, hidden in the unusual "diagonal-acrostic" device, paraphrases Col. 3:3 as "My Life Is Hid In Him That Is My Treasure":

My words & thoughts do both expresse this notion,
That *Life* hath with the sun a double motion.
The first *Is* straight, and our diurnall friend,
The other *Hid,* and doth obliquely bend.
One life is wrapt *In* flesh, and tends to earth.
The other winds towards *Him,* whose happie birth
Taught me to live here so, *That* still one eye
Should aim and shoot at that which *Is* on high:
Quitting with daily labour all *My* pleasure,
To gain at harvest an eternall *Treasure.*

The text, thus poetically expressed, enacts itself: it is hidden in the verse, treasured mnemonically, and revealed each time the verse is read. Chana Bloch has written sensitively of the way in which Herbert's speaker personalizes the text's application and, in so doing, does not "consume" but on the contrary fulfills himself.[20] The reader's experience of the poem is of an order only possible if the "poem-text" exists in a form where poem and text are seen to be integrally related to each other; the text, so versified, brings about what it represents. The expository surrounding, together with the text whose placing and structure explicate that surrounding visually as well as thematically, interact to form a poem. Neither the text nor its exposition, taken separately, seem to afford the pleasure given by the poem as a whole.

Several poems in *The Temple* center around a motto, ostensibly in much the same way as "Coloss. 3.3." centers around its text. However, closer examination of these other poems reveals that the motto is not always wittily annexed into the poem as a whole, so that one does not always have the sense of the entire structure's depending for its technical fulfillment on the interaction between poem and motto. Instead it is almost as if Herbert, having shown

20. Chana Bloch, *Spelling the Word: George Herbert and the Bible,* pp. 34–36.

us in a poem such as "Coloss. 3.3." what a truly integrated relationship between poem and scriptural text might involve, challenges his readers in, for example, the two "Jordan" poems (1633, pp. 48 and 95); he substitutes for the brilliance of the relationship in "Coloss. 3.3." a flagrantly less spectacular one in which a word ("love") or a form of address ("My God, My King") is made to do the work that the scriptural text does in "Coloss. 3.3." In the much-discussed "Jordan" poems, as in "The Posie" (1633, p. 177), the context for the claims made for the motto is the same: the motto, sometimes even repeated, is clearly set off against the devices of poetic rhetoric:

> Invention rest,
> Comparisons go play, wit use thy will:
> *Lesse then the least*
> *Of all Gods mercies,* is my posie still. ("The Posie" [9–12])

In "The Posie," the motto is invested with a modesty that it would be dangerous to attempt to defuse. In itself, however, together with the more neutral instances to be found in the "Jordan poems," the motto in "The Posie" is not unique to Herbert, although his use of the strategy that it represents is highly characteristic. It is now common currency that the renunciation in a poem such as "Jordan" [II] has a clear antecedent in Sidney's *Astrophel and Stella*[21] and that Herbert's takes sacred, not secular, form. Less frequently examined are the claims that Herbert makes for his mottoes. He does not simply portray himself, in poems such as "Jordan" [I] and [II] or "The Posie," as finding the solution to the lures of artfulness in a genuine appeal to his own heart, as Sidney does. Nor does he picture himself as asserting only that the motto embedded in the poem completes the poem and renders the entire structure possible, as he does with the text of "Coloss. 3.3." Herbert goes further still in the "Jordan" poems and "The Posie," claiming technical excellence for the combination of motto and surrounding frame, yet at the same time suggesting that the

21. See Louis L. Martz, *The Poetry of Meditation: A Study in English Religious Literature of the Seventeenth Century,* pp. 261ff, and Sir Philip Sidney, *The Poems of Sir Philip Sidney,* ed. William A. Ringler, Jr., p. 165.

motto actually supersedes the poem. The motto therefore not only completes the poem but is presented as its substitute. It is held to be genuine because it is not artful. (The modesty of the motto serves as an analogy to Sidneian claims for the worth of what is going on in the heart of the poet.) Yet even though it is a motto, it is also regarded as possessing in superior measure the kind of value normally accorded to poetic language.

"The Forerunners" (1633, pp. 170–71) offers a particularly ambivalent use of the poetic motto, and to consider it briefly at this point may help to highlight some of the difficulties that this aspect of Herbert's art presents his readers with. The poem's repetition of the motto "Thou art still my God" punctuates a renunciation of poetic language and technical skill that is intimated in the graying of the poet's hair, the appearance of the "harbingers" of age:

> The harbingers are come. See, see their mark;
> White is their colour, and behold my head.
> But must they have my brain? must they dispark
> Those sparkling notions, which therein were bred?
> Must dulnesse turn me to a clod? (1–5)

It is hard to know how to take the declamatory tone of the opening lines, particularly as during the course of the poem Herbert bids, more colloquially, a detached farewell to the devices of poetic expression:

> Yet if you go, I passe not; take your way:
> For, *Thou art still my God*, is all that ye
> Perhaps with more embellishment can say,
> Go birds of spring. (31–34)

The phrase "I passe not" picks up the colloquial sense also used at line 9 ("I don't care") and meshes it, in the context of 31, with a sense such as "this will not finish my career as a poet." Yet while there is much technical skill at this level of expressive economy, there are also more puzzling features, such as the inane rhyme-words of this couplet and its self-conscious ambivalence:

> He will be pleased with that dittie;
> And if I please him, I write fine and wittie. (11–12)

The uncertainty of the poet's will to submit to the renunciation ("Farewell sweet phrases, lovely metaphors. / But will ye leave me thus?" [13–14]) is reflected in a rhetorically expressed uncertainty of focus, so that we are made to doubt the poet's grasp of technique at the same time as wondering what his attitude to the threatened loss of his gift would "really" be. Clearly there is a subtle mimetic effect behind all this, which we may admire, but the poem's very evasiveness seems to allow us to make only limited claims for "Lovely enchanting language, sugar-cane, / Honey of roses" (19–20): it adumbrates, but does not discover, verbal truths:

True beautie dwells on high: ours is a flame
But borrow'd thence to light us thither. (28–29)

"Fine" language is evidently not regarded as absolutely necessary to Herbert's poetic purpose, and the manner in which this belief is stressed in "The Forerunners" and the "Jordan" poems and elsewhere in *The Temple* has led many readers to the view that Herbert is a practitioner of the plain style of writing. Not all Herbert's commentators mean the same thing, however, when they use the term. The work of Arnold Stein has already been cited; although he has described the plain style as "far easier to recognise and admire than to describe or define,"[22] this is unduly cautious. In a more recent essay, Leah S. Marcus has distinguished a specifically Anglican plain style, characterizing it as "more effective, more playful in tone than the Puritan, more austere and hortatory than the Catholic."[23] For Anglican practitioners, there were clear guidelines for its use, and Marcus has shown that by the seventeenth century it had come to be associated with didactic and homilectic writing and with exhortations to accept unquestioningly the teaching of the established Church. Marcus therefore provides a historical context for Herbert's sophisticated departure from established practice, a departure that has frequently been sensed critically, and she has expressed this sophis-

22. See Arnold Stein, *George Herbert's Lyrics*, p. xiii.
23. Leah S. Marcus, "George Herbert and the Anglican Plain Style," in *"Too Riche to Clothe the Sunne": Essays on George Herbert*, p. 180.

tication in terms of a demonstration on Herbert's part of "the immense cost and complexity of the task of *achieving* simplicity" (Marcus, p. 185; emphasis added). Certainly Herbert's practice of plainness is intensely problematic, and it will be clear that the preceding discussion reflects a wide recognition that many of Herbert's lyrics are self-consciously artful in their seeming concern to demonstrate the unattainability of plainness. Indeed, the immensely varied structure of *The Temple* has led commentators to suggest that one impulse behind their writing was the creation of as many varieties of poetic structure as there are settings; be this as it may, only one consecutive pair of poems in *The Temple* ("The Invitation" and "The Banquet") are similar in metrical form and rhyme scheme, and far more forms are unique to particular poems than are not.[24] Any attempt to apply criteria of plainness, of whatever kind, to Herbert's poetry is thus fraught with some difficulty.

Simplicity

Michael Gallagher has recently drawn attention to this difficulty.[25] Analyzing "A Wreath," Gallagher sees a "seeming contradiction . . . between content and performance, between what [Herbert] is saying and how he is saying it" (Gallagher, p. 506). It does seem evident that an account of a "form-and-content correspondence" in this poem is not really adequate to its reader's experience, since although at one level the poem represents, and describes, a wreath, the conclusion arrived at by the poem's argument is that the "poore wreath" is being opposed to a "crown of praise": the form of the poem forces the reader to go in other directions than that pointed to by the words. The aims of the poem seem divided; Gallagher characterizes "A Wreath" as "a prayer for simplicity and at the same time a poem of intricate workmanship." It ends:

24. See Albert McHarg Hayes, "Counterpoint in Herbert," pp. 43–60.
25. Michael P. Gallagher, "Rhetoric, Style and George Herbert," pp. 495–516.

Give me simplicitie, that I may live,
So live and like, that I may know thy wayes,
Know them and practise them: then shall I give
For this poore wreath, give thee a crown of praise. (9–12)

Gallagher considers that such poems "undermine any . . . limited interpretation" of them as "simply an attack on the complex styles of secular love-poetry" (Gallagher, p. 506). It is not an attractive solution to the problem to impute insincerity to Herbert, and Gallagher postulates an alternative:

> There is a danger of misinterpreting such poems unless it is understood that the plainness and simplicity of which they speak is primarily an interior and spiritual one. . . . 'Give me simplicitie, that I may live' is the prayer of an extremely artful poem but there is no real contradiction between the simplicity and the art: they belong to two different realms. (Gallagher, p. 507)[26]

"A Wreath" seems to me to be a formal concession of the impossibility of the exchange to which it draws attention ever taking place within the medium of poetry. However well it is written, poetry remains *verba* not *res,* and as such it is incapable of rising to the requirements of "a crown of praise"; these requirements are conditional to "simplicitie," which is the one thing that poetic language seemingly does not offer. It would not be too fanciful to read the wreath as figurative of a hermeneutic circle and to suggest that escape may be represented by the strategy of saying that the simplicity requested in the poem, and the art with which this request is accompanied, "belong to two different realms."

Herbert's search for what Gallagher calls "a style . . . which would unite holiness and art" is reflected in Gallagher's comments on "Church-monuments" (1633, pp. 56–57), a poem that has come to be seen by critics since Yvor Winters as one of the subtlest examples of form-and-content correspondence in *The Temple*:[27] it treats

26. Again, it is interesting to note that Gallagher resorts to the term "misinterpretation" in a context such as this.

27. Yvor Winters, *Primitivism and Decadence: A Study of American Experimental Poetry,* and M. M. Mahood, "Something Understood: The Nature of Herbert's Wit," p. 135 (note 10 above). Fish, *Self-Consuming Artifacts,* analyzes the poem rigorously (pp. 164–69). The remarks on punctuation in "Church-monuments" that follow should be balanced against Mario A. Di Cesare's recent defense of the authority of Bodleian MS Tanner 307; see *GHJ* 6 (1983): 23.

dissolution, of body and monuments, into dust, and as Joseph Summers puts it, the poem's "series of clauses and participial phrases, each relating to a word in some preceding clause or phrase, threaten to dissolve the sentence structure" (Summers, p. 135). The movement of the sentences cuts across the division of lines and stanzas, a practice "found in no other poem in *The Temple*" (Summers, p. 133). Gallagher's analysis of this poem goes further into the idea of dissolution, and he sees in the poem a movement towards a plainer style than that offered by the first few lines. He reads the language of the first part of the poem as reflecting the pomposity and grandeur of the monuments: "Whereas the second part not only tells of the humbling and destruction of the proud monuments, but shows it forth in its change of tone and style. . . . It is only in the second half that the truth is experienced in the language of the poem" (Gallagher, p. 515). Gallagher considers that the first part of the poem "merely plays" with "the truth of the undermining facts" (p. 515). In reading a form-and-content correspondence in this poem, we are certainly encouraged to see the declamatory opening crumbling into simpler diction as the poem proceeds; Gallagher interestingly draws attention, for instance, to the difference between "While that my soul repairs to her devotion" (1) and "while I do pray" (17). The claims to sincerity made by lines such as the following require examination:

> Deare flesh, while I do pray, learn here thy stemme
> And true descent; that when thou shalt grow fat,
>
> And wanton in thy cravings, thou mayst know,
> That flesh is but the glasse, which holds the dust
> That measures all our time; which also shall
> Be crumbled into dust. Mark here below
> How tame these ashes are, how free from lust,
> That thou mayst fit thy self against thy fall. (17–24)

The language, at first sight certainly more straightforward than that of the opening lines of the poem, can also be seen as astonishingly mannered in its deployment if not in its choice of diction. In accepting the notion that the structure of the poem enacts what the poem describes, a reader is committed to the difficult task of accounting for the crumbling effect by means of analytic description. The end of the poem's third stanza (18) is marked only by a comma, and the line-endings of the last stanza are so lightly pointed that only two apart from the last are marked by any form of punctuation at all. Moreover, the one sentence-break in the extract quoted occurs in the middle of a line, so that it is certainly not as if the whole sense is being run into one sentence. Apart from this, two further breaks occur in the middle of lines in this extract (18, 21), both more heavily pointed than anything at the end of any but the last of these lines (24). Nevertheless, rhyme words recur insistently, regularly, and remorselessly ("know . . . below"; "dust. . . lust"; "shall . . . fall"). The presence of an occasional internal rhyme ("blast . . . last") complicates matters further. The reader is persistently encouraged by this poem to apply the description "formal" to it; yet it simultaneously suggests within intense formality the potential for the abandonment of poetic form. Nevertheless, against this disconcerting linguistic experience, Herbert's readers are somehow encouraged to claim "plainness" for the poem. What sort of plainness is this, particularly in view of the poem's claim to sincerity or even "truth"?[28]

The experience a reader of such a poem is faced with has been acutely described by Winifred Nowottny:

> The moment the formal relations visibly affect the articulation of the sense—that is, the moment it is perceived that formal relationships take precedence in determining the diction—we have a situation where for some readers the sense is discredited and revulsion rather than pleasure occurs; such a reader feels himself to be confronted with a form of language whose elaboration interferes with transmission from the poet to himself.[29]

The sense in which transmission is interfered with, however, depends on the kind of conventions against which the poem is being read. Something of the complexity of the issues a poem such

28. Helen Vendler's comments on "Antiphon" [II] (1633, p. 85), in *The Poetry of George Herbert*, pp. 209-212, are perhaps comparable to some of these remarks on "Church-monuments."

29. Winifred Nowottny, *The Language Poets Use*, p. 127.

as "Church-monuments" raises in this context may be indicated if we briefly note Herbert's apparently bizarre exploitation of the potential of poetic expressiveness in a poem such as "Businesse" (1633, pp. 105–106). "Businesse" is rarely discussed, probably because it is among the small but important handful of Herbert poems—"Trinitie Sunday" is another—where the mimetic intention and the expressive effect clash in such a way as to make it extremely hard to know whether to regard the result as a success or rather (as I suspect many of its readers would) an interesting failure. In "Businesse," vapidity becomes an important mimetic and expressive device, so that in the following stanza the last line, addressed to the soul about Christ, is in narrative terms completely superfluous:

He so farre thy good did plot,
That his own self he forgot.
Did he die, or did he not? (23–25)

Reflection of the content of "Businesse" in its diction may indeed lead us to describe the result in terms of revulsion. Yet although by a comparable token, "Dulnesse" ought to be a dulling experience, the pattering rhythm and at times inane diction of "Businesse" constitute a problem for Herbert's reader for which it is not really possible to see an analogue in a poem such as "Dulnesse." In the case of "Church-monuments," the conventions in question are hard for the reader to describe, since the form seems to crumble. Even so, the smooth, leisurely movement of the poem seems to question any account of it as bringing about "revulsion." I am unable to reconcile my impressions of an expressive rhetoric in a poem such as "Church-monuments," which, because of the difficulty in deciding against which conventions to read the poem, is opaque to the point of reticence, with Gallagher's impressions of a truth emerging out of the verse and carried in a developing plainness of diction.

Although it is clear that all these examples constitute a range of varieties of expressive effect that may be termed "mimetic," I have not yet attempted to account for their nature by relating the range to the varying distances that Herbert's lyrics posit between the reader and the transaction in a given case. It does seem to have emerged, however, that the less direct the reader's apprehension of relationship to the transaction of a given lyric, the more acute is his perception of the exquisiteness of Herbert's deployment of his remarkable arsenal of form-and-content correspondence. In the poems we have been regarding as, in their expressiveness, Herbert's most rhetorically opaque, the balance is most delicately sustained in favor of that pleasure (rather than revulsion) that springs from an apprehension of form-and-content correspondence. Despite the variety of Herbert's arsenal, it is still possible to claim plainness for his achievement in *The Temple,* and one of the reasons for this apparent paradox lies in Herbert's perplexing fascination for the embedded text or motto and for the implications of its use. Indeed, Herbert's fondness for the device gives an interesting twist to any conclusions we can draw from our readings of those poems that we may consider his most opaque; although the conceit of the text embedded in the matrix of the poem adds to our apprehension of rhetorical opacity in his verse, Herbert more than once claims that the briefer and less "textlike" (in fact, the more ostensibly "motto-like") his mottoes become, the stronger are their claims to poetic merit. As a result, Herbert is capable of actually positing the self-sufficiency of the more motto-like mottoes as poems, in place of the lyrics in which they have been employed.

Let us now attempt to focus the issues so far raised by considering "A true Hymne," a poem that raises the problems referred to as acutely as any yet mentioned, and to push our discussion further in the direction of a conclusion as we notice the manner in which Herbert's motto is itself superseded in this poem by means of a postulated divine intervention. The motto "My joy, my life, my crown!" both opens the poem and, as motto, occurs in the last line of the first stanza; its simplicity of statement is comparable with the mottoes of "Jordan" [I] and "The Forerunners." It is placed, in this poem, in the context of one of the rather rare instances in *The Temple* where the speaker simultaneously addresses both himself and the reader in his offering of the motto to God. Response to the motto should be to "slight not these few words," and Herbert then advances reasons for this assertion:

If truly said, they may take part
Among the best in art.
The fineness which a hymne or psalme affords,
Is, when the soul unto the lines accords. (7–10)

These reasons, given in lines 9–10, remind us of "The Windows" and once more highlight the paradox in which man is seen as an unworthy instrument of divine communication; by extension the qualities of poetic expressiveness, even in the most technically gifted hands, are all man possesses, yet precisely the qualities that show his unworthiness, being in effect witty and complex and at the same time drawing attention to their own inadequacy. The poet whose "words onely ryme" may be dissatisfied; yet, as in "The Forerunners," simplicity is sought and offered as some kind of poetic and religious ideal. As Herbert expresses matters in "The Forerunners":

if I please him, I write fine and wittie. (12)

That line is double-edged, since the causal relation suggested by the word order ("if . . . [then] . . .") can in fact be reversed, permitting several readings of the line: "In order to please him, I must write well"; "In the act of pleasing him, I inevitably write well"; and even "I please him even though I do not write well." This last possibility matches the tone of "I passe not"; it is paradoxical because it is a poetically couched concession that the poet aspires towards a state in which he is no longer concerned with the business of writing well, and as such it is a statement of an ideal of simplicity that is falsified by the poem in which it is expressed. As such, too, it is comparable with the reader's experience of "A Wreath."

The reader of "A true Hymne" finds a prescription for poetic success in the last stanza:

Whereas if th'heart be moved,
Although verse be somewhat scant,
God doth supplie the want.
As when th'heart sayes (sighing to be approved)
O, could I love! and stops: God writeth, *Loved*.[30] (16–20)

30. Here I have departed from the 1633 reading, since there is a crux that is discussed in Appendix 1.

The supplying of want by God is conditional here ("*As when* th'heart sayes"), and intervention with the word "Loved," which completes the poem, remains possibility rather than actuality. Perhaps that possibility, when the heart "stops," is only achieved with the death of the speaker in a state of Grace. In effect, however, the words of the poem suggest that intervention remains a possibility; but the intervention itself within the poem is actual, and consequently the experience of the poem in its entirety is comparable with that of "Paradise." The ending of "A true Hymne" evidences a quite extraordinary tense-change: the "As when . . ." introduces a conditional tense, supported by the "writeth" of the divine response, but this is no sooner postulated than it has become a reality in terms of the poem. Yet the present-tense potential of the word "writeth" is only fully given by the last word, "Loved," since this fulfills the expectations of completion of rhyme set up by the metric structure of the preceding three stanzas. This suggests, as does "Coloss. 3.3.," that human words and divine motto taken together make up a poem. Yet that suggestion is simultaneously confirmed and undermined in "A true Hymne." On the one hand, a claim is made for "My joy, my life, my crown!," yet on the other, God's motto, "Loved," simple in itself, completes the poem in a device of remarkable technical virtuosity. Positing its own motto's potential superiority to the lyric of which it is a part, "A true Hymne" seems yet again to be setting out to exclude its reader from the central expressive transaction (in what way can "My joy, my life, my crown!" possibly be regarded as a poem in which the reader can participate?), but the reader's experience is that the divine intervention defines that transaction in a manner that the reader could not predict until the poem is complete. Indeed, the divine intervention *is* the poem's completion. The reader's response must be couched in terms of a simultaneous recognition of resignation on the poet's part and of the poet's own wit and virtuosity.

Human and divine dialogue

So far in this chapter we have been considering examples of

Herbert's poetic expressiveness that, when conceived of as sacramentally offered up to God, present their human readers with a source of difficulty characterized by a complex of elements, none in themselves necessarily especially problematic. All readers, and not just students of literature, quickly become adept at recognizing poetic fictions and may even without difficulty indulge in what are really quite sophisticated exercises, such as identifying the complexity of a poetic fiction couched as dramatic monologue, where, for instance, one of the participants in a conversation may have to be supplied imaginatively by the reader. And one does not even have to be literate to gain imaginative purchase on the propriety of a situation where a speaker is overheard praying or meditating. Difficulty seems to arise in the context of Herbert's poetry when the addressed Divine is conceived of as overstepping the proprieties that the imagination traditionally exercises and is granted not simply a reply, but a reply that is thought of as contributing to, completing, and even enhancing the poetic status of the imaginative construct. The result is a situation in which the elements of the entire poem—Herbert's surrounding context and God's divinely revealed text—must be taken together if the poem's integrity is to be ensured; yet in terms of the fictions that the poems are constantly positing, that integrity humiliates the poet. A reader's strategy for escape from this unacceptably problematic outcome may constitute an act of interpretation that releases him from the terms of the fiction. The ensuingly rational response will be to maintain that, if God's poetic replies enhance the poem and humiliate the poet, then this state of affairs itself constitutes a fictional conceit in which attention is drawn, through and by means of an apparent humiliation, to the poet's own artistry. This would form an acceptable strategy only, however, if we could be sure that Herbert did not "really" believe the terms of his own fiction. Since we cannot be sure of this, we cannot be sure how we are to respond. In the end, conceiving ourselves as excluded from commerce between Herbert and God, able only to watch and listen to it, we may overhear words that "signify" to us but cannot be imagined to signify to God. Acknowledging the opacity of the poems' rhetorical expressiveness may constitute an act of interpretation that ensures that as readers we are not drawn into an endless recession of possibilities whose instability rests on the status of poetic fictions.

Recognition of Herbert's scrupulousness in conscripting God into participation in his verse implies clear and challenging attitudes to his own selfhood. Let us rapidly survey three poems that explore these attitudes but through very different kinds of fictional construct. "Artillerie" (1633, pp. 132–33) presents anecdotally the paradox of an argument with God, in which Herbert reproaches God for reproaching him. The disposal of the "starre," which Herbert brushes from his lap, is seen to represent sensible conduct by the domestic standards that may here be self-mockingly employed; by divine standards Herbert's action is seen, curiously enough, to be foolish. The opaque sign of the star is "explained" and then immediately turned around on God by means of the device of Herbert's reproaching God for ignoring his own communication. Herbert challenges God through his very revelation: "Thy promise now hath ev'n set thee thy laws" (24). An apparent resolution through "parley" (27) is rejected: "There is no articling with thee" (31). "The Holdfast" (1633, p. 137) and "Clasping of hands" (1633, p. 151) are comparable in that both explore human and divine status through virtuosic use of personal pronouns ("ours/his," "thine/mine"). There are two interlocutors in "The Holdfast"; both represent statements of Christian orthodoxy. Both are arguably if not facets of the Divine then at least of what is not the speaker. The first interlocutor presents the unconsoling nature of the poem's theological insight, whereas the second humanizes it ("all things were more ours by being his"). This is a form of that equivocal predication of which Heather Asals has written so well: "ours" is defined by its existence in terms of "his," more precisely than it could ever be in terms of itself.[31] The same can be maintained of the play on "thine" and "mine" in "Clasping of hands." The difference between the two poems can best be illustrated by pointing to the indirect speech form that Herbert selects for "The Holdfast," so

31. Heather Asals, *Equivocal Predication: George Herbert's Way to God*, p. 86.

that the reader is necessarily left in some uncertainty as to whether a line such as "We must confesse, that nothing is our own" actually represents what the first interlocutor ("one") *said,* or what—with its very characteristic ontological play on "nothing"—Herbert's speaker paraphrases that voice as having said. The syntactic expression is consistent with Herbert's elsewhere, and so is the thought; the poem enacts a very strange retreat in its octave and the first part of its sestet where what is in effect indirect speech is presented as though it were direct. In the case of "Clasping of hands" there are no other interlocutors in the poem, which constitutes a meditation in which the insight is arrived at logically rather than granted intuitively or by revelation. William V. Nestrick has demonstrated the importance in this poem of the challenging restrictions of the rhyme-scheme: the poem's entire stock of rhyme words, deployed through twenty lines, is "thine/mine" and "more/restore." Nestrick clearly articulates the differences between the two stanzas: the first culminates, as he puts it, in a recognition of "the need for the other to define the separate self," whereas the second posits "the equation of separate identities" in terms of "a total absorption of the one into the other."[32]

The scrupulousness with which notions of human selfhood and God's ownership are defined in these three poems provides a context for discussion of "Dialogue" and "Love" [III]. In postulating dialogue whose totality makes up the poem, they constitute the epistemological and ontological boundaries of the form-and-content correspondence discussed so far and push the human reader's difficulty to its farthest point. A. D. Nuttall is among those who have noticed that dramatization of the part of God is a potentially blasphemous action, and Herbert does not help us out of the difficulty by giving "God's communications . . . a high finish and a certain metrical form in order that they may harmonise with the rest."[33] Nuttall shows why what he calls "the escape through fiction"—the strategy of defending Herbert's poetic prac-

32. William V. Nestrick, " 'Mine' and 'Thine' in *The Temple,*" in *"Too Riche to Clothe the Sunne,"* ed. Summers and Pebworth, p. 120.
33. Nuttall, *Overheard by God,* p. 6.

tice in terms of its status as poetic fiction—is untenable precisely because of the example of the "Jordan" poems, which enact rejection but postulate a nonpoetic alternative to poetic language in the context of the poem and as an integral part of its form. Involving as it does the discovery of concepts of possession outside normal human experience, "Dialogue" explores that love sometimes termed *caritas*.[34] The divine reply in "Dialogue" is unusual in the sense that divine "words" are customarily read (that is, interpreted) by Herbert once his perceptions and understanding are clear. The poem's forthrightness may indicate to Herbert's reader a particularly clear, almost ecstatic intuition of God's presence. The third stanza ends with Herbert's seeing the apparent uselessness of entering into a relation with God, realizing as he does the soul's unworthiness:

I disclaim the whole designe:
Sinne disclaims and I resigne. (23–24)

The divine reply is interrupted by what the reader is encouraged to see as a moment of revelation; he is encouraged to do so because expectations built up at other points in *The Temple* suggest that when another voice completes a poem, some kind of realization has been conceded. Here it is possible to read Herbert's interruption as his own acceptance of the gift of divine love—despite everything. This acceptance miraculously, though appearing to break up the antiphonal symmetry of the poem, simultaneously completes it. The reader's discernment of a disturbing change of voice seems to be subordinated to his satisfaction at a completed cadence; the series of running rhymes[35] is not, after all, disrupted, so that the human creation of the poem has been wrecked but miraculously completed by a human voice, and this is taken to signify acceptance of divine love:

That is all, if that I could
Get without repining;

34. See Rosemond Tuve, "George Herbert and *Caritas*," in *Essays by Rosemund Tuve*, ed. Thomas P. Roche, Jr., pp. 167–206.

35. An alternative contemporary spelling, "desart," reflects its pronunciation; the stress is on the second syllable.

And my clay my creature would
Follow my resigning.
That as I did freely part
With my glorie and desert,
Left all joyes to feel all smart — —
Ah! no more: thou break'st my heart. (25–32)

Herbert's reader must, however, ask whether this ending is not too mannered for the extremely disconcerting emotions in play: the poet is, after all, subjecting himself in writing of this sort to an utter humiliation. For what is enacted in "Dialogue" is God's demonstration to Herbert that poems that in human terms most triumphantly affirm their technical virtuosity are, in divine terms, failures; they can be rewritten not simply by a divine hand but as the result of an interruption by Herbert that miraculously disrupts, yet recreates.

"Love" [III] (1633, p. 183) is in several respects an extreme case, constituting as it does the final poem in "The Church" and offering dialogue with God characterized by an absence of the kinds of formality we have so far been able to observe. Elsewhere in the 1633 edition of *The Temple* there are typographical indications to suggest that direct speech is issuing from a divine voice, whether as discursive dialogue or as motto. The mode of "Love" [III], however, is mixed: nowhere else in *The Temple* is there dialogue in which the divine voice is framed by markers such as "said" while the human voice is not. The absence of the expected italics may denote a sense of achievement, in that the poem's narrative is related in a past tense; yet we have arrived at that identification of lover and beloved, toward which Herbert's lyrical progress in "The Church" may be said to have striven. And it may be argued that other varieties of formal elements are present in the poem, such as a "reversed" hierarchy of the senses, in which there is a progression—albeit a hesitant one—from the highest, sight, through touch, to the basest, taste.

In view of all this, most of Herbert's commentators have unquestioningly considered that the poem's narrative takes place in heaven, particularly as it concludes not only "The Church" but a short sequence of overtly eschatological poems as well ("Death,"

"Dooms-day," "Judgement," and "Heaven" [1633, pp. 180–83]). Yet as Chana Bloch has shown, it is not necessary to assume an exclusively celestial context for the poem, "though it gains in complexity if we read it with the [preceding] sequence in mind."[36] Bloch has drawn attention to the intensely traditional elements in the poem, arguing that it demonstrates how Herbert can make such elements "speak with his own voice" (Bloch, p. 100). For Bloch, Stanley Fish's reading of the poem, in which conflict is reenacted rather than resolved,[37] is inadequate in its failure to come to terms with the positive counterbalance to man's sinful insufficiency that serious attention to scriptural and liturgical sources may reveal. Such counterbalance is necessary, in Bloch's view, because only then is the true "tension of ideas . . . which Herbert carries over from his sources" (Bloch, p. 108) allowed to emerge. The poem's mode of existence is then seen to be such that it reflects, through intensely compact allusiveness to tradition, a movement "through the historical stages of religious consciousness, from the Old Dispensation to the New, before [the guest] can resolve his difficulties. . . . When the problems posed by the Old Testament are finally resolved by Christ, Herbert's poem tells us, those ancient words find their true fulfillment" (Bloch, pp. 104–7).

Two elements, one of particular applicability to this poem, the other bearing more generally on my approach to *The Temple*, emerge from Bloch's sophisticated reading of "Love" [III]. First, Bloch offers a sensitive and reasoned approach to the poem's eroticism, a quality all too few readers have explicitly allowed its opening lines:

> Love bade me welcome: yet my soul drew back,
> Guiltie of dust and sinne.
> But quick-ey'd Love, observing me grow slack
> From my first entrance in,
> Drew nearer to me. (1–5)

Rochester's parody implicitly admits this quality; however, with-

36. Bloch, in *Spelling the Word*, p. 101.
37. Stanley E. Fish, *The Living Temple: George Herbert and Catechizing*, pp. 131–36.

out Bloch's kind of reasoning, the expression of spiritual abasement in sexual terms that—in our own century—John R. Mulder, writing of the soul's "detumescence," has noticed, is likely to seem perverse to many readers.[38] Yet in the innocent-sensuous languor of these lines there is more than a suggestion that Love is responding to the soul's impotence with the awareness that ideally characterizes erotic manners. Bloch's reading of the poem, endorsing this suggestion, not only locates its expression of tact firmly in Herbert's allusive treatment of the Song of Songs, but suggests that "in this respect the Bible has *freed* [Herbert's] imagination to more direct expression than he would otherwise have attempted."[39]

Second, Bloch's reading of "Love" [III] does a great deal to suggest the characteristic nature of Herbert's deployment of scriptural and liturgical sources and serves to remind us that it was their unresolved debate over the very nature of this deployment that so occupied the energies of William Empson and Rosemond Tuve. I believe that Bloch's view of Herbert's attitude to tradition takes too little account of the disturbing effect that this attitude exerts on the reader of his poetry. At the same time, I have tried to argue that those poems that seem to assert Herbert's speakers' intuitively mystical apprehension of divine presence most strongly and clearly through dialogue are far from being, as Bloch perhaps too readily claims of "Love" [III], his most reassuring to this reader. I have been focusing so far in this chapter upon Herbert's characteristic deployment of the texts or mottoes in his poems, and their very Herbertian extension into the device of dialogue, as imparting reticence and opacity to the poems in which they occur. It is my final task to consider what is implied in our understanding of the kind of relationship that may be said to hold between the elements of a poem that seem to act as a foreground for this opacity and the rest of the poem. There is no doubt that in sensing such

38. See Jeremy Treglown, "The Satirical Inversions of Some English Sources in Rochester's Poetry." Mulder is one of Herbert's few readers to have explicitly admitted this aspect of "Love" [III]; see "George Herbert's *The Temple*: Design and Methodology," p. 43.

39. Bloch, *Spelling the Word,* p. 111.

relationship a reader is affected in some way, and Winifred Nowottny has usefully written of "linguistic excitement," a term that does seem to convey a great deal of the essence of the experience of engaging with any poem: "This linguistic excitement is an excitement about encounters between relationships, and . . . these can be set up among any of the elements present in the poems" (Nowottny, p. 221). The stating of relationships implied in a poetry such as Herbert's has to do with the conveying of realities that it would be otherwise hard to conceive of intellectually. In Herbert's lyrics the reader is concerned more emotionally not just with what is said but very much with the way it is said. On the one hand, therefore, it may be held that the quality I have been terming "opacity" is something that it is necessary for Herbert's reader to discern if the richness of a linguistic experience that not only states relationships, but also describes and alludes to them, is to be apprehended with pleasure and satisfaction. It may indeed be, as Nowottny claims, that this has to do with a realization "that poems give what life does not" (Nowottny, pp. 221–22). Yet on the other hand, it may be equally valid, although more disturbing, to suggest that only through a realization of the existence of such relationships can the essence of Herbert's poetry be grasped; that is to say, this is the only level at which we as human readers can read Herbert's poetry.

In order to pursue the implications of this suggestion, a suggestion that may turn out to be one of limitation rather than enablement, we must locate it in terms that Herbert would have understood. For the Renaissance the idea of relationship was familiar through the existence of what has been termed "wit philosophy." Its theoretical formulations are often felt to have been the result of hindsight, and some extremely useful work on continental European (particularly Italian and Spanish) *seicento* theory is now available. From this it emerges that wit philosophy may be defined as the seeing and stating of relationships throughout the cosmos, where God is seen as the creator of a wit exercised through these apprehensible relationships. Man is capable of discernment; human wit is seen as "a quasi-divine aptitude which apprehends relationships that are either expressed or exist potentially through the wit of the Creator"; this aptitude in men can produce "an orderly yet surprising beauty in poetry . . . as does God himself in creation."[40] A passage in the *Disputatio de Sacra Scriptura* of William Whitaker, which was first published in Latin at Cambridge in 1588 and reprinted in 1590 and 1600, is of particular interest here.[41] During its course, Whitaker asserts that the "whole complete sense" (*totus & integer sensus*) of a given signification is realized when the "mutual relationship between the sign and the thing signified" (*mutua relatio inter signum & rem signatam*) is apprehended.[42]

This assertion compares interestingly with one result of S. L. Bethell's conflation of the later writings of the Spanish theorist Balthasar Gracián and the Italian theorist Emanuele Tesauro. What emerges from the conflation is that wit is distinct from rhetoric, in that "in Rhetoric the figure B exists solely to explicate the subject A, whereas in wit a mutual relationship AB is presented" (Bethell, p. 34). What Whitaker calls "the whole complete sense" may therefore be described as being "set forth" (*proponitur*) wittily. I have indicated some of the ways in which, in given Herbert poems, the motto or comparable element for which poetic status is claimed and the whole poem or poetic context are related to each other, and how the reader perceives this relationship. I now suggest that an understanding of the implications of a witty setting forth of "the whole complete sense" may account for the opacity sensed by Herbert's reader as a result of both his and Herbert's own acts of interpretation. And I suggest further that man's "quasi-divine aptitude" for discerning divinely given relationships discovered throughout God's Creation is analogous to the reader's aptitude

40. S. L. Bethell, "Gracián, Tesauro, and the Nature of Metaphysical Wit," p. 35. See also J. A. Mazzeo, *Renaissance and Seventeenth Century Studies*.

41. See Charles K. Cannon, "William Whitaker's Disputatio de Sacra Scriptura: A Sixteenth-Century Theory of Allegory," pp. 129–38. Neither Bethell nor Mazzeo mentions Whitaker's work. George L. Scheper, "Reformation Attitudes toward Allegory and the Song of Songs," pp. 554–55, considers that Whitaker's pronouncement represents a development from medieval (particularly scholastic) exegetic theory rather than constituting anything startlingly original. This might be contrasted with Barbara K. Lewalski's claims for Whitaker in *Protestant Poetics and the Seventeenth Century*, pp. 201–221.

42. William Whitaker, *Disputatio de sacra scriptura . . .* , p. 302 (sig. V8^r).

for discovering and apprehending relationships of formal elements to each other and to the whole in a given poem. The idea that poetic creation imitates both the act of divine creation (the work of foundation) and the clothing of *res* in *verba* in the Incarnation (the work of restoration) supports this suggestion. Yet at the same time it must be realized that the totality of form and content, as this relationship is seen to emerge in Herbert's most reticently opaque lyrics, is something that affects to satisfy the reader's deepest hermeneutic needs and urges but *in doing so* placates and rebuffs him. In fact, the most opaque of Herbert's lyrics may be held to operate by means of a strategy that pushes the reader off and away from an intolerable area of strident—spiritual—conflict. The reader is thereby made to surrender any vicarious claim to participation in such conflict; instead, participation occurs at the level of his being granted the linguistic excitement that resides in the pleasure and satisfaction of signs correctly read and relationships apprehended in all their elegance of conception.

Conclusion

To regard Herbert's poetic expression of his apprehended relation to God in the way this book has suggested is seriously to question Rosemond Tuve's claim for the complete adequacy, in reading *The Temple,* of a "willingness to learn Herbert's language." Bethell (p. 29) considers that the Tuvean approach to a statement such as "Cleopatra is a serpent" would be to say that the only function of a serpent is to explain Cleopatra, whereas *seicento* theory would say that Cleopatra also explains the serpent and that the reader is interested in both; that is, that a mutual objective relationship is presented. Whitaker's treatise asserts that such a mutuality sets forth "the whole complete sense" of a relationship. Tuve's view of Herbert's engagement with the cosmos, however, relegates this mutuality to too subordinate a position. According to Tuve, Herbert

> writes in symbols because he thus sees the world, both outside and

> inside himself; he sees it as a web of significances not as a collection of phenomena which we may either endow with significance or leave unendowed. He writes not of events and facts, but of meanings and values, and he uncovers rather than creates those meanings. He "reads" them in the universe, of which he is a humble but undetachable part. Things, experiences, and events convey values to him just as metaphors convey them—by presenting significances which escape more literal statement.[43]

To be sure, such a summary is ostensibly in keeping with Augustinian sign theory. Yet at the same time it is possible to see that, in the light of criteria that were evidently known to the Renaissance, Tuve's recension of Augustine's theory surrenders the complexity and implication of those criteria in favor of belief in a language of "significances" that must be deciphered or decoded. This is a dangerous assertion, for "events and facts" and "meanings and values" are not mutually exclusive; it is not necessary to say that Herbert writes not in one mode but in another. "Things, experiences, and events" certainly do carry an opaque but divinely given significance that man, the reader of God's signs, discovers; *but the act of interpretative discovery also involves discovery about the nature of these things.* They are not simply to be seen as tokens or counters; Herbert's act of interpretative discovery of God's text and the reader's act of interpreting Herbert's text together serve to suggest a great deal of the sense in which poetry has from time to time been regarded as a "making."[44]

A reader's encounter with George Herbert's poetry, then, surely leads to the creation as well as the discovery of meanings. A full realization of this would go a long way toward resolving the controversy between Empson and Tuve over "The Sacrifice" in particular and reading George Herbert in general.[45] The points that

43. Tuve, *A Reading of George Herbert,* pp. 103–104.

44. For the English Renaissance the definitive statement is Sir Philip Sidney's *An Apology for Poetry,* or *The Defence of Poesy, passim.*

45. Robert Ellrodt, in *L'Inspiration personelle et l'esprit du temps chez les poètes métaphysiques anglais,* vol. 1, pp. 312–23, has attempted at some length to come to terms with this problem. He, too, finds that Tuve's claims cannot stand as they are, arguing from an interesting discussion of Herbert's poetic sensibility that "The Sacrifice" does in fact offer more in the way of dramatic contrast than do its medieval liturgical and lyric sources.

these two readers raised can most effectively be presented by reading one stanza of "The Sacrifice":

> *O all ye who passe by, behold and see:*
> Man stole the fruit, but I must climbe the tree;
> The tree of life to all, but onely me:
> Was ever grief like mine? (201–4)

When Empson first wrote of this stanza, neither he nor, more surprisingly, Hutchinson later, noticed the affinity of the poem to medieval Holy Week tradition in the liturgy. However, Empson did recognize that the quotation of 201 is from Lam. 1:12, given in full for the first time in the poem, and in his remarkable analysis commented that Christ

> climbs the tree to repay what was stolen, as if he was putting the apple back; but the phrase in itself implies rather that he is doing the stealing, that so far from sinless he is Prometheus and the criminal. Either he stole on behalf of man (it is he who appeared to be sinful, and was caught up the tree) or he is climbing upwards, like Jack on the Beanstalk, and taking his people with him back to Heaven. The phrase has an odd humility which makes us see him as the son of the house; possibly Herbert is drawing on the medieval tradition that the Cross was made of the wood of the forbidden trees. Jesus seems a child in this metaphor, because he is the Son of God, because he can take the apples without actually stealing (though there is some doubt about this), because of the practical and domestic associations of such a necessity, and because he is evidently smaller than Man, or at any rate than Eve, who could pluck the fruit without climbing. This gives a pathetic humour and innocence (except ye receive the Kingdom of Heaven as a little child, ye shall in no wise enter therein); on the other hand, the son stealing from his father's orchard is a symbol of incest; in the person of Christ the supreme act of sin is combined with the supreme act of virtue. Thus in two ways, one behind the other, the Christ becomes guilty.[46]

It is worth bearing in mind that Rosemond Tuve's objection to these comments first appeared nearly twenty years after the first publication of *Seven Types of Ambiguity*:

> "He climbs the tree to repay what was stolen, as if he was putting the apple back," says Empson, later commenting that this makes Christ

46. Empson, *Seven Types of Ambiguity,* p. 269.

smaller, more childlike, than Eve, who could reach the apple without climbing; "but the *phrase in itself implies rather* that he is doing the stealing." Does it imply this? Perhaps a critic has to decide whether or not it makes any difference to us that it could not have implied this to Herbert . . . It is not possible to read the many, many uses of this liturgically common contrast and think that Jesus seems a child or an apple-stealer in them—if words, tone, context, can convey anything at all trustworthy to us ever; nor is it possible then to read Herbert and feel that his use differs from these others in words or tone or context. This reservation seems to me relevant to one's way of reading the poem. (Tuve, pp. 30–31)

Empson subsequently took exception to the general strictures in his reply in the *Kenyon Review* 12, the journal in which a shortened form of Tuve's *Reading* had first appeared:

> Generation after generation of poets and liturgists had handled this theme, no doubt, but [Tuve] does not actually quote even one of them who clashes in plain words, as Herbert does, the idea of the mercy and yearning love of Christ against the idea of his terrible and inevitable revenge. . . . Surely the act of making "explicit" these very remarkable parts of a tradition is worth notice; it might even be worth calling a new style.[47]

Care is necessary in order that what is at issue here may be isolated. Tuve does not suggest that Empson's interpretation of this stanza is as such impossible, nor even, in so many words, invalid; instead, she asserts that it does not square with a traditional handling of paradoxes illustrated by the stanza and as such manifestly unknown to Empson. Of the "reservation" that she has for Empson's reading, she writes that it

> does not seem relevant if a critic merely wishes to discover what a poem can mean to him, can become under his hands. This is a valuable activity, and it is only too bad that it is generally accompanied by implications that this meaning is "the meaning" and that one may praise the (original) author for it. One should rather praise the critic, who is the author of another and different poem—and why should he not be? The more good poems in the world the better. But he should acknowledge his paternity. (Tuve, pp. 31–32)

Tuve therefore admits as a valid activity the "creation" as well as

47. William Empson, "George Herbert and Miss Tuve," p. 735.

the discovery of meanings, both in the word and in the world. However, for her the creation of poetic meaning constitutes an act of interpretation as a result of which the reader is to be considered "the author of another and different poem." I have tried to present a case that suggests that Tuve's view is, in the final analysis, a reductive one to take of the creation of meanings. In earlier chapters of this book I have surveyed what I consider to be the principal areas in which the creation of Herbert's poetic meanings can be said to result from his ultimately sacramental acts of interpretation as God's initially reluctant reader, and I have argued that there are historical grounds for my approach. My claim in this chapter has been that Herbert's interpretative act in creating meaning is analogous to, and perhaps ultimately inseparable from, his reader's inevitable mimetic response to the poet's "quasi-divine aptitude" for sensing and creating relationships. The reader's renunciation of a claim to participation in spiritual conflict in the interests of discerning relationship can be seen to enact Herbert's sacramental offering up of his verse. Discovery of significance—the discernment of relationships—is the provenance of the reader, just as Herbert, the reader of God's opaque signs, learns to discover significance in what he perceives. Herbert expresses the satisfaction offered by his act of interpretation in terms of the *topoi* of Providence and Grace. Yet in the Augustinian devotional tradition in which Herbert has been identified, his expression involves an acknowledgment of the opacity of what Providence and Grace signify; the response they encourage and of which they are manifestations has already been inscrutably forestalled and "prevented."

Empson's last word[48] on the lines from "The Sacrifice" (since it later appears, scarcely changed, in a note to the third edition of *Seven Types of Ambiguity*) is a self-conscious documentation:

> Quite detachedly, tasting these wonderful lines with as clean a palate as I can, I find I cannot now clear away a feeling that the Christ in torment is made to appear, with ghastly pathos, as an adventurous boy. (*Kenyon Review* 12:738)

48. But see also William Empson's "Herbert's Quaintness."

If what Herbert achieved in this poem is innovative in the way Empson wished to claim, we may well be forced to concede that the innovation is more usefully seen in terms of a "wit-philosophy" current in the thought of Herbert's age than with such critical equipment as the twentieth century has been able to supply. The assertion that man's aptitude for apprehending relationships is quasi divine implies a concession to man's fallen, interpretative nature residing in the admission that if poetic language can be said to grant truths at all, it can only do so imitatively. Poetry may be a "making," but for Herbert, as both a reader and a writer aware of man's Fall, it mimics the divine act of creation. To acknowledge this mimicry is to admit that the poet's act in concealing the artfulness of his poetry is at once an act of interpretation and an expression of the uneasy equilibrium that in a fallen world must always exist between our readings of that poetry and the poet's own readings of the opaque but divinely authored text that surrounds him. This admission plunges the reader into an experience whose nature has been documented in our own century in verse: W. H. Auden's wryly disillusioned lines may be appropriated here as giving word, with more sureness of touch than that granted to the critic or even reader alone, and perhaps as only a great poet who is also a thinker can, to the issues that have been the concern of this book:

> For given Man, by birth, by education,
> Imago Dei who forgot his station,
> The self-made creature who himself unmakes,
> The only creature ever made who fakes,
> With no more nature in his loving smile
> Than in his theories of a natural style,
> What but tall tales, the luck of verbal playing,
> Can trick his lying nature into saying
> That love, or truth in any serious sense,
> Like orthodoxy, is a reticence?[49]

49. W. H. Auden, from "The Truest Poetry Is the Most Feigning," in *Collected Poems*, p. 471.

Appendix 1

A Note on the Text of *The Temple*

For more than thirty years after its first appearance in 1941, F. E. Hutchinson's edition of *The Temple*[1] was unquestioningly regarded as standard. During the last decade, however, some of this consensus has been eroded. Since I have decided against using Hutchinson's edition in this book, some account of the state of scholarship on the text of *The Temple* is due. Hutchinson's premise was that, of the complete versions of the text, the Bodleian manuscript (MS Tanner 307) "brings us nearer the author's text than anything else that survives, and therefore its readings have the first claim on our respect" (*Works,* p. lxxi). In admitting the "deficiencies" of this text, however, and in commending the "unusual excellence" of the first edition of 1633 (*Works,* p. lxxiv), Hutchinson was in effect forced to collate the text of the Bodleian manuscript with that of the first 1633 edition wherever he found "evident slips" in the former (*Works,* p. lxxiii); in each of twenty-eight such cases Hutchinson admitted that the reading of the incomplete Williams manuscript (MS Jones B 62) supported the 1633 reading. In another case, Hutchinson actually preferred the Williams reading to both the Bodleian and 1633 readings.

In 1973, J. Max Patrick published a strong attack on what he considered to have been Hutchinson's eclecticism in producing a text that no one in the seventeenth century actually saw, unlike either of the first two 1633 editions, whose greater authority he accordingly proposed. Whereas Hutchinson had defended his text on the basis of its more closely representing the author's intention than had any previous edition, Patrick suggested that even this intention may have been wrongly deduced.[2] Instead, he asserted that Walton's account of the dying Herbert's sending a "little book" to Nicholas Ferrar, through Edmond Duncon, was unreliable in that it constituted "a supposed message [that] was ingeniously composed by Walton some thirty years after the event on the basis of material which Ferrar composed on the basis of the poems themselves after Herbert had died" (Patrick, p. 9). A year after the appearance of Patrick's paper, in 1974, there was implicit support for his case in the edition of *The*

1. Referred to throughout as *Works*; see George Herbert, *The Works of George Herbert.*

2. See J. Max Patrick, "Critical Problems in Editing George Herbert's *The Temple*" What Herbert actually intended as the "final version" is in itself a conception that Stanley E. Fish's approach (*The Living Temple: George Herbert and Catechizing*) surrounds with such uncertainty that one is perhaps hesitant to suggest anything.

Temple published by C. A. Patrides, which is based largely on the first 1633 edition. Yet since then there has also been dissent. In her 1977 biography of Herbert, Amy Charles rejected Patrick's case on the basis of there being insufficient documentary evidence to support it. She declared herself "entirely in agreement" with Hutchinson and censured Patrick for omitting to mention John Ferrar's account of how his brother Nicholas received the poems from Herbert.[3] Patrick's view was that, rather than the manuscript of *The Temple,* what Duncon may have been given was that of *The Countrey Parson,* and that Herbert had sent the poems on to Ferrar or to the press at Cambridge somewhat earlier. In consequence, according to Patrick, it was highly conceivable that the licensing, typesetting, and proofreading had all been undertaken while Herbert was still alive. This part of Patrick's case is now questionable, since in erroneously considering Walton's account of the Herbert-Duncon transaction to be its only record, his claim that it is "of very doubtful reliability" is seriously undermined. Furthermore, Daniel W. Doerksen has since examined the documentary evidence afresh and not only concludes that Walton is to be trusted here because his account is indeed endorsed by that of John Ferrar, but proposes in addition a publication date for *The Temple* of September 1633, six months after Herbert's death.[4]

Patrick's case is undermined, to be sure, by this evidence and its implications. But it is not destroyed in its entirety, although the conclusions he draws must remain more than ever at the level of hypothesis. As such, they do offer an attractive solution to two problems, one major and one minor, that Hutchinson—while troubled by them—does not seem to me satisfactorily to account for. In summarizing these, I suggest that there

3. Amy M. Charles, *A Life of George Herbert,* p. 182, n.11. John Ferrar's account is printed in B. Blackstone, ed., *The Ferrar Papers,* p. 59.

4. Daniel W. Doerksen, "Nicholas Ferrar, Arthur Woodnoth, and the Publication of George Herbert's *The Temple* 1633." Doerksen's remarks should also be read in the light of Amy Charles's introduction to her 1977 facsimile edition of the Williams MS (see George Herbert, *The Williams Manuscript of George Herbert's Poems*), her recent article "The Original of Mr George Herbert's Temple," and Mario Di Cesare's defense of the Bodleian MS, "The Bodleian Manuscript and the Text of Herbert's Poems." These last two articles are due to appear, in expanded form, as part of an introduction to a facsimile edition of the Bodleian MS (Delmar, NY: Scholars' Facsimiles and Reprints). Although I do not agree with its conclusions, Di Cesare's essay is a balanced presentation of the case against the claim for the exclusive authority of the 1633 editions. The points about mislineation in 1633^1 are more substantial than are the analytical deductions from the differences in punctuation between the Bodleian MS and 1633^1. Much of the evidence presented by Di Cesare could equally well support a case, such as I have hypothesized, for a lost fair copytext. Nevertheless, to the two cases of error in 1633^1 that I present in this book should be added Di Cesare's argument that "The Thanksgiving" (line 11) and "The Collar" (line 21) are indeed incorrectly punctuated in that edition, although the argument does not, I believe, affect the concluding paragraph of my Appendix 1.

are not yet sufficient grounds for dismissing out of hand the remaining, admittedly hypothetical, aspect of Patrick's case.

Hutchinson's major problem, over which he expressed some concern, was with the time within which "many events" would have to have been "crowded," if one accepted Walton's account (*Works*, p. lxxii). Indeed, he committed himself to accepting that in the thirteen months between late February 1632/33 (the date Walton's account refers to) and March 25, 1633/34, the following events occurred: Ferrar read Herbert's manuscript, had it copied, and sent it to Cambridge to the licensers, of whom at least one (and possibly two or three) read a considerable way into it, since on Walton's account of the matter the vice-chancellor not only objected to the couplet in "The Church Militant" (1633, pp. 184–91) about religion passing "to the *American* strand" (pp. 235–36), but withdrew his objection only "after some time and some arguments," Ferrar refusing to omit the lines.[5] The type for the first edition was then set meticulously, proofread, and copies of this edition sold, after which, for the preparation of a second edition also bearing the date 1633, the type of the first edition was broken up and this second edition published. Patrick's argument—that it is inconceivable that all this could have taken place within a little over a year—remains strong on this point. It is hardly affected (indeed, if anything it is strengthened still further) by Doerksen's suggested publication date of September 1633 for the first edition.

But it does not seem to me an indispensable part of the case to assert that Herbert did not hand over *The Temple* to Duncon in order to postulate with Patrick that a (now lost) fair copytext—not necessarily identical to that submitted for licensing, from which the printers would set up the type—had already found its way to Cambridge. The licenser's copy and the "little book" may then indeed have been MS Tanner 307; Amy Charles rightly stresses that Walton's description reflects his knowledge of Herbert's poems in their published form only, rather than proving his mendacity: "any of the seventeenth-century editions was, indeed, a little book."[6] For until documentary evidence emerges to disprove the possibility of a lost fair copytext, the crucially weak link in Hutchinson's case must really be his claim for the status of MS Tanner 307—that is, his assumption that the Cambridge printers set the type from it. To contest this claim is not only to be freed from the implausible crowding of events in the period after Herbert's death and to suggest that the reason Herbert did not bother to correct the slips in MS Tanner 307 was that it had itself been made from a fair copy; it is also to resolve the more minor problem

5. Izaak Walton, *The Life of Mr. George Herbert*, p. 75. The lines remain obscure but have recently been placed, by David Norbrook, *Poetry and Politics in the English Renaissance*, p. 220, in the context of the Bohemian crisis of 1621/22.

6. Amy M. Charles, *A Life of George Herbert*, p. 182, n.12.

that Hutchinson voiced (and that he somewhat unconvincingly overrides): that MS Tanner 307 is a clean copy, with no printer's ink on it. Hutchinson had to resort to the rather desperate tactic of considering it "not inconceivable that, if this fine copy were put in the compositor's hand with an injunction to treat it with special care, it might escape injury" (*Works,* p. lxxii). The hypothesis raises interesting implications for the authority of the second edition of 1633: was this prepared by collating the postulated fair copytext with the first 1633 edition?

The case must be scrutinized rigorously. The first and second 1633 editions are sufficiently authoritative for me to have decided to use the former in this book but not, I suggest, flawless. I shall present two cases in which I believe it could be argued that Herbert's intention is not realized in the 1633 editions. I refer to both cases in the text of this book.

In "Man" (1633, pp. 83–85), Hutchinson's reading seems to give the sense required:

For Man is ev'ry thing,
And more: He is a tree, yet bears more fruit;
A beast, yet is, or should be more:
Reason and speech we onely bring. (7–10)

Hutchinson felt that there was "no greater textual difficulty in *The Temple*" (*Works,* p. 508) than the choice between his reading "more fruit" and the Bodleian manuscript "no fruit" (8). The latter makes less sense, it can be argued, because it misses the point that in writing the lines Herbert is in effect handing over his claims of wit to God (see Chapter 4).[7] The Williams manuscript, the only one with alterations in Herbert's hand, is the basis for this reading; as I have mentioned, in cases where Hutchinson sensed an obvious slip in the Bodleian manuscript reading and collated it with the 1633 editions, he found that his decision was supported by the Williams manuscript. The problem that presents itself here is that if the Bodleian manuscript "no fruit" is an error, it is one that can be corrected only with reference to the Williams manuscript, since the 1633 editions on this occasion agree with the Bodleian reading. Although the Williams reading makes better sense, it is of course possible that Herbert altered the line, since it might be assumed that the lost fair copytext probably read "no fruit"; however, this assumption is more open to question than that Herbert missed an error in the Williams manuscript. In other words, the Williams reading cannot seriously be queried, since it is certain that Herbert saw it, as it contains his corrections elsewhere. There is no evidence at all, rather it is unlikely, that Herbert saw the Bodleian man-

7. Cf. Diana Benet, *Secretary of Praise: The Poetic Vocation of George Herbert,* pp. 142–43, n. 2, who prefers "no fruit" on the basis of an "implied characterization of the Christian as a fruitless tree" in "Affliction" [I] and "Employment" [II].

uscript, so that on the face of it, "no fruit" should be less favored. But since the 1633 edition also reads "no fruit," two possibilities should be considered. Either the reading represents Herbert's changed intention, or the compositor uncharacteristically (but not impossibly) misread the copytext, which Herbert's earlier editor A. B. Grosart (1874) speculated read "mo fruit" (though Hutchinson felt that it was "unlike Herbert to use an obsolescent form" [*Works*, p. 508]). While it may therefore be felt that the presence of "mo" avoids a repetition of "more" three times in two lines, this does not seem to me an overriding objection, and in view both of the better sense and of the uncertainty attending this particular reading in the 1633 text, we should therefore, I urge, read here "more fruit."

In "A true Hymne" (1633, pp. 162–63) there is a crux in the last stanza, and here I quote from the Bodleian manuscript itself:[8]

Whereas if y'heart be moued,
Although verse be somewhat scant,
God doth supply ye want.
As when th'heart sayes (sighing to be approoued)
O, could I love! & stops: God writeth, Loued. (16–20)

In line 17, "the" is missing, and Hutchinson considered that this was a slip, since the omission affects the meter. No version of the poem exists in the Williams manuscript, and so in this case the 1633 reading could not be verified or otherwise by referring to this manuscript. Coburn Freer seems to have been the first to have noticed the implications of this "slip" (though he mistakenly attributes the omission of "the" to the 1633 text as well); he considers it "much more likely" that the quoted reading represents Herbert's intention: "The missing article is not just a trick of demonstration. By leaving out *the*, Herbert makes clear that the 'scantness' is purely technical; it is not a deficiency of spirit that God makes up—only a mere article is missing—but a deficiency of numbers. The skip in the meter determines the meaning of the line."[9] It is quite possible that the compositor was in error here, perhaps falling prey to his expectations and catching "the" from the surrounding lines. The inconsistent orthography of the Bodleian manuscript version seems to reduce the possibility of such error and to raise instead the question of Herbert's own orthography. Certainly if 17 is read without "the," the word "although" assumes trochaic weight and has the effect of dramatically reminding the reader

8. *The Temple* ["The Original of Mr George Herbert's Temple; as it was at first Licenced for the Presse"], fol. 124^r (p. 256 deleted), Bodleian MS Tanner 307. Here I have kept to the writer's orthography (the MS is not in Herbert's hand), and have altered only the superscribed "e" in "ye" (18).

9. Coburn Freer, *Music for a King: George Herbert's Style and the Metrical Psalms*, p. 128.

that supplying of want is actually conditional to the heart being "moved"; furthermore, 18 now makes exquisite sense, allowing its reader to discover simultaneously that God supplies "the" and that this wanted "the" completes the line. The last couplet may then be read as a full realization of this speculative assertion.

In both cases, then, it could be said that the 1633 reading is plausible but not as effective as when this reading is emended, with some manuscript authority, as shown. Such emendations should be thought of less as undermining any case for the authority of the 1633 editions than as suggesting that the compositor of these beautiful pieces of work was in rare instances capable of error. The quality of the 1633 editions is so exceptionally high that it is necessary to be aware of this possibility. The readings I have proposed cannot be proved to represent Herbert's "final intention," but I have tried to show why I think they do.[10]

10. For the defender of the authority of the first 1633 edition, the missing line in the seventh stanza of "The Size" (pp. 131–32) (absent also from the Bodleian MS and therefore from Hutchinson) is admittedly a vexing error but does not in itself destroy the proposed hypothesis. Charles (*A Life of George Herbert*, p. 184) assumes that the copyist of MS Tanner 307 "failed to catch the pattern, or was distracted"; what is missing, however, is a "tag" of four syllables and while it admittedly spoils the stanza pattern, it does not destroy the sense. This would provide an additional argument against Herbert's having carried out the entire proofreading of 1633^1, but we need not assume that the line was not already missing from a lost fair copy, from which the Bodleian MS copyist(s) merely reproduced the error, as did the 1633 printer. The stanza reads, in 1633:

> Wherefore sit down, good heart;
> Grasp not at much, for fear thou losest all.
> If comforts fell according to desert,
> [..................]
> They would great frosts and snows destroy:
> For we should count, Since the last joy.

An editor would be justified in emending, I think, according to one of two suggestions offered by Charles. Thus "On one and all," or "On great and small" (the latter, surely, being far more likely, as it does not duplicate the rhyme word of the stanza's second line), may be placed between the square brackets, so that the stanza conforms to the pattern of the rest.

Appendix 2

A table of page numbers in three editions of *The Temple*

This table has been included for ease of reference. The editions in question are: that used throughout this book, that is, the first edition of 1633 (see page numbers under column headed "1633"); F. E. Hutchinson (ed.), *The Works of George Herbert* (2d ed.; Oxford: Clarendon, 1945) (see under column headed "Hutchinson"); C. A. Patrides (ed.), *The English Poems of George Herbert* (London: Dent, 1974) (see under column headed "Patrides"). As the reader will have gathered from Appendix 1, Patrides adheres closely to the first 1633 edition, whereas Hutchinson bases his edition on Bodleian MS Tanner 307; the textual differences are nowhere greater than in the specific cases discussed in Appendix 1. Titles are given in the form in which they appear in 1633: numberings of all poems that share the same titles (except the first two "Love" poems and "The H. Scriptures") are given, as editorial interpolations, between square brackets.

		Page number in:	
Title of poem	"1633"	"Hutchinson"	"Patrides"
The Church-porch	1	6	33
Superliminare	17	25	46
The Altar	18	26	47
The Sacrifice	19	26	48
The Thanksgiving	27	35	56
The Reprisall	28	36	57
The Agonie	29	37	58
The Sinner	30	38	58
Good Friday	30	38	59
Redemption	31	40	60
Sepulchre	32	40	60
Easter	33	41	61
Easter wings	34	43	63
H. Baptisme [I]	36	43	64
H. Baptisme [II]	36	44	64
Nature	37	45	65
Sinne [I]	37	45	65
Affliction [I]	38	46	66
Repentance	40	48	68
Faith	41	49	69

		Page number in:	
Title of poem	"1633"	"Hutchinson"	"Patrides"
Prayer [I]	43	51	70
The H. Communion	43	52	71
Antiphon [I]	45	53	72
Love I	45	54	73
[Love] II	46	54	73
The Temper [I]	46	55	74
The Temper [II]	47	56	74
Jordan [I]	48	56	75
Employment [I]	49	57	76
The H. Scriptures. I	50	58	76
[The H. Scriptures] II	50	58	77
Whitsunday	51	59	78
Grace	52	60	78
Praise [I]	53	61	79
Affliction [II]	53	62	80
Mattens	54	62	80
Sinne [II]	55	63	81
Even-song	55	63	81
Church-monuments	56	64	82
Church-musick	57	65	83
Church-lock and key	57	66	83
The Church-floore	58	66	84
The Windows	59	67	84
Trinitie Sunday	59	68	85
Content	60	68	85
The Quidditie	61	69	86
Humilitie	61	70	87
Frailtie	62	71	88
Constancie	63	72	89
Affliction [III]	64	73	90
The Starre	65	74	90
Sunday	66	75	91
Avarice	69	77*	93
Ana[Mary/Army]gram	69	77	93

*Hutchinson departed from the order of MS Tanner 307 at this point and followed that of 1633. In the manuscript this little poem is less persuasively inserted between "Church-musick" and "Church-lock and key," probably for reasons of space, since elsewhere the two texts are, from the point of view of order, identical.

Title of poem	"1633"	Page number in: "Hutchinson"	"Patrides"
To all Angels and Saints	69	77	94
Employment [II]	70	78	95
Deniall	71	79	96
Christmas	72	80	96
Ungratefulnesse	74	82	97
Sighs and Grones	75	83	98
The World	76	84	99
Coloss. 3.3.	77	84	100
Vanitie	77	85	100
Lent	78	86	101
Vertue	80	87	103
The Pearl	81	88	103
Affliction [IV]	82	89	105
Man	83	90	106
Antiphon [II]	85	92	108
Unkindnesse	86	93	108
Life	87	94	109
Submission	87	95	110
Justice [I]	88	95	110
Charms and Knots	88	96	111
Affliction [V]	89	97	111
Mortification	90	98	112
Decay	91	99	113
Miserie	92	100	114
Jordan [II]	95	102	116
Prayer [II]	95	103	117
Obedience	96	104	118
Conscience	98	105	119
Sion	99	106	120
Home	99	107	120
The British Church	102	109	122
The Quip	103	110	123
Vanitie [I]	104	111	124
The Dawning	104	112	125
Jesu	105	112	125
Businesse	105	113	125
Dialogue	107	114	127
Dulnesse	108	115	127
Love-joy	109	116	128
Providence	109	116	129
Hope	114	121	133

Title of poem	"1633"	Page number in: "Hutchinson"	"Patrides"
Sinnes round	114	122	134
Time	115	122	134
Gratefulnesse	116	123	135
Peace	117	124	136
Confession	118	126	137
Giddinesse	119	127	138
The bunch of grapes	120	128	139
Love unknown	121	129	140
Mans medley	123	131	142
The Storm	125	132	143
Paradise	125	132	143
The Method	126	133	144
Divinitie	127	134	145
Ephes. 4.30	128	135	146
The Familie	130	136	147
The Size	131	137	147
Artillerie	132	139	149
Church-rents and schismes	134	140	150
Justice [II]	135	141	150
The Pilgrimage	135	141	151
The Holdfast	137	143	152
Complaining	137	143	153
The Discharge	138	144	153
Praise [II]	140	146	155
An Offering	141	147	156
Longing	142	148	157
The Bag	145	151	159
The Jews	146	152	160
The Collar	147	153	161
The Glimpse	148	154	162
Assurance	149	155	163
The Call	150	156	164
Clasping of hands	151	157	164
Praise [III]	151	157	165
Josephs Coat	153	159	166
The Pulley	153	159	166
The Priesthood	154	160	167
The Search	156	162	168
Grief	158	164	170
The Crosse	158	164	170
The Flower	160	165	171

Title of poem	"1633"	Page number in: "Hutchinson"	"Patrides"
Dotage	161	167	173
The Sonne	162	167	173
A true Hymne	162	168	174
The Answer	163	169	174
A Dialogue-Antheme	164	169	175
The Water-course	164	170	175
Self-condemnation	165	170	176
Bitter-sweet	165	171	176
The Glance	166	171	177
The 23 Psalme	167	172	177
Marie Magdalene	168	173	178
Aaron	168	174	179
The Odour	169	174	180
The Foil	170	175	181
The Forerunners	170	176	181
The Rose	172	177	182
Discipline	173	178	183
The Invitation	174	179	184
The Banquet	175	181	185
The Posie	177	182	186
A Parodie	177	183	187
The Elixer	178	184	188
A Wreath	179	185	188
Death	180	185	189
Dooms-day	181	186	189
Judgement	182	187	190
Heaven	182	188	191
Love [III]	183	188	192
The Church Militant	184	190	193
L'Envoy	192	199	200

Selected Bibliography

Works listed here are only those footnoted (or otherwise alluded to in my text above) in abbreviated form. For convenience this bibliography has been divided into two sections: the first ("Primary") lists works that first appeared in or before 1700 (later editions of such works are therefore included in this section); and the second ("Secondary") lists works that first appeared after 1700. Where more than one item appears under a given name, these have been listed alphabetically by title. Neither part is in any way intended to be exhaustive; for a fuller list of recent Herbert criticism than can be offered here, see *The English Poems of George Herbert,* edited by C. A. Patrides; Jerry Leath Mills, "Recent Studies in Herbert"; and, above all, John R. Roberts, *George Herbert: An Annotated Bibliography of Modern Criticism 1905–1974.* A supplement to Roberts's work is forthcoming.

Primary

Adams, Thomas. *Workes.* London, 1629.

Ambrose (St.). *Opera Omnia.* 4 vols. Ed. J.-P. Migne. Paris, 1845. [*PL* 14–17.]

Andrewes, Lancelot. *XCVI Sermons.* London, 1629.

Aquinas. See below under Thomas Aquinas (St.).

Augustine (St.). *The Confessions of the Incomparable Doctour S. Augustine. Translated into English* [by Sir Toby Matthew]. [London], 1620.

——— [attrib.]. *A Heavenly Treasure of Confortable Meditations and Prayers written by S. Augustin . . .* [Trans.] *Antony Batt.* Saint Omer, 1624.

———. *Opera Omnia.* 16 vols. Ed. J.-P. Migne. Paris, 1841–1849. [*PL* 32–47].

Bartas, G.de. *Les Oeuvres de G. de Saluste S[ieur] du Bartas.* Paris, 1611.

Beza, Theodore. *Job expounded by Theodore Beza, partly in manner of a Commentary, partly in manner of a Paraphrase.* Cambridge, n.d. (1589?).

Blackstone, B., ed. *The Ferrar Papers.* Cambridge: Cambridge University Press, 1938.

Bonaventura (St.). *Opera Omnia.* 10 vols. Quaracchi: Collegi S. Bonaventurae, 1882–1902.

——— [attrib.]. *Soliloquies.* London, 1655.

Brown, Carleton, ed. *English Lyrics of the XIIIth Century.* Oxford: Clarendon, 1932.

———. *Religious Lyrics of the XIVth Century.* 2d ed. Oxford: Clarendon, 1952.

———. *Religious Lyrics of the XVth Century.* Oxford: Clarendon, 1934.

Browne, Sir Thomas. *Works.* 4 vols. Ed. Geoffrey Keynes. London: Faber & Faber, 1964.

Calvin, John. *Sermons of Master John Calvin, upon the booke of Job. Translated out of French by Arthur Golding.* London, 1574.

Cramer, Daniel. *Emblemata Sacra. Hoc est, decades quinque emblematum ex Sacra Scriptura, de dulcissimo Nomine & Cruce Jesu Christi.* Frankfurt, 1624.

Donne, John. *The Divine Poems.* Ed. Helen Gardner. Oxford: Clarendon, 1952.

———. *Sermons.* 10 vols. Ed. Evelyn M. Simpson and George R. Potter. Berkeley: University of California Press, 1953–1962.

G[oodman], G. *The Creatures Praysing God: or, The Religion of Dumbe Creatures.* London, 1622.

Hall, Joseph. *The Arte of Divine Meditation.* London, 1607.

———. *Works.* London, 1625.

[Harvey, Christopher]. *Schola Cordis, or the Heart of it selfe gone away from God. . . .* London, 1647.

———. *The Synagogue, or, Shadow of the Temple.* London, 1640.

Heinsius, Daniel. *Emblemata Aliquot Amatoria.* n.p. [?Amsterdam], n.d. [?1624].

Henshaw, Joshua. *Horae Succisivae, or, Spare Houres of Meditation.* 2d ed. London, 1631.

Herbert, George. *The English Poems of George Herbert.* Ed. C. A. Patrides. London: Dent, 1974.

———. *The English Works of George Herbert.* 3 vols. Ed. George Herbert Palmer. London: Hodder & Stoughton, 1905.

———. "The Original of Mr George Herbert's Temple: as it was at first Licenced for the presse." MS Tanner 307. Bodleian Library, Oxford.

———. [*The Temple,* "Bodleian MS"]. A facsimile reproduction of MS Tanner 307 with an introduction by Mario di Cesare and Amy M. Charles. Delmar, NY: Scholars' Facsimiles and Reprints, in press.

———. *The Temple. Sacred Poems and Private Ejaculations.* [1st ed.]. Cambridge, 1633.

———. *The Temple. Sacred Poems and Private Ejaculations.* 2d edition. Cambridge, 1633.

———. *The Temple. Sacred Poems and Private Ejaculations.* [facsimile of 1st 1633 ed.]. London: Scolar Press, 1968; reptd. 1973.

———. [*The Temple,* "Williams MS"]. MS Jones B 62. Dr. Williams Library, London, WC1.

———. [*The Temple,* "Williams MS"]. *The Williams Manuscript of George Herbert's Poems.* A facsimile reproduction with an introduction by Amy M. Charles. Delmar, NY: Scholars' Facsimiles and Reprints, 1977.

———. *The Works of George Herbert.* Ed. F. E. Hutchinson. 2d ed. Oxford: Clarendon, 1945.

Hooker, Richard. *Of the Lawes of Ecclesiastical Politie.* [Books I-IV]. London, n.d. [1593?].

———. *Of the Lawes of Ecclesiastical Politie. The Fift Booke.* London, 1597.

Hugh of St. Victor. *Opera Omnia.* 3 vols. Ed. J.-P. Migne. Paris, 1854. [*PL* 175–77.]

Hugo, Hermann. *Pia Desideria.* Antwerp, 1624.

Imitatio Christi. The Imitation of Christ. Trans. Richard Whitford (1530). Ed. Edward J. Klein. New York: Harper & Bros., [1941].

King, Henry, *Poems, Elegies, Paradoxes, and Sonnets.* [facsimile of London, 1657, ed.]. London: Scolar Press, 1973.

La Perrière, Guillaume de. *Le Théâtre des bons engins.* Paris, n.d. [1539?].

Meditationes vitae Christi. Trans. Nicholas Love (1430?). Ed. L. F. Powell. London: Frowde, 1908.

Mornay, Philippe de. [Philip of Mornay]. *A Woorke concerning the trewnesse of the Christian Religion. . . .* Trans. Sir Philip Sidney and Arthur Golding. London, 1587.

Ochino, Bernard. *Certayne Sermons of . . . Bernadine Ochine.* London, n.d. (1550?).

Patrologiae cursus completus . . . series . . . Latina. [Referred to throughout as *PL.*] 221 vols. Ed. J.-P. Migne. Paris, 1844–1864.

P[arsons], R[obert]. *A Booke of Christian Exercise, appertaining to Resolution. . . . Perused . . . by Edm. Bunny.* London, 1584.

Philo Judaeus. *Philo.* Trans. F. H. Colson and G. H. Whitaker. 10 vols. The Loeb Classical Library. London: Heinemann, 1929–1962.

Quarles, Francis. *Emblemes.* London, 1635.

Raleigh, Sir Walter. *The History of the World.* London, 1614.

Sales, François de. *Introduction to a Devoute Life.* Trans. I. Y. 3d ed. Rouen, 1614.

Scupoli, Lorenzo. *The Spiritual Combat.* [Translation]. London: Burns & Oates, 1935.

Sidney, Sir Philip. *An Apology for Poetry* [or *The Defence of Poesie* (1595)]. Ed. Geoffrey Shepherd. Manchester: Manchester University Press/New York: Barnes & Noble, 1973.

———. *The Poems of Sir Philip Sidney.* Ed. William A. Ringler, Jr. Oxford: Clarendon, 1962.

Sylvester, Joshua. *Bartas: His Devine Weekes and Workes.* London, 1605.

Taylor, Thomas. *Meditations from the Creatures.* 2d ed. London, 1629.

Thomas Aquinas (St.). *Questiones quod libetales.* Ed. Raymundi Spiazzi. 8th ed. Rome: Marietti, 1949.

———. *Summa contra Gentiles.* Rome: Desclee & Co., 1934.

———. *Summa Theologiae* [*Summa Theologica*]. [Latin text and English translation]. 60 vols. Ed. Thomas Gilby. London: Eyre & Spottiswoode, 1964–1976.

Vaenius, Otho. *Amorum Emblemata.* Antwerp, 1608.

Van Haeften, Benedictus. *Schola Cordis, sive aversi a Deo cordis, ad eumdem reductio, et instructio.* Antwerp, 1629.

Vermigli, Peter Martyr. *The Common Places . . . Translated and partly gathered by Anthonie Marten.* London, 1583.

Walton, Izaak. *The Life of Mr. George Herbert.* London, 1670.

Weemse (or Wemyss), John. *The Workes . . . in Three Volumes.* London, 1636.

Whitaker, William. *Disputatio de sacra scriptura . . . .* Cambridge, 1588.

Williams, John. *A Sermon of Apparell.* London, 1620.

Secondary

Adams, H. M. *Catalogue of books printed on the Continent of Europe, 1501–1600, in Cambridge libraries.* Cambridge: Cambridge University Press, 1967.

Adler, J. H. "Form and Meaning in Herbert's 'Discipline.'" *N&Q* 203 (1958): 240–43.

Alvarez, A. *The School of Donne.* London: Chatto & Windus, 1961.

Asals, Heather. *Equivocal Predication: George Herbert's Way to God.* Toronto: University of Toronto Press, 1981.

———. "George Herbert and Hugh of St Victor's 'Soliloquium.'" *N&Q* 214 (1969): 368–70.

Auden, W. H. *Collected Poems.* Ed. Edward Mendelson. London: Faber & Faber/New York: Random House, 1976.

Auerbach, Erich. *Mimesis: The Representation of Reality in Western Literature.* Trans. Willard R. Trask. Princeton: Princeton University Press, 1953.

Bainton, Roland, H. *Studies on the Reformation.* London: Hodder & Stoughton, 1964.

Bell, Ilona. " 'Setting Foot into Divinity': George Herbert and the English Reformation." *Modern Language Quarterly* 38 (1977): 291–41.

Benet, Diana. *Secretary of Praise: The Poetic Vocation of George Herbert.* Columbia: University of Missouri Press, 1984.

Bethell, S. L. "Gracián, Tesauro, and the Nature of Metaphysical Wit." *Northern Miscellany* 1 (1953): 19–40.

Blackstone, B., ed. *The Ferrar Papers.* Cambridge: Cambridge University Press, 1938.

Blanchard, Margaret M. "The Leap into Darkness: Donne, Herbert and God." *Renascence* 17 (1964): 38–50.

Blau, Sheridan D. "The Poet as Casuist: Herbert's 'Church-porch.'" *Genre* 4 (1971): 142–52.

Bloch, Chana. *Spelling the Word: George Herbert and the Bible.* Berkeley: University of California Press, 1985.

Bloom, Harold. *The Anxiety of Influence.* Oxford: Oxford University Press, 1973.

Booty, John E. "George Herbert: *The Temple* and *The Book of Common Prayer.*" *Mosaic* 12 (1979): 75–90.

Bowers, Fredson. "Herbert's Sequential Imagery: 'The Temper.'" *Modern Philology* 59 (1962): 202–13.

Burnaby, John. *Amor Dei: A Study of the Religion of St Augustine.* London: Hodder & Stoughton, 1938.

Butt, John. "Izaak Walton's Methods in Biography." *Essays and Studies by Members of the English Association* 19 (1933/1934):67–84.

Cannon, Charles K. " 'William Whitaker's *Disputatio de Sacra Scriptura*: A Sixteenth-Century Theory of Allegory." *Huntington Library Quarterly* 25 (1962): 129–38.

Carnes, Valerie. "The Unity of George Herbert's *The Temple*: A Reconsideration." *ELH* 35 (1968): 505–26.

Charity, A. C. *Events and Their Afterlife: The Dialectics of Christian Typology in the Bible and Dante.* Cambridge: Cambridge University Press, 1966.
Charles, Amy M. *A Life of George Herbert.* Ithaca, N.Y.: Cornell University Press, 1977.
———. "The Original of Mr George Herbert's Temple." *GHJ* 6 (1983): 1–14.
———. "The Williams Manuscript and *The Temple.*" *Renaissance Papers* (1971): 59–77.
Clark, Ira. " 'Lord, in Thee the *Beauty* Lies in the *Discovery*': 'Love Unknown' and Reading Herbert," *ELH* 39 (1972): 560–84.
Clements, A. L. "Theme, Tone, and Tradition in George Herbert's Poetry." *English Literary Renaissance* 3 (1973): 264–83.
Coleridge, S. T. *Biographia Literaria.* 2 vols. London, 1817.
Colie, Rosalie L. *Paradoxia Epidemica: The Renaissance Tradition of Paradox.* Princeton: Princeton University Press, 1966.
———. *The Resources of Kind: Genre Theory in the Renaissance.* Berkeley: University of California Press, 1973.
Collinson, Patrick. *The Religion of Protestants: The Church in English Society 1559–1625.* Oxford: Clarendon Press, 1982.
Curtius, E. R. *European Literature and the Latin Middle Ages.* Trans. Willard R. Trask. London: Routledge & Kegan Paul, 1953.
Daniélou, Jean. *The Lord of History.* Trans. Nigel Abercrombie. London: Longmans, 1958.
———. *From Shadows to Reality.* Trans. Dom Wulstan Hibberd. London: Burns and Oates, 1960.
D[avenport], A. "Five Notes on George Herbert." *N&Q* 197 (1952): 420–22.
Davies, H. Neville. "Sweet Music in Herbert's 'Easter.' " *N&Q* 213 (1968): 95–96.
Di Cesare, Mario A. "The Bodleian Manuscript and the Text of Herbert's Poems." *GHJ* 6 (1983): 15–35.
Doerksen, Daniel W. "Nicholas Ferrar, Arthur Woodnoth, and the Publication of George Herbert's *The Temple,* 1633." *GHJ* 3 (1979/80): 22–44.
Eliot, T. S. *For Lancelot Andrewes: Essays on Style and Order.* 1928; reissued London: Faber, 1970.
Ellrodt, Robert. *L'Inspiration personelle et l'esprit du temps chez les poètes métaphysiques anglais.* 3 vols. Paris: José Corti, 1960.
Elsky, Martin. "Polyphonic Psalm Settings and the Voice of George Herbert's *The Temple.*" *Modern Language Quarterly* 42 (1981): 227–46.
Empson, William. "Donne and the Rhetorical Tradition." *Kenyon Review* 11 (1949): 571–87.
———. "George Herbert and Miss Tuve." *Kenyon Review* 12 (1950): 735–38.
———. "Herbert's Quaintness." *New Statesman* 65 (1963): 18.
———. *Seven Types of Ambiguity.* 3d ed. London: Harmondsworth, 1973.
———. *The Structure of Complex Words.* London: Chatto & Windus, 1951.
Fish, Stanley E. "Letting Go: The Reader in Herbert's Poetry." *ELH* 37 (1970): 475–94.

———. *The Living Temple: George Herbert and Catechizing*. Berkeley: University of California Press, 1978.
———. *Self-Consuming Artifacts: The Experience of Seventeenth-Century Literature*. Berkeley: University of California Press, 1972.
Ford, Ford Madox. *Parade's End* [1924–1928]. Collected ed. New York: Alfred A. Knopf, 1961.
Foucault, Michel. *The Order of Things* [Translation of *Les Mots et les Choses*.] London: Tavistock Publications, 1970.
Freeman, Rosemary. *English Emblem Books*. London: Chatto & Windus, 1948.
Freer, Coburn. *Music for a King: George Herbert's Style and the Metrical Psalms*. Baltimore: The Johns Hopkins University Press, 1972.
Furbank, P. N. *Reflections on the Word "Image."* London: Secker & Warburg, 1970.
Gallagher, Michael P., S.J. "Rhetoric, Style and George Herbert." *ELH* 37 (1970): 495–516.
Gilman, Ernest B. "Word and Image in Quarles' *Emblems*." *Critical Inquiry* 6 (1980): 385–410.
Gilson, Etienne. *The Philosophy of St Bonaventure*. Trans. Dom Illtyd Trethowan and F. J. Sheed. London: Sheed & Ward, 1938.
———. *The Spirit of Medieval Philosophy*. Trans. A. H. C. Downes. London: Sheed & Ward, 1950.
Gombrich, E. H. *Icones Symbolicae*. London: Phaidon, 1972.
Grant, Patrick M. *The Transformation of Sin: Studies in Donne, Herbert, Vaughan, and Traherne*. Montreal: McGill-Queen's University Press, 1974.
Graves, Robert. *Poetic Unreason and Other Studies*. London: Cecil Palmer, 1925.
Gray, Douglas. *Themes and Images in the Medieval Religious Lyric*. London: Routledge & Kegan Paul, 1972.
Greenwood, E. B. "George Herbert's Sonnet 'Prayer': A Stylistic Study." *Essays in Criticism* 15 (1965): 27–45.
Grimm, Harold J. *The Reformation Era, 1500–1650*. New York: Macmillan, 1954.
Halewood, William H. *The Poetry of Grace: Reformation Themes and Structures in English Seventeenth Century Poetry*. New Haven: Yale University Press, 1970.
Harman, Barbara. *Costly Monuments: Representations of the Self in George Herbert's Poetry*. Cambridge, Mass.: Harvard University Press, 1982.
Hayes, Albert McHarg. "Counterpoint in Herbert." *Studies in Philology* 35 (1938): 43–60.
Henkel, Arthur, and Albrecht Schöne. *Emblemata: Handbuch zur Sinnbildkunst des XVI. and XVII. Jahrhunderts*. Stuttgart: Metzler, 1967.
Hirsch, E. D., Jr. *Validity in Interpretation*. New Haven: Yale University Press, 1967.
Kermode, Frank. *Shakespeare, Spenser, Donne*. London: Routledge & Kegan Paul, 1971.
Kinnamon, Noel J. "A Note on Herbert's 'Easter' and the Sidneian

Psalms." *GHJ* 1 (1978): 44–48.
———. "Notes on the Psalms in Herbert's *The Temple.*" *GHJ* 4 (1981): 10–29.
Labriola, Albert C. "Herbert, Crashaw, and the *Schola Cordis* Tradition." *GHJ* 2 (1978): 13–23.
Lampe, G. W. H., and K. J. Woollcombe. *Essays on Typology.* London: SCM Press, 1957.
Lewalski, Barbara K. *Protestant Poetics and the Seventeenth Century Religious Lyric.* Princeton: Princeton University Press, 1979.
Luscombe, D. E. *The School of Peter Abelard.* Cambridge: Cambridge University Press, 1969.
Mahood, M. M. "Something Understood: The Nature of Herbert's Wit." Stratford upon Avon Studies 11 (Metaphysical Poetry). Ed. Malcolm Bradbury and David Palmer. London: Arnold, 1970, pp. 123–48.
Martz, Louis L. *The Poetry of Meditation: A Study in English Religious Literature of the Seventeenth Century.* Rev. ed. New Haven: Yale University Press, 1962.
Mazzeo, J. A. *Renaissance and Seventeenth Century Studies.* London: Routledge & Kegan Paul, 1964.
McLelland, Joseph C. *The Visible Words of God: An Exposition of the Sacramental Theology of Peter Martyr Vermigli.* Edinburgh: Oliver & Boyd, 1957.
Miller, Perry. *The New England Mind: The Seventeenth Century.* Rev. ed. Cambridge, Mass.: Harvard University Press, 1954.
Mills, Jerry Leath. "Recent Studies in Herbert." *English Literary Renaissance* 6 (1976): 105–18.
Mulder, John R. "George Herbert's *The Temple*: Design and Methodology." *SCN* 31 (1973): 37–45.
Munz, Peter. *The Place of Hooker in the History of Thought.* London: Routledge & Kegan Paul, 1952.
The New Catholic Encyclopedia. 15 vols. Ed. at the Catholic University of America, Washington, D.C. New York: McGraw-Hill, 1967.
Norbrook, David. *Poetry and Politics in the English Renaissance.* London: Routledge & Kegan Paul, 1984.
Novarr, David. *The Making of Walton's "Lives."* Ithaca, N.Y.: Cornell University Press, 1958.
Nowottny, Winifred. *The Language Poets Use.* London: Athlone Press, 1962.
Nuttall, A. D. *Overheard by God: Fiction and Prayer in Herbert, Milton, Dante and St John.* London: Methuen, 1980.
Ong, Walter, S.J. *The Barbarian Within, and other Fugitive Essays and Studies.* New York: Macmillan, 1962.
Otto, Rudolf. *The Idea of the Holy.* [*Das Heilige*]. Trans. John W. Harvey. 2d ed. London: Oxford University Press, 1950.
Patrick, J. Max. "Critical Problems in Editing George Herbert's *The Temple.*" *The Editor as Critic and the Critic as Editor.* Ed. J. Max Patrick and Alan Roper. Los Angeles: William Andrews Clark Memorial Library, 1973.

Patrides, C. A., ed. *George Herbert: The Critical Heritage.* London: Routledge & Kegan Paul, 1983.

Praz, Mario. *Studies in Seventeenth-Century Imagery.* 2d ed. 2 vols. Rome: Edizioni di Storia e Letteratura, 1964.

Quinn, Dennis. "Donne's Christian Eloquence." *ELH* 27 (1960): 276-97.

Richards, I. A. Review of Helen Vendler, *The Poetry of George Herbert. TLS* 28 (1975): 1417.

Rickey, Mary E. *Utmost Art: Complexity in the Verse of George Herbert.* Lexington: University of Kentucky Press, 1966.

Roberts, John R. *George Herbert: An Annotated Bibliography of Modern Criticism 1905–1974.* Columbia: University of Missouri Press, 1978.

Ross, Malcolm M. *Poetry and Dogma.* New Brunswick: Rutgers University Press, 1954.

Rubey, Daniel. "The Poet and the Christian Community: Herbert's Affliction Poems and the Structure of *The Temple.*" *SEL* 20 (1980): 105–23.

Sanders, Wilbur. "'Childhood is Health': The Divine Poetry of George Herbert." *Melbourne Critical Review* 5 (1962): 3–15.

———. "Herbert and the Scholars." *Melbourne Critical Review* 4 (1961): 102–11.

Scheper, George L. "Reformation Attitudes toward Allegory and the Song of Songs." *PMLA* 89 (1974): 551–62.

A Short Title Catalogue of Books Printed in England, Scotland and Ireland and of English Books Printed Abroad 1475–1600. Comp. A. W. Pollard & G. R. Redgrave. London: The Bibliographical Society, 1926.

Short Title Catalogue of Books printed in England, Scotland, Ireland, Wales, and British America, and of English Books printed in other countries 1641–1700. 3 vols. Comp. Donald Wing. New York: Columbia University Press, 1945–1951.

Smalley, Beryl. *The Study of the Bible in the Middle Ages.* 2d ed. Oxford: Blackwell, 1952.

Stambler, Elizabeth. "The Unity of Herbert's *Temple.*" *Cross Currents* 10 (1960): 251–66.

Stein, Arnold. *George Herbert's Lyrics.* Baltimore: Johns Hopkins University Press, 1968.

Stewart, Stanley. *The Enclosed Garden: The Tradition and the Image in Seventeenth-Century Poetry.* Madison: University of Wisconsin Press, 1966.

Strier, Richard. *Love Known: Theology and Experience in George Herbert's Poetry.* Chicago/London: University of Chicago Press, 1983.

Summers, Claude J., and Ted-Larry Pebworth, eds. *"Too Riche to Clothe the Sunne": Essays on George Herbert.* Pittsburgh: University of Pittsburgh Press, 1980.

Summers, Joseph [H.] "From 'Joseph's Coat' to 'A True Hymne.'" *GHJ* 2 (1978): 1–12.

———. *George Herbert: His Religion and Art.* London: Chatto & Windus, 1954.

Taylor, Mark. *The Soul in Paraphrase: George Herbert's Poetics.* The Hague: Mouton, 1974.

Thomas, Keith. *Man and the Natural World. Changing Attitudes in England*

1500–1800. London: Allen Lane, 1983.

Thomas, Keith. *Religion and the Decline of Magic: Studies in Popular Beliefs in Sixteenth- and Seventeenth-Century England*. London: Weidenfeld & Nicolson, 1971.

Treglown, Jeremy. "The Satirical Inversions of Some English Sources in Rochester's Poetry." *RES* 24 (1973): 42–48.

Tuve, Rosemond. *Essays by Rosemond Tuve*. Ed. Thomas P. Roche, Jr. Princeton: Princeton University Press, 1970.

———. *A Reading of George Herbert*. London: Faber, 1952.

Unrau, John. "Three Notes on George Herbert." *N&Q* 213 (1968): 94-95.

Vendler, Helen. *The Poetry of George Herbert*. Cambridge, Mass.: Harvard University Press, 1975.

Walker, D. P. *The Ancient Theology: Studies in Christian Platonism from the Fifteenth to the Eighteenth Century*. Ithaca, NY: Cornell University Press, 1972.

Walker, John D. "The Architectonics of George Herbert's *The Temple*." *ELH* 29 (1962): 289–305.

Wallerstein, Ruth. *Studies in Seventeenth Century Poetic*. Madison: University of Wisconsin Press, 1950.

Whiting, Paul R. "Two Notes on George Herbert." *N&Q* 210 (1965): 130–31.

Williams, Arnold. *The Common Expositor: An Account of the commentaries on Genesis, 1527–1633*. Chapel Hill: University of North Carolina Press, 1948.

Williams, Raymond. *The Country and the City*. London: Chatto & Windus, 1973.

Wind, Edgar. *Pagan Mysteries in the Renaissance*. Reissue of 1958 ed. Oxford: Oxford University Press, 1980.

Winters, Yvor. *Primitivism and Decadence: A Study of American Experimental Poetry*. New York: Arrow Editions, [1937].

Wood, Chauncey. "A Reading of Herbert's Coloss. 3.3." *GHJ* 2 (1979): 15–24.

Woolf, Rosemary, *The English Religious Lyric in the Middle Ages*. Oxford: Clarendon, 1968.

Zinn, Grover A., Jr. "Book and Word: The Victorine Background of Bonaventura's Use of Symbols." *Volumen Commemorativum anni septies centenarii a morte S. Bonaventurae Doctoris Seraphici*. Rome: Collegio S. Bonaventura, 1974, vol. 2, pp. 143–69.

Index